MW00577111

SECRETS
OF THE
FATHER

———BOOK THREE———

Understanding the Almighty

SERIES

John A. Naphor

Secrets of the Father
Book Three of *Understanding the Almighty* Series

© 2016 John A. Naphor

Published in Succasunna, New Jersey, by CORNERSTONE PUBLISHING.

www.godculture.net

CORNERSTONE PUBLISHING can bring a live speaker to your event. For more information please visit www.godculture.net

Book cover design and interior formatting by BookStylings.com

Dedication

This book is dedicated to the one and only living God, Yahweh, my Father in heaven. Your *"love suffers long and is kind;"* your *"love does not envy; does not parade itself, is not puffed up; does not behave rudely, does not seek its own, is not provoked, thinks no evil; does not rejoice in iniquity, but rejoices in the truth."* Your love *"bears all things, believes all things, hopes all things, endures all things."* Your *"love never fails."* (1 Corinthians 13:4-8) You are incapable of disappointing. You are ever present and all powerful. *"Apart from You I can do nothing."* (John 15:5)

TABLE OF CONTENTS

Introduction

WARNING! WHAT YOU ARE ABOUT TO READ MAY OFFEND YOU...

Before I begin revealing the Lord's divine secrets to you, please allow me to lay the foundation of why our Father chose to hide them in the first place. I must caution you though, if you are not in touch with God's Spirit you may become highly offended toward what I am about to say. Keep in mind, however, that although the following introduction may sound like a political discourse, it is not intended to be one. Unfortunately, or fortunately, depending upon your cultural perspective, religion and politics have come crashing together in modern times.

As a result, the laws of God often times clash with the laws of a particular society.

Regardless of how this makes you feel, I can assure you that what you are about to read is absolute biblical truth. Truth is always black and white. Yes or no is the very nature of the truth, and, therefore, Jesus clearly warns us to *"let your 'Yes' be 'Yes,' and your 'No,' 'No.' For whatever is more than these is from the evil one."* (Matthew 5:37) Due to His cut and dry nature, God is an offense to those who do not believe. Jesus is, *"a stone of stumbling and a rock of offense"* (1 Peter 2:8) to those who are disobedient to the word of His message.

With that in mind, I am sure you have noticed that something has gone terribly wrong in the world? It seems like much of humanity has gone completely insane and just like Elvis, if I did not know better I would think that God has left the building.

Consider the following: *Planned Parenthood* has not only participated in America's demonically influenced holocaust, they have recently been busted profiting from the sale of human body parts in what may be America's most vile historical secret, the vicious slaughter of nearly *sixty million* unborn human souls.

Tragically, the conversation has not headed in the direction of morality. Theology rarely enters the mind of the wicked. The debate has not even entered the realm of right and wrong. The highly politicized issue of infanticide now rests solely upon legality. Think about it; the debate is whether or not killing baby's, (yes, that is what abortion is) which is undoubtedly among the most heinous of crimes against humanity, is legal or illegal. America is actually debating the legality of not just killing an unborn human being, but whether or not it is permissible to dismember the child and sell the dissected body parts for profit. And we call ourselves a civilized nation? Do you really believe God approves of this abomination?

Sadly, the controversy has been raging on for more than fifty long years. With each passing day the devil rips one more piece from the heart and soul of the American people. As a result, *"the love of many has grown cold,"* (Matthew 24:12) as the masses attempt to justify the breaking of God's great commandment, *"thou shall not murder."* (Exodus 20:13)

In what is absolute proof that our nation has completely sold itself to evil, the prevailing majority has voted in favor of murder for profit. Do not forget that it is not just the sellers of body parts who are rolling in the dough. It is also the death mongering doctors who daily renege on their hippocratic oath to save human lives at any cost. They teach the practice of death above the saving of human life and reap tremendous profits from the bloodbath as well. Therefore, the crimson voice of Roe vs. Wade cries out from the ground like the slain blood of Abel who was killed by his brother Cain. (Genesis 4:10) Do not believe for one second that the cry of innocent blood has not reached the throne of almighty God.

As science continually proves that life absolutely, 100% of the time, begins at conception, we continually toss the truth aside for the sake of what can only be classified as a government sponsored genocide. If that were not enough, we then have the nerve to refer to ISIS as savages. Does this not make us every bit as gruesome? ISIS has not dismembered nearly the number of human beings as the "civilized" people of the West. If they are savages, and they are, what are we? To promote, legalize and lie about the murder of sixty million innocents is utter barbary. Now add to it the number of fetus' murdered throughout Europe and China. Labeling and legalizing it is nothing more than outright hypocrisy and lying to ones self. The world, my friend, has become a dangerous place, particularly for those residing in the womb.

Therefore, it is undeniable that global governments and world educational systems are operating under the spirit of antichrist. (1 John 4:3) They have lied to the public and may have even condemned their citizenry to the lake that burns with fire and brimstone. If you do not believe this, check out what Jesus has to say concerning the matter.

"When the Son of Man comes in His glory, and all the holy angels with Him, then He will sit on the throne of His glory. All **the nations** will be gathered before Him, **and He will separate them one from another,** as a shepherd divides his sheep from the goats. And He will set the sheep on His right hand, but the goats on the left. Then the King will say to those on His right hand, 'Come, you blessed of My Father, inherit the kingdom prepared for you from the foundation of the world: for I was hungry and you gave Me food; I was thirsty and you gave Me drink; I was a stranger and you took Me in; I was naked and you clothed Me; I was sick and you visited Me; I was in prison and you came to Me.'

"Then **the righteous** will answer Him, saying, 'Lord, when did we see You hungry and feed You, or thirsty and give You drink? When did we see You a stranger and take You in, or naked and clothe You? Or when did we see You sick, or in prison, and come to You?' And the King will answer and say to them, 'Assuredly, I say to you, inasmuch as you **did it** to one of **the least of these** My brethren, **you did it to Me.'**

"Then He will also say to those on the left hand, **'Depart from Me, you cursed, into the everlasting fire prepared for the devil and his angels:** for I was hungry and you gave Me no food; I was thirsty and you gave Me no drink; I was a stranger and you did not take Me in, naked and you did not clothe Me, sick and in prison and you did not visit Me.'

"Then they also will answer Him, saying, 'Lord, when did we see You hungry or thirsty or a stranger or naked or sick or in prison, and did not minister to You?' Then He will answer them, saying, 'Assuredly, I say to you, inasmuch as you **did not** do it to one of **the least of these,** you **did not do it to Me.'**

And these will go away into everlasting punishment, but the righteous into eternal life."

—Matthew 25:31–46

As you will undoubtedly have noticed, Jesus was quite concerned about the well being of those least able to take care of themselves (classified by the *"least of these"*). From Jesus' perspective, the spiritual justification of the entire nation (not just the personal justification of the individual) is predicated upon how that nation treats its poor, needy, oppressed and defenseless.

That begs the following question; if the nations are to be justified by their treatment of the poor, the needy, and even those imprisoned, (notice that Jesus did not qualify the prisoner's guilt or innocence) how much greater is that nation's responsibility toward the most defenseless members of all—its unborn children? Do you think Jesus will simply excuse such behavior? When you stand before God, do you believe that Jesus will excuse the false doctrine of "the Bible does not address abortion," simply because the terminology did not exist in the days of antiquity? Nowhere in scripture do I see any evidence of Jesus excusing the intentional killing of any human being, whether young, old, or unborn.

The Bible does, by the way, address the issue. If you are motivated enough to seek the truth, put this book down right now and check out Exodus 21:22–25. God undoubtedly speaks concerning the matter.

Therefore, according to the above scriptural reference, the life of a fetus is most certainly on an equal plane to the adult living outside the womb. Therefore, aborting a baby is on equal par and thus, akin to re-crucifying the Lord of glory. It is the killing of the innocent. When any act of violence or oppression, or just outright apathy, is performed against those cast off from society, the act is considered to have been perpetrated against the Lord Jesus Christ. The nation's, including its leaders and constituents that both participate and support such vile acts, will not be counted guiltless.

I have heard and understand all of the arguments. For just a moment, forget about rape, incest or the life of the mother, although Jesus never qualified either as spiritual justification to sin. According to *Right to Life,* statistics show that rape and incest make up less than 1% of all abortions. The physical and/or psychological health of the mother comprise less than 5%. Keep in mind, however, that a psychological evaluation is not required for the "procedure." Apparently, in the new normal of our blood-thirsty American culture, "I don't want it" is more than an adequate mental state for the diagnosis of psychological pain in suffering.

What about about serious birth defects? Surely this must be an adequate means to justify the systematic slaughter of 60 million unborn human beings. Is it? Studies have shown that the very highest estimates comprise less than 6% of all abortions. I would imagine the majority of these occur when the "mother" is above the age of forty. At 6%, however, I am giving all you "pro-choicers," or "abortionists," and keep in mind that "choice," which is a variation of the word "choose," means it is a choice to "terminate," or better stated, "kill" your baby, more than a fair benefit of the doubt.

With that truth in mind, is the vast minority of the so called "valid" reasons to terminate a pregnancy really a reason to blanket kill any baby, anywhere, anytime, and for any reason? with no questions asked? At least the birth defect argument takes into account the quality of life of the child. Many, "defective" children, however, go on to live quite happy lives. Severity, is certainly something to take into account, but truthfully, severe birth defects make up a minuscule percentage of abortions.

Conversely, and if you are an abortionist you might want to sit down for the following revelation of truth. The overwhelming reason comprising the vast majority of abortions, making up a whopping 82%, is simply as a means of birth control. The top three reasons cited are: 1) being unready for responsibility, otherwise known as, selfishness. 2) The inability to afford a baby, also known as, selfishness. and 3) concern about how a baby might change their life, which is merely a reworded form of selfishness.

Let's get real for a moment. Having a baby will undoubtedly change your life. I can guarantee you, however, that it will be for the better, even if it is difficult. The two most selfish acts I can possibly think of are suicide and abortion. If you cannot figure out why, you are in serious need of a "heart" transplant. Therefore, keep reading.

Do you find this heresy as tragic as I do? Unfortunately, most do not. Humanity has become willing to kill another human being for the sake of a new car. Equally as tragic is the fact that the majority supporters of the violence are women—those who are traditionally the most compassionate members of society. In truth, men rarely consider the issue. That is, until they either get a woman pregnant or run for political office. The vast majority of women, on the other hand, breathe fire when someone challenges the issue. What can possibly be in store for the world when even the women thirst for innocent blood?

Amazingly, and what can be considered as none other than absolute proof of our barbary, is the simple truth that even after having been exposed, *Planned Parenthood* still has the majority support of the death mongering, spiritually defunct public they have somehow duped into believing the most heinous of all lies; that a baby is not alive until he/she breathes his/her first breath; and somehow, the only issue on the public docket is the destruction of our 2nd Amendment rights.

What about the rights of our baby's? Doctors have killed infinitely more children than guns—by a margin of nearly 220:1. 1.1 million baby's were aborted in the year 2015. Does that mean we should take away all doctor's, as well? In truth, all of the gun control talk, along with a plethora of other politically motivated issues, is merely a mask to cover the real problem. The hearts of the American people have grown cold.

Did you know that according to American law, a double homicide only results if the the murdered pregnant woman delivers the baby as a result?

In other words, if the baby does not take at least one breath, it is not even considered alive. I am still trying to figure out if that is just absurd or evil. My personal opinion is both. Does anyone having birthed or fathered a child believe their now walking, talking, living, loving, child was lifeless in the womb? For anyone containing even half a brain it is not too difficult to figure out who the real father of today's abortion loving, God hating, today's man or woman is. (See John 8:44 if you are yet to figure it out)

The beginning of life is an interesting proposition when you consider that the bloodthirsty radical left *and right wing* abortionists also began as a mere "clump of cells." Talk about hypocrisy! Perhaps they should suck out their own brains, or what is left of them after having ingested all the mind bending hallucinogenic drugs that have undoubtedly distorted their ability to comprehend reality, or even worse, has eradicated the gray matter that contains both conscience and morality.

Incredibly, the same degenerate and hypocritical generation that accused our Vietnam veterans of being baby killers now fills the modern-day mass grave known as the petri dish to overflow, with no regard for human life. They kill baby's without conscious and chalk it up to progress—and, of course, a woman's right to choose. After sixty *million* deaths, you tell me who the real baby killers are. When will enough be enough?

Perhaps you are thinking that I am "a little" angry. The truth is, I am not angry. I am sad. I suppose I am a bit outraged by all of this, but what the heck . . . Why aren't you? I grieve for the American public and am outraged that as a society we have become so enlightened by progress that we can "lovingly" approve of any and every lifestyle regardless of what God's Word says about it. The problem progresses even further as one considers that we no longer respect the descending opinion.

In today's new age cultural normalism we must shove the same sinful ideology down the throat of nearly every American child with complete disregard for their parents will. To further our spiritual descent into the murderous abyss, we demonize the Christian and "compassionately" kill the only human beings unable to defend themselves. Of course I am outraged by such an avoidable tragedy. Who wouldn't be? Well . . . I guess we all know the answer to that.

I would imagine that Yahweh is not all that thrilled with it either. In fact, I am pretty sure He is downright furious about it—to the point of judgment. Jesus' Matthew 25 discourse, as noted above, eliminates any and all doubt about that. Do not, however, mistake God's anger with hatred, a lack of love, or even apathy. God's anger is derived from a holy passion. It is an intense desire to be in loving fellowship with the *"apple of His eye,"* (Deuteronomy 32:10 and three others) who just happen to be the masses of humanity defying His perfect will.

Therefore, in a carefully calculated rage of loving anger He lashed out at the sin separating Him from the object of His affection and spilled His own blood on the cross at Calvary. Perfect love is God's answer to judgment. Thankfully, God loves the sinner, of whom I am chief. Yes, I completely recognize my own sinful lack of righteousness. Therefore, my societal outrage drives me to reveal the truth of true love by any means necessary, which sometimes includes a good tongue lashing directed toward the blind. If that takes the form of a political rant . . . well . . . so be it.

Read the Fine Print

The abortionists, by the way, are not the only death mongers making headlines these days. In complete and total defiance of God's will, ISIS, Al-Qaeda, Boko Haram and a whole host of others are crucifying Christian and Muslim "infidels" alike—lopping off their heads, burning some in cages, drowning others, throwing homosexual's from the rooftops and mowing down nightclubs and city streets full of innocents. Incredibly, the cowardly governmental leaders of the present-day free world are attempting to dupe us by another slight of hand. They claim that the viciously homocidal terrorist brand of jihad known as Radical Islam is "un-Islamic," as if it has no basis in the Qu'ran or Sunna. This too, is a lie.

Therefore, here is my advice to anyone who has heretofore been too apathetic to discover the truth on your own. Read the Qu'ran! Read the Sunna, which is comprised of the Hadith and the traditions of Islam. Study Islamic history. You will very quickly discover that ISIS, Boko Haram and their plethora of homicidal counterparts are the only groups authentically practicing the brand of Islam that Mohammed originally intended.

The goal of Allah is crystal clear as laid out in the Qu'ran and the Sunnah. Eliminate the infidel. Mohammed's life mirrored ISIS on a far greater scale than anyone is willing to admit. It, by the way, in no way resembled the life of Jesus Christ. The two are diametrically opposed to one another in doctrine. The question is, are you willing to believe what you read or has political correctness vanquished your truth meter?

That's Not All

As if that were not enough, the conformity of the apathetically godless Western parent, who in cahoots with the equally godless governments of the world, is producing such a violent generation that school shootings, gang violence, and both suicidal and homocidal tendencies have become common place . . . and all anyone is concerned with is global warming?! Oh, excuse me, climate change.

Congruently, the God hating, evolutionist liars dominating the educational systems of the world will not even accept a smidgen of blame for spreading their global deception, which eradicates the value of human life. They have legislated God out of the public, convinced the delusional masses that their nearest of kin descended from a banana, then stand before the camera's even more stupefied with every mass killing. Being devoid of any and all answers, they attempt to cover their ignorant rebellion against Yahweh by claiming guns are the problem and not their singled celled ousting of the only place human life value can possibly exist—almighty God.

Although I agree that owning an AK-47 is more than a bit over the top, no gun ever pulled its own trigger. That takes the product of a *No Child Left Behind* the *Common Core* curriculum to accomplish such a lofty task. Am I the only one to recognize that America entered into judgment the day the Supreme Court legalized murder in the passing of *Roe vs. Wade?* From that day forward, America has continuously reaped the fruit of our embryonic bloodshed.

I don't know, perhaps it is just easier to bow before the atheistic minority and kill baby's; or to cowardly hide behind the erroneous interpretation of separating church from state. How else could we have arrived at such a horrific place? Perhaps if we continue to sing God Bless America, while at the same time ousting Him from the pledge of allegiance, everything will be okay. It's progress, isn't it? Although it is politically incorrect to say, it appears that Reverend Jeremiah Wright wasn't really that far off. Is God damning America?

> *"And even as they did not like to retain God in their knowledge, **God gave them over to a debased mind,** to do those things which are not fitting; **being filled** with all unrighteousness, sexual immorality, wickedness, covetousness, maliciousness; full of envy, murder, strife, deceit, evil-mindedness; they are whisperers, backbiters, haters of God, violent, proud, boasters, inventors of evil things, disobedient to parents . . ."*
> **—Romans 1:28**

In America, racism has also been freshly set ablaze by the radical baby boom, hippy, mentored Generation X brand of politician's who are still too high to notice they are forty years beyond the *folly of their youth.* (Proverbs 22:15) As a result, the masses have so little regard for authority that disrespect has become the very least of the pubic's ever increasing vulnerabilities.

Incredibly, those in charge have attempted to solve the problem by legalizing marijuana and letting all the drug dealers out of prison. No wonder the Police cruiser has become a war zone surpassed only in its peril by the inner city streets of Chicago, Baltimore and St. Louis, Missouri. The law abiding citizen is under attack. They (both the Police and the inner city resident) may as well be in Iraq dodging roadside IED's. At least they would be on the lookout for stray bullets and ambushes in Iraq.

Police shootings have become as common as blaming the police for producing criminal behavior. Our precious children are paying the price with far too many meeting their Maker in the once sacred, but now Godless, classroom. Can you tell me again why *"thou shall not murder"* (Exodus 20:13) should be taken off the classroom wall? Can it really be that offensive? even to an atheist? Our kids seem to have forgotten the Golden Rule. In truth, it was never taught to a generation that worships at the altar of self. Amazingly, such anarchy seems to have support from the rainbow colored Whitehouse on down.

When gazing upon the chaos that has become the modern world, it is no wonder the biblically ill-informed masses feel God does not possess the power, nor even the desire, to intervene in the affairs of men. The politician's of the world have convinced humanity that intervention is their job. Dependence upon government has become a worldwide epidemic. The rapidly expanding one-world governmental rule has made its abode in the place that was once reserved for the living God.

Silence Is Golden

With all that I have said thus far, do you still question why God has allowed the world to fall into such an irreparable state chaos? and this is just the beginning, folks! The world is going to get much worse before God blows it to smithereens. Does all this really mean that God has left the building?

Seriously, if I did not know better I would think God has gone AWOL. (Absent Without Leave).

To the untrained eye, or perhaps, even better stated, to the un-covenanted eye, it appears that God has no interaction in the affairs of men. Therefore, look deep within yourself. Do you believe this is true? If so, why? What happened? Where did God go and why did He leave? or could it be . . . that just as in times past, God has simply gone silent due to a rebellious and iniquitously sinful generation of humanity?

With that in mind, allow me to let you in on our initial secret. Are you aware that God did not speak to the Israelites for over two hundred-thirty years during their time of slavery in Egypt? In fact, it had been so long that God had to re-identify Himself when sending Moses to deliver them from the hands of Pharaoh. Seriously, He had been silent for so long that there was not a person alive who had ever heard His voice. As a result, they had no idea who He was or what He might say. Does that sound familiar? For those alive today, I often wonder.

There were also four hundred years of silence between the biblical books of Malachi and Matthew—the end of the Old and the beginning of the New Testament. As you can see, God going silent is not unprecedented throughout human history. I am sure the ancient Israelite felt the same way modern man feels today. Where is God? Why did He leave? Does He care about our suffering? Is He even real?

When viewed from this perspective, it is no wonder that God has gone off the grid. Our world is being run by iniquitous world leaders concerned only with political power, personal gain and where to garner their next vote. The President's primary concern has abandoned the will of the people and has shifted to the vanity of legacy . . . Congress, with re-election . . . and local government's with attaining a higher office. Where does serving the people fit into the agenda?

The answer is, it does not. Hence, today's politician wets his finger and holds it in the proverbial air to check the direction of the politically fueled, pop cultural wind. If it is blowing in the direction of the LGBTQ we approve same-sex marriage. When the wind blows toward the sexual revolution, we legalize abortion. If the wind blows in the direction of a failing economy we construct Weapons of Mass Destruction and start a war (or a police action to avoid either Congress or the political fallout of the actual declaration). When the whirlwind of self-interest leaves our nation bankrupt, we raise taxes, increase the spending budget and enslave the next generation with an unpayable national debt.

What about the people? Does anyone care? Do you realize that the spiritual climate of every nation will depend upon the integrity of those in power? This is a societal truism from the days of antiquity. The pattern has reoccured from the idolatry of ancient Israel, to the orgy's of the Roman Empire. While unrecognized by so many, it continues on through the wiles of American slavery, all the way to the present historical legacy we are currently leaving to our self-centered, "me first," rapidly expanding Ritalin induced, Bi-Polar, abortion loving children. Hence, God has been involuntarily silenced. He has declined to speak to a world that has stopped their ears.

I will never forget the day that God put the world into perspective for me. Often times, we are simply unable to see God and His incredible plan for humanity through all of the chaos. As many of you undoubtedly feel, I too was having, and sometimes still do, something of an aversion to all of the illegal immigration problems that America and many of the Western country's throughout the world are experiencing today.

A dear friend of mine, who happens to be from Jamaica, the island of, not the region of Queens, New York, where Saint John's University is located, heard me grumbling in my frustration with today's political leaders.

He said to me, "John, you claim to be a preacher of the gospel and aim to make disciples of all nations, is that correct?" I wish I could convey his accent. It seemed so much more powerful when spoken in Patois.

I said, "Of course, God means everything to me."

He then replied, "Then why do you question His sovereignty?"

Being a little taken aback I replied, "What on earth are you talking about?"

That is when he set me straight. He chided, "We no longer have to leave our own borders to make disciples of all nations. God is bringing them *to* us."

That is when it hit me. I cannot even begin to tell you how correct he was—and still is. *"The truth had made me free."* (John 8:32) Let me give you an example. At the time of this writing there is a refugee crisis going on in Syria. Many of the refugees are being emigrated throughout the world. America happens to be one of the nations they are being placed in. Incredibly, however, and what makes it so scary, is there also happens to be a crisis going on with ISIS at the same moment in history. With that said, I completely understand the reservation on the part of the American people, and other Western nations, of allowing the Syrian refugee to enter our nations, particularly when ISIS has already announced their intention to be hiding amongst them.

But God is sovereign. Every nation that He allows to be established is for the purpose of His glory. The region of the world these refugees are coming from, and a large portion of all Muslim people for that matter, is a region known as the 10/40 window. It is a summation the longitudinal and latitudinal coordinates of the region of the world that is least likely to be reached for the gospel, and, therefore, has the greatest number of non-Christians on the planet.

It also happens to be incredibly dangerous for Western missionaries to enter, or any missionary for that matter, and often times quite ineffective for those that do. Very few Westerners speak the Arabic and other Middle Eastern languages, nor understand the culture. To survive long enough to speak one word of truth in their native tongue, the gospel often times must be disguised as humanitarian aid or some form of relief. Communication and cultural violence are major hindrances throughout the Middle East and parts of Asia.

Trust me when I tell you that I am aware of such cultural violence first hand. As our car recently wound its way through a mountainous region of Flores, Indonesia, we were stopped on the road to allow the local police the proper room to disperse. Apparently, several family members of this primarily "Christian" region had gotten into a land dispute. The disagreement escalated to roughly sixty people and only came to a conclusion when one of the family members shot and killed another with a bow and arrow. Several others were wounded.

Our driver and his local friend simply laughed it off and said, "Don't worry. That's normal here." What? I thought dodging the myriad of fallen boulders on the winding, two lane "spaghetti road" being expressed as normal was a bit strange, but this brought normal to whole new level. Normal to "Orang Flores," (Flores people) was not only *abnormal* to me, it was more than a bit disconcerting to my wife, as well! Apart from that, however, Flores is absolutely breathtaking. I would recommend it to anyone with a bit of an adventurous heart.

So what does God do? Before I tell you, let me fill you in on the first real secret (it's actually the second) you are going to encounter in this discourse. Secret numero uno is that *God is not causing all of the chaos.* That job has been undertaken by a rebelliously sinful humanity. In fact, the exact opposite is true. God will do anything in order to save you; including, but not limited to, entering the natural realm as human flesh to die for your sin. That in itself is incredible; but what does that have to do with the unreached people of the Middle Eastern world?

It is simple and leads us directly to secret number two. *God is relocating them*—just like any loving father would! Most Christians will never have to leave the borders of their native lands to reach the rest of the world. If God stupefies the political leaders of the world, which He undoubtedly has, it is for the purpose of salvation. It is for the mission of bringing the 10/40 window, and any other unreached people groups, right into the midst of the currently, but perhaps not for long, religiously free Western world for the purpose of evangelizing them.

That means as Christians, we can now reach the Middle East in our own language, within the bounds of our own cultures, in peace, for the most part, and in the middle of our own city's, towns and neighborhood's. If you ask me, that is incredible and completely illustrates the sovereignty of God. If man cannot see it, it is simply a matter of ignorance on the part of sinful humanity. Will there be challenges and dangers? Aren't there always? The real question is; will today's modern-day Christian take up the mantle and complete the preordained mission?

There lies the problem. Most of "God's people" have never heard His voice, and, therefore, either refuse to or are unable to answer His call. Either, we have become so blinded by prejudice, racism and cultural bias that we are unable to see the forest for the trees, or we rely on the never ending educational process that never leads to any significant action. We seem to run the gamete on opposite sides of the spectrum. We either ignore God's Word, or we become so bound up in its intricacies that we become as those who are *always learning and never able to come to the knowledge of the truth.*" (2 Timothy 3:7)

That, therefore, leads to my next question. Has God really gone silent? Perhaps, in such a self induced state of numbness and human chaos, He just cannot be heard above the noise. Can it be that modern man is so stubborn that God is beating His head off a proverbial stiff-necked wall of rebellion? As you might imagine, that can only go on for so far before anyone, let alone the God of the universe, begins not only to withdraw, but to judge.

God, however, is the epitome of love. The good news is that He is still willing to speak to anyone willing to listen. That is the essence of the gospel. The gospel is the good news to a fallen world. Therefore, read on.

In the following pages you are about to encounter the wondrous Ancient of Days.

As you draw closer to His presence you will begin to hear His *"still small voice"* (1 Kings 19:12) whispering His precious secrets into your unstopped ears. If you are willing to listen and to diligently pursue His presence, He will reveal to you the mysteries of life. You may not realize it, but God still has plenty to say. Therefore, let's complete the final stage of our journey together. In the following pages, you are about to discover God's ultimate truth: **Humanity desperately needs God.** Therefore, let's move on and into the future together. It is time to reveal the long awaited *Secrets of the Father.*

CHAPTER 1

The Temple Lies in Ruin

(THE SECRET OF REBUILDING THE TEMPLE)

Several days ago I was playing golf with a good friend of mine. We were enjoying the beautiful day, joking about the ineptness of our golf swings and generally having a great time enjoying the company of friends and the beauty of creation. Golf is a funny game though. I have become utterly convinced that apart from those talented enough to grace the professional tours, no one is really any good at golf. Some are better than others, but in truth, most cheat. Check that, we all cheat.

I am yet to meet an honest amateur golfer. We move our ball, kick it away from trees and out of divots. We continuously forgive obvious penalty's—all in a sick and twisted effort to delude ourselves from the truth and make ourselves feel better. I once heard of a gentleman who cleverly crafted a hole in the pocket of his cotton dockers. When no one was looking he would slide a ball down his pant leg. Somehow, no matter how errant his shot, he always found his ball—until the day he was discovered.

Come to think of it, golf is a lot like life in general. We human's will do nearly anything to mask our pain and hide from the cruel realty known as the human experience. Regardless of the level you play at, and just like the game we call life, golf is ultimately a test of one's integrity. What was your real score? is a reality that every golfer leaves the course knowing, regardless of what is written on the scorecard. I am quite certain that all you golfers know exactly what I am talking about. I cannot be the only cheater, can I?

For those of you ready to judge me according to my confession, consider the following; golf works just like the Levitical law. With the law, if you are guilty of breaking one, you are guilty of breaking them all. There is a symbiotic relationship between the law that never depreciates with time. Thus, we are all in need of a Savior.

With golf, if you have ever cheated once, guess what? You are a cheater. How is that for a reality check? That also happens to be an intrinsic value that never depreciates with time either, and, therefore, we *still* need a Savior, even if it is merely to save us of from the sin of our lying, cheating, self-deprecating and foul-mouthed golf swing. With all that said, are there any honest golfers left standing? Let's take that one step further. Are there really any honest human beings left standing? Unfortunately, apart from Jesus Christ *"we have all gone astray."* (Isaiah 53:6, Psalm 14:3 and Romans 3:12)

Anyway, the birds were singing, the sun was shining and God was showing off the beauty of His magnificent glory . . .

Always on our Lips

There was one member of our foursome, however, who was not having the same grand experience. He was not embracing the peace and tranquility available in *"the secret place of the most High."* (Psalm 91:1) After his third or fourth errant shot (mind you it was only the third hole) he cried out, "God damn it . . . Jesus Christ!" You see, golf also works like life in the following regard, as well.

Most golfers think they are much better than they actually are. Does this ring a bell for you? We delude ourselves into the magical fantasy that today I will somehow break eighty, when in reality I know I am going to spray it off the tee at some point. Perhaps, even, all day long. I am a nineties golfer. On a very good day I will shoot in the eighties. I have a much better chance of shooting one hundred and two than seventy-eight. Once I grasp this reality, while simultaneously coming to the realization that only twenty percent of golfers worldwide can break one hundred without cheating, I enjoy the game much more. Most of the time, however, my mind plays in the seventies but my body just does not seem to agree. My, how *"the spirit is willing but the flesh is weak."* (Matthew 26:41)

Therefore, when the truth of our impotence sets in, the resulting frustration is often times uncontainable. Thus, we cry out in inexplicable horror as we realize the one thing we have known deep in our hearts all along. We suck at golf.

On this particular day, however, after the third or fourth round of blasphemous insults directed at the Lord of glory, my friend, who also happens to be a lover of Yeshua (that's Jesus in Hebrew), could not contain himself either. He immediately turned to me and declared, "Isn't it amazing how God's name is on everyone's lips."

With a bit of a start in my eyes I replied, "Wow! I never looked at it that way, but you are right. You never hear anyone cry out, 'Allah damn it, or Mo-ham-med!' No one ever cries out, 'Maya mother of Buddha, or even, Lucifer damn it!'"

I mean, c'mon, we do not even call for the devil to damn our lives. Yet we hear the masses crying out for God to perform the devil's duty on a daily basis. How did God damning our lives become an every day part of speech?

Anyhow, as soon as the words crossed my lips the Lord spoke to me. What He said stunned me at first, but within a millisecond of time I realized He was right. Therefore, I immediately turned to my friend and reiterated Jehovah's words, "It's perverted praise."

That is what taking the Lord's name in vain is—perverted praise. It perfectly matches the devil's modus operandi, as well. He showed up in the wilderness to tempt God (Jesus Christ) not to worship Him. The devil cannot create. The devil never said, "Let there be light." In fact, he did not even say, "Let there be darkness." It was God who *divided the light from the darkness."* (Genesis 1:4) God is the creator. *"I form the light, and create darkness: I make peace, and create evil:* **I the Lord do all these things."** (Isaiah 45:7) Incredibly, and what most people never come to realize in a lifetime of biblical study is that Satan is not even responsible for the genesis of evil.

Because Satan has no creative abilities and because he is corrupt to the very core of his existence, all he *can* do is pervert that which God has created. In case you are yet to notice, his point of reference begins with both you and me. This was true in the Garden of Eden and it is still true today. Incredibly, and just in case you are yet to notice this as well, it all stems from the most basic form of worship—revering the name of our holy Father, Yahweh. Satan is completely opposed to it.

In other words, the devil puts *his* twisted words in *our* more than willing mouths. He then recedes back into the dark shadows of deprecation and watches man's mouth aimlessly run amuck. Regrettably, the masses of ignorant humanity, *"unable to tame our own tongue"* (James 3:8) are more than happy to cooperate. Thus, we walk right into Lucifer's ambush and unwittingly condemn our own lives by demeaning *"the King of all kings."* (Revelation 19:16)

"God," which is not His name, but is the sanctified description of the Holy One of Israel, angrily vociferates from our sin-stained lips and culminates into the curse of Deuteronomy chapter twenty eight, "damn it!" Regrettably, for a theologically ignorant humanity who is completely unaware of what they just said, damnation is exactly what we get . . . in this life or the next. Perhaps, even both.

With no prior thought or venerable fear of our Maker, we flippantly *"trample the Son of God underfoot, count the blood of the covenant by which we are sanctified a common thing, and insult the Spirit of grace."* (Hebrews 10:29) We ignorantly transform the *"name above all names"* (Philippians 2:9) into a common curse word. "Jesus Christ!" Like so many before and so many yet to come, *Another One Bites the Dust.* Doo-doo doot . . . doot . . . doot . . . Mission accomplished. Our irreverent insolence has empowered the fury of Lucifer and irreparably desecrated our own unrepentant lives. "God damn it."

When you think about it, the devil has been attempting to damn every one of us—God, the angels in heaven, and a totally outmatched humanity since the day iniquity was found in him. (Ezekiel 28:15) Why is this a problem? What does taking the Lord's name in vain have to do with our eternal destiny? Have you considered that God is not the dammer? God is the blesser. Do you realize that God's holy name is to be revered, sanctified and glorified, not thrown into the cesspool of our gluttonous, gutter mouthed, cultural filth?

Furthermore, *"do you not know that you are the temple of God and that the Spirit of God dwells in you?"* (1 Corinthians 3:16) Psalm 84:4 proclaims, *"Blessed are those who dwell in your house; they are ever praising you."* Therefore, I must conclude that since we are the temple of God and that His Spirit dwells in us, the perversion of His name constructs a twisted view of His countenance and directly leads to the ruination of God's temple. We are committing spiritual suicide by the insolence of our own mouths.

Do you realize that the Lord, who is the most holy, powerful, and loving being in all of creation, is worthy of honor and praise? Yet, day after day passes with us nonchalantly dishonoring the name and reputation of our King. Why does this happen? To find out, let's refer the words of the prophet Haggai for revelation.

> *"Is it time for you yourselves to dwell in your paneled houses, and this temple to lie in ruins?' Now therefore, thus says the Lord of hosts:* **'Consider your ways!'"**
> —**Haggai 1:4–5**

Broken Down

The prophet Haggai instructs us to do something life changing in just three simple words, *"Consider your ways."* Have you ever thought about the pandemonium that exists in the world today? Consider what graces the news on a daily basis. We are continuously bombarded with news of wars, homicide, rape, sex, drugs, violence, fraud, and most recently, the sale of human body parts being harvested from the most innocent of all humanity, completely healthy aborted baby's. The list goes on and on ... and that is just within the trinity of the United States government. Yes, it is Congress and the President, who in conjunction with the Supreme Court that create, interpret and implement the nation's laws.

With that said, here is another news flash. The court is not supreme, nor is any world government institution. Yahweh alone, holds that position and judgment is in His hands. I know that you all want to hear me say that God is a God of prosperity, love and mercy; and that it was the God of old that carry's out judgment. If that is what you believe you had better reopen your Bible. Although God is all of these to the obedient, He will judge the disobedient one hundred percent of the time—even in the New Testament!

I am only half joking, by the way, when I say that Congress has become a haven for the debaucherous. Apart from the sixty million abortions or so, I have not heard of a homicide in Congress since Gary Condit was accused in 2001 of killing Sandra Levy. However, the remaining daily acts of immorality conjoined with the legislative encouragement to commit such heinous crimes against Jehovah, most certainly apply. Consider the implication this has on society as a whole. Ponder the effect on the totality of world affairs when the planet's most powerful dignitaries are the chieftain's of sin and murder.

The world has become an absolute disaster and it is all due to one simple truth. The temple of God lies in ruin. In other words, our spiritual lives are a mess. We are the temple of the living God and just as in Haggai's day, the people are too apathetic to care about the unintended consequences. *"Where there is no vision the people perish."* (Proverbs 29:18)

Just like any property left unattended, nature, human nature in this case, which also happens to be sin nature, takes over. With the weeds left unchecked sin grows uncontrollably, thus transforming the temple of the Lord into an unrecognizable ruin. Within a generation of time the temple is swallowed up with no semblance of its prior existence visible to the naked eye.

As a result, the world wreaks of chaos, suffering and pain while being totally blind to the truth of the decaying ruin that lies hidden beneath the surface of human flesh. With no restoration plan laid, the Lord of Hosts speaks, *"Saying: 'This people says, "The time **has not come,** the time that the Lord's house should be built."'"* (Haggai 1:2) Thus, the temple of God degrades into abject ruin as we witness the crumbling wreckage manifest into the manifold crimes against humanity—and incredibly, no one seems to care. Man's heart has become an impenetrable stone.

If you do not believe that, consider your own reaction to the last mass shooting you heard? Were you as outraged and horrified as you were from the first? Before you answer, look deep within yourself. Did you have the same reaction to Orlando, Florida, or San Bernardino, as you did to Columbine, or even Sandy Hook? The nature of the crime has not changed. The human heart, however, has been desensitized. Sin has stolen our humanity. Did the slaughter of twenty, yes, count them, twenty, five and six year old children at Sandy Hook leave an indelible mark upon your soul that no measure of personal pleasure and hedonism can erase? Does your sorrow still burn as molten hot outrage against the powers of darkness? Did it ever?

We live in a world that has become indifferent at best and more often than not, rebellious toward the Lord of glory. If you do not believe that, consider how acceptable premarital sex has become. Have you considered how disgusted God is by such a harrowing act against your own body, in which He is intended to reside, by the way? Do you now realize what sex outside of marriage is and Who you are really violating?

"Flee sexual immorality. Every sin that a man does is outside the body, **but** *he who commits sexual immorality* **sins against his own body,"** and thus, the Lord, who by the power of the Holy Spirit is intended to be adjoined to your body—and his or her body that you are fornicating with. (1 Corinthians 6:18) When placed in its proper context, sex outside the covenant of marriage is pretty horrifying. Wouldn't you now agree?

Why does this happen? How could we have drifted so far from morality? The majority of the masses are ignorant of both God's laws and where the Spirit of God truly dwells. Therefore, we have progressed to the point of being totally clueless in regard to what is, and is not, acceptable to the creator of all that exists.

Therefore, we build majestic church buildings, complete with theatrics that rival the highest quality broadway plays—all in an attempt to usher in the presence of God. All too often, however, our worship is really nothing more than playacting, the recitation of a few fabled lines as nothing changes once we exit the building. Unfortunately, the joke is on God as the essence of Yahweh exits the minds of the cast for the next six days, twenty-two hours and thirty minutes. "But I went to church on Sunday . . ."

Unbeknownst to far too many, the Spirit of the Lord does not dwell within the four walls of the institutional church. God left the building the day the veil was torn in two. Although we are not to *forsake the assembling of ourselves together,"* (Hebrews 10:25) where are our hearts? Have we become a people that *"honor God with our lips, but our hearts are far from Him?"* (Isaiah 29:13 and Matthew 15:8) Only you know the answer.

Humanity has created innumerable rituals and traditions. We continuously search for artifacts and relics . . . all in a vain attempt to connect to our creator. The Lord, however, does not reside in man-made relics or historical artifacts. The Spirit of the Lord resides in you. *You* are the temple of God. Fancy clothes, expensive jewelry, nor any material possession can hide the dilapidation of the Lord's temple. The world is in disrepair. The unanimous approval of sin cries out as a heavenly testimony that the temple of God has fallen into abject ruin.

He's Not Here!

I recently had a conversation with a friend of mine who was struggling with not feeling the presence of God during our Sunday worship. He was feeling things had become a bit dry and even brought the matter before our Senior Pastor. During the course of conversation the Lord quickened my Spirit and I was able to disclose to him that he has been **"looking for Love in all the wrong places." —Johnny Lee**

The presence of God no longer emanates from *"the temple made with hands."* (Acts 7:48) We are the temple. As I just stated, God left the box (the Arc of the Covenant) the day Jesus died and the veil separating the Priests from the Most Holy Place was torn in two. Jesus' life, death and resurrection reconnected you to Yahweh. Therefore, due to the infilling of the Holy Spirit, the presence of God radiates from *you.* Perhaps even better stated, the presence of Jehovah is disseminated from *us,* the body of Christ.

I fully realize that there is a corporate anointing and/or presence of God experienced by the gathering together of believers. (Matthew 18:20) If, however, we are not feeling the presence of God, the trouble is not stemming from the building in which we worship. The problem may not even be in the heart of your fellow believer. The dilemma lay within the heart of each and every one of us, the individuals who have been disconnected from the King of all kings through un-repented sin, pride, ego, jealousy, or just plain old fashioned rebellion. In other words, if you cannot feel, or even better stated, experience the presence of God, it is because *your* temple lay in ruin. Therefore, I would give you the same advice that the prophet Haggai gave Israel so long ago—*"Consider your ways!"*

Run Away!

There is no denying that the world is continually drifting from the presence of God. Consider what has gone on in the "church" over the past sixty-five years or so. *The Associated Press* estimated the total from settlements of sex abuse cases in the Roman Catholic Church taking place from 1950–2007 to be more than $2 billion. *BishopAccountability* reports that figure reached more than $3 billion in 2012. The true extent of the worldwide problem of Priestly pedophilia remains virtually unknown. Not to the victims, however. They are fully aware of the devastation.

The even greater atrocity is how the Roman Catholic Church responded when they discovered the transgression. Rather than do the right thing and prosecute those involved, the church simply moved the pedophile Priests to a new location, and thus, sicced them on a brand new population of innocent children. In other words, the church refused to repent of their sin, rebelled against God, and callously subjected the multitudes to their perversion. Think about what was done. Do you understand the extent of the atrocity committed?

"Pride goes before destruction, and a haughty spirit before a fall." (Proverbs 16:18) With such detestable sin having been left unchecked to this day, my advice to anyone gracing the four walls of the Roman Catholic Church is to run as fast and far from this power hungry atrocity as your weak-kneed spiritual legs can take you. There is no religious institution worthy of a swim in the Lake of Fire. It is blindingly obvious that these modern-day Pharisees are infinitely more concerned with maintaining political support and power than saving the precious souls that are lost in their pews. *"For they loved the praise of men more than the praise of God."* (John 12:43) The love of prideful self-directed praise will result in cover up every time.

I know how offensive that may sound to so many of you, but hey, truth is truth and sin is sin. If the leaders refuse to repent where does that leave the people in the pews? They say ignorance is bliss. That defense, however, will not hold water before the *"judgment seat of Christ."* (2 Corinthians 5:10) *"For there is nothing covered that will not be revealed, nor hidden that will not be known."* (Luke 12:2)

While all may seem well at the time, do not forget that God sees the affairs of men. *"I the LORD search the heart and examine the mind, **to reward each person according to their conduct, according to what their deeds deserve.**"* (Jeremiah 17:10) I don't know about you, but that scares the hell out of me—literally! Knowing that God will recompense me for approving of such matters (Romans 1:32) would drive me as far from that heresy as humanly possible. But that is just me. What truly matters is you.

What has been the result of their apostasy? On the surface very little. Their coffers are still overflowing. Rather than flee the Roman Catholic Church like the plague, the congregants have chosen to ignore the church's sin. They have reacted exactly as the Jews of Haggai's day. *"The time **has not come**, the time that the Lord's house should be built,"* (Haggai 1:2) has been the response. In other words, the reaction from the congregation has thus far been, "Let the temple lay in ruin. It is not my responsibility to fix it." Do you realize that according to Romans 1:32, (as cited above) deliberate inaction makes one complicit to the crime?

What has gone on beneath the surface, however, is a radically different story. Make no mistake, the Roman Catholic Church has fallen. Elvis *has* left the building! The Holy Spirit of God, if He ever was there, has left the Roman Catholic Church. How do you think the devil so easily crept in? As a result, they are merely left with a plethora of empty rituals that make God want to spew. (Revelation 3:16) The proof is in their worldwide decision to implement a cover up and place their own political and financial interests above the well being of countless innocent and defenseless children, which, by the way, was decided from the Pope on down.

Keep in mind that I am speaking to the institution as whole. I am fully aware of the wonderful Roman Catholics who have and continue to make our world a better place—standing firm against abortion, feeding the poor, and educating our children. My prayer is that they would accept Jesus as their personal Savior and hold the Pharisaical church leaders, whom they answer to, accountable.

The Vatican is rich with gold but devoid of the Spirit. Therefore, their seats remain packed with a people refusing to recognize the "born again" experience that every believer must secure (John 3:3), and thus, have ventured down a one way path that ends with the destruction of fire and brimstone. Do not, however, believe for one second that they are alone. There are a multitude of "churches" that will be "walking the line" to the *Great White Throne* judgment, with them. (Revelation 20:11–12)

Consider how many denominations have decided to ordain homosexual and lesbian Pastors, in conjunction with performing same-sex weddings. They claim such lifestyles are not sinful. My question is; are we reading the same Bible? or do you subconsciously "white out" that which your sin-stained spirits rebelliously disagree with? In truth, any insubordination to the Bible will edit God out of *any* church. Therefore, just like the Roman Catholic Church, if your congregation or denomination is encouraging, or even condoning, the practice of any form of sin, it is time to find a new congregation. Run for the hills, even if you have to leave Justin Bieber or Kanye West behind. My advice is not to *Keep Up With the Kardashian's*, but to outrun them. When Jesus returns it will not be pretty for those in opposition to Him, whether or not they falsely bear His name.

Toebah

The Word of God, in both the Old and New Testaments, for example, is abundantly clear on its stance regarding homosexuality and all sexual sin, for that matter. It also has plenty to say regarding those who not just condone, but also approve of those practicing such licentiously sinful behavior.

> *"For the wrath of God is revealed from heaven **against all ungodliness and unrighteousness of men,** who suppress the truth in unrighteousness, because what may be known of God is manifest in them, **for God has shown it to them . . ."***
> **—Romans 1:18–19**

> *"For this reason God gave them up to vile passions. For even their women **exchanged the natural use for what is against nature.** Likewise also the men, **leaving the natural use of the woman,** burned in their lust for one another, **men with men committing what is shameful,** and receiving **in themselves** the penalty of their error which was due . . . who, knowing the righteous judgment of God, that those who practice such things are deserving of death, not only do the same **but also approve** of those who practice them."*
> **—Romans 1:26–27 and 32**

Does this not describe the current state of America and the West, who not only condone such vile acts, but have actually both encouraged and normalized such vile behavior? Check out what the Levitical Law has to say about such sin and keep in mind the word, "abomination" for just a few moments. The English definition of the word abomination is; *a vile, shameful, or detestable action, condition, habit, lifestyle, etc . . .* In Hebrew, it comes from the word, "toebah," or "toevah" and do not let the LGBT fool you. I recently heard there is now a "Q" for "questioning" attached to the end—LGBTQ.

Personally, I do not quite get the "questioning" part. I am pretty sure one knows whether or not they are attracted to the opposite sex. Anyway, regardless of how the LBGTQ positions themselves, "toebah" means "morally disgusting."

Although "toebah" is often times used in reference to idolatry, thrusting your own will above the will of God *is* idolatry. Claiming that homosexuality is not sinful, and thus, directly contradicting the Word of God, or in other words, creating your own version of the law, *is* elevating one's own morality above the morality of God. This, in effect, is an attempt to raise ones-self to a higher position of authority than the creator. That is the textbook definition of idolatry. It is the basis of every form of humanism and more than a few world religions.

Therefore, do not forget the meaning of "toebah"—that which is "abominable." You will see this word appear again shortly apart from the Book of Leviticus. In fact, you are about to see the Greek form of it cross the lips of Jesus, Himself. (Although, He originally spoke it in Aramaic.) When you do, it will permanently establish the matter regarding those who will never see the kingdom of God.

*"You shall not lie with a male as with a woman. It is an **abomination (toebah)**."*
—Leviticus 18:20

*"If a man lies with a male as he lies with a woman, both of them have committed an **abomination** (toebah). They shall surely be put to death. Their blood shall be upon them."*

—Leviticus 20:13

As you read this, keep in mind, 1) that I am not calling for the death of the homosexual, 2) Leviticus 18 and 20 clearly establish the practice of homosexual behavior as an abomination before the Lord, and 3) the grace of Jesus Christ is available to all. However, there is a fourth issue, which also happens to be one of the great Secrets of the Father. *Repentance must occur for grace to abound.*

While we are on the subject, many claim (former United States President Jimmy Carter included) that Jesus Christ would condone homosexuality, or that He never addressed the subject. Of course, no one can point to chapter and verse to support their twisted position—but I can, and I will.

First and foremost, show me one place in the Word of God where Jesus advocated or even condoned sin. He was certainly willing to forgive sin, but repentance on the part of the transgressor is always required. As an example, think about the woman caught in adultery. Although Jesus stated, *"neither do I condemn you,"* He immediately qualified His forgiveness by demanding that she *"go and sin no more."* (John 8:11–12)

"Go and sin no more" equates to repentance, which means to "turn away" from your old sinful life. In fact, Jesus said to the man healed at the *Pool of Bethesda,* and I quote, *"See, you have been made well. **Sin no more, lest a worse thing come upon you."*** (John 5:14) Repentance is a requirement to be taken seriously. The lack of such results in tremendously destructive consequences. Can you now see what is really going on?

Furthermore, Jesus never directed anyone to break the laws of Moses. Jesus was very clear regarding His doctrine when He proclaimed, ***"Do not think that I came to destroy the Law** or the Prophets. **I did not come to destroy** but to fulfill. For assuredly, I say to you, **till heaven and earth pass*** *away, one jot or one tittle **will by no means pass from the law** till all is fulfilled."*

*"Whoever, therefore, breaks one of the least of these commandments, **and teaches men so,** shall be called least in the kingdom of heaven; **but whoever does and teaches them,** he shall be called great in the kingdom of heaven. For I say to you, that unless your righteousness **exceeds** the righteousness of the scribes and Pharisees, **you will by no means enter the kingdom of heaven."** (Matthew 5:17–20)

Think about this logically. The grace of Jesus Christ does not permit us to break the law. We are not permitted to worship and serve other gods. We are not allowed to murder, steal, or covet our neighbor's wife. The idea that the law no longer applies to the New Testament believer is completely absurd.

Although it is true that Jesus Christ has fulfilled the law, that does not mean that we now get to break the law. It means that when we are in Christ the penalty defined under the law no longer applies. We have been freed from its effects. It means Jesus paid the redemption price for you by dying on the cross for your sin. Jesus became your atoning Lamb, having His blood spilled to eradicate your transgressions.

It also means that when one is in Christ they become a new creation, with a new nature, that no longer desires sin. Therefore, it is no longer the desire of the redeemed to break the law. The born again believer detests sin. The disciple of Jesus Christ has found the narrow gate leading us to eternal life, not the broad and destructive pathway into iniquity, and thus, perdition.

Therefore, when the temple of God is restored in the grace of Jesus Christ, the penalty of sin (defined by the law) no longer applies. We can finally live in the grace of 1 John 3:9, which states, *"Whoever has been born of God **does not sin,** for **His seed remains** in him; **and he cannot sin,** because **he has been born of God."***

It is not that the law is no longer valid. It is the truth that those who are in Christ, who have refurbished the temple of God in their hearts, have been freed from the law's effects. True repentance turns a man's desire away from, not toward sin. Repentance, therefore, is a man's entry point into the kingdom of God. Repentance is the restoration of God's holy temple. Without a turning away from one's sinful life, which is what repentance is, the grace of God is non-existent. If you do not believe that, check out Hebrews 10:26–31:

> *"For **if we sin willfully** AFTER we have received the knowledge of the truth, **there no longer remains a sacrifice for sins,** but a certain fearful expectation of judgment, and fiery indignation which will devour the adversaries. Anyone who has rejected Moses' law dies without mercy on the testimony of two or three witnesses. Of how much worse punishment, do you suppose, will he be thought worthy who has **trampled the Son of God underfoot, counted the blood of the covenant by which he was sanctified a common thing, and insulted the Spirit of grace?** For we know Him who said, 'Vengeance is Mine, I will repay,' says the Lord. And again, **'The Lord will judge His people.'** It is a fearful thing to fall into the hands of the living God."*
>
> **—Hebrews 10:26–31**

Furthermore, Jesus was abundantly clear in His stance on sexual immorality, which the practice of homosexuality clearly is. In fact, as we just discovered, the law regards such lifestyle's as toebah. They are an abomination. (Leviticus 18 and 20)

Do not forget that Jesus Christ is the author of the Book of Revelation which states, *"But the cowardly, unbelieving, **abominable,** murderers, **sexually immoral,** sorcerers, idolaters, and all liars shall have their part in the lake* *which burns with fire and brimstone, which is the second death."* (Revelation 21:8)

In this case, the word "abominable" is a translation of the Greek word, "bdelugma." It is the Greek version of toebah and also means something that is abominable. The root of the word actually means: *to stench—to emit a foul odor.* In other words, and these are Jesus' words, not mine, those who live abominable lifestyle's stench to God. They emit a foul odor in the Spirit that God detests!

Once again, I must clarify that God loves the individual. The stench of sin, however, is abominable in His sight. It is certainly forgivable upon repentance, but when left unchecked, it is loathsome. To whom does this apply? To find out, one must simply look up the scriptures regarding toebah. In addition to the idolatrous, guess who else we come across? That is correct, according to Leviticus 18 and 20, Romans 1, et.al., those practicing *and approving* of homosexuality.

It's Your Call

Finally, Jesus was clear that marriage was to take place between one man and one woman. *"And He answered and said to them,* **'Have you not read** (Ignorance of God's Word is still the underlying problem.) *that He who made them at the beginning* **'made them male and female,'** *and said,* **'For this reason** *a man shall leave his father and mother* **and be joined to his wife,** *and the two shall become one flesh'? So then, they are no longer two but one flesh. Therefore,* **what God has joined together let not man separate.'"** (Matthew 19:4–6)

Did Jesus address homosexuality? You are darn right He did! Incredibly, He addressed, homosexuality, adultery, fornication and every form of sexual immorality, including divorce, in one fell swoop. Therefore, as you can now clearly see, as humanity continues to drift further and further from the truth of God's Word, the temple of the Holy Spirit perpetually falls into ruination . . . and we wonder why God refuses to speak.

Therefore, it is time to rebuild the temple. It is time to reunify the body of Christ. If we do not, God will remain silent and humanity will continue to believe in an absentee God. What we have here is a double edged sword. As former Federal Reserve Chairman **Alan Greenspan** proclaimed about the United States economy, **"We are in a conundrum."** God will not speak until America (and the rest of the world) turns, but America (and the rest of the world) will not turn until God speaks. Do not fret about this. In truth, we do not have to wait for God to speak. He already has.

> *"God, who at various times and in various ways spoke in time past to the fathers by the prophets,* ***has in these last days spoken to us by His Son . . ."***
>
> **—Hebrews 1:1**

The question is; will you listen? Just like the ancient Israelites we are wandering about the wilderness with just enough God to feed our belly's and assure that our sandals do not wear out. (Deuteronomy 29:5) Apart from that, however, and also just like the Israelites, we are forty years into a three day journey through the wilderness. Our glutton is being spewed from our mouths like the quails Israel demanded in the Egyptian desert. Can we ever be delivered from such heresy? Not only can we, I believe our time of redemption draws near. God is on the verge of permanently rebuilding His holy temple.

If you are feeling a bit convicted right now, do not fret. Our time of trial is actually necessary. Do not forget that it was in the wilderness that God delivered the pattern necessary to construct the tabernacle. It was also in the wilderness that God first engaged His beloved Israel. Therefore, if you would like to encounter our holy Father, come with me. I would like to introduce you to the Messianic archetype, also known as, Moses. While we are at it, I may as well show you the secret of *discovering God in the wilderness.*

CHAPTER 2

Turning to See God

(THE SECRET OF THE WILDERNESS)

Have you ever considered how Hollywood, and the media in general, has affected our theology of the Bible? In fact, simply being a part of Western culture has effected the way we see the Word of God. Most do not realize that the Bible is a Middle Eastern oriented book and literally revolves around one main city, Jerusalem. Therefore, when we read the Word of God, we should always keep this integral secret in mind. *The current Western world view is non-existent in our Father's eyes.*

Although you most likely have not considered this, I certainly have and thus have found that many people in the Christian community get upset by the Hollywood version of biblical events. The church has misunderstood the essence of Hollywood's existence. Hollywood is not out to make disciples. They are not attempting to glorify God, even when they produce a religious movie. Therefore, I more often than not, get a kick out of the blatant acts of "poetic license" (I'm giving them the benefit of the doubt) used by those creating biblical action movies as opposed to an actual historical recounting of events. Do not forget that Hollywood's ultimate goal is to make a profit (not a prophet) and *not* to lead the individual watching to Christ.

Most recently, we have been graced with such Hollywood gems as *Noah*, as well as, *Left Behind*. Is "not even close" an accurate description of the theatrical parallels between Hollywood and "the Good Book?" Thankfully, every once in a while we see a Spirit filled gem such as *War Room*, which is an outstanding depiction of the power of prayer, hit the Silver Screen. Does this mean America is turning the tide? Although I would love to believe so, the support is waining. It is far too difficult to kick against the pop culture goads.

The best example of Hollywood's shaping of Christianity, however, are the various depictions of Moses, and perhaps the most famous of all is *The Ten Commandments*. Although I love the movie, in my opinion Yule Brenner is the greatest of all Pharaoh's, (even if he is a white man in Africa) how many of us believe Moses was the incredibly handsome and linguistically talented individual portrayed by Charlton Heston? Who can forget the image of Moses standing before the Red Sea . . . staff in hand . . . arms outstretched . . . majestically gazing upon Israel while the mighty waters of the Red Sea begin heaping into cavernous walls of salvation? The glorious image of the prophet is permanently etched into the banks of my earliest biblical memories.

After studying the Word of God, however, I have come to realize that quite a bit of caricature has been injected into the Moses of our most prized Hollywood treasure. Come to think of it, *The Prince of Egypt,* a cartoon movie directed at children, is a more accurate depiction of the true Moses of the Bible. Don't even get me started on the world's distorted view of Jesus Christ, particularly in regard to His return. That will require a whole new book series.

Anyway, I absolutely adore the biblical account of the Exodus and came across something rather amazing as I was pondering scripture the other day. Allow me to share a revelation with you that can never be exegeted from watching even the greatest of Hollywood films.

Unbeknownst to most, buried deep inside the Book of Exodus is a secret that will change your life for eternity. If you are willing to apprehend it, or should I say, if you are willing to apprehend *Him,* your spiritual life will never be the same. You will be forever altered by the presence of almighty Jehovah. Therefore, I would like to invite you to journey back in time with me. Our destination lies deep inside the desert abyss of Midian, specifically at the foot of Horeb, the Mountain of God. You might want to take your shoes off for this. What lies ahead is holy ground. You are about to witness an incredible encounter while simultaneously discovering the secret of Moses and the "burning bush."

"Now Moses was tending the flock of Jethro his father-in-law, the priest of Midian. And he led the flock to the back of the desert, and came to Horeb, the mountain of God. And the Angel of the Lord appeared to him in a flame of fire from the midst of a bush. So he looked, and behold, the bush was burning with fire, but the bush was not consumed. Then Moses said, 'I will now turn aside and see this great sight, why the bush does not burn.' So when the Lord saw that he turned aside to look, God called to him from the midst of the bush and said, 'Moses, Moses!'"
—Exodus 3:1–4

The Real Moses

Let's start with a little background information on who Moses was at this point in his life. Moses was not the majestic figure portrayed by Charlton Heston. At this point, he was eighty years old. Yes, you read that correctly, eighty years old. Moses was already old when he met Jehovah. He was no longer a prince and he was yet to become a prophet. Just like David, he was a shepherd. (Are you beginning to see a divine theme?)

In truth, Moses was old, ordinary and most likely, just like so many of us, bored and frustrated with whom he had become. Think about that for just a moment, Moses was an ordinary eighty year old man when God decided to call him to perform the greatest work apart from the redemption provided by our Messiah. In fact, Moses is a foreshadowing of our Messiah.

By the way, the Passover, in conjunction with the Promised Land of Israel, was the purpose Moses was called to, not the splitting of the Red Sea, nor any other miracle. The miracles were simply a means to the end of entering into the Promised Land. I am always amazed how the Passover has taken a back seat to the various wonders performed by the hand of Moses. Our tendency to seek God's hands while ignoring His face is legendary and continuously discloses the narcissistic nature of humanity.

The Passover was the pinnacle of miraculous wonder in Moses' day. It was an incredible foreshadowing of the redemptive work that would later be wrought through the blood of Jesus Christ. Do not forget that Jesus *"is the image of the invisible God, **the firstborn** over all creation?"* (Colossians 1:15)

The greatest miracle of Moses' prophetic reign was the liberation from the Angel of Death through the miraculous blood stained doorways of Goshen. While the pangs of death stung the first born of Egypt, all was well with Israel. The blood of the lamb triumphed over death, just as it would for all those grafted into Israel (Romans 11:17) some fifteen hundred years later in Calvary; and just as we are *currently* witnessing, God's chosen people were destined to be gathered together throughout the bounds of the Promised Land.

Let that in itself be the revelation of a divine secret. Moses ministry was for the purpose of salvation. He was a Messianic archetype. Therefore, keep in mind that God does not care about your age. God can use you if you are eight, eighty, one hundred eighty, or anything above or below. God can and will use you when He wants, where He wants, and how He wants with only one prerequisite necessary. You must be willing to put Him first. Talent does not matter, looks do not matter and as you are about to find out, linguistic elegance is irrelevant in the Kingdom of God. God is sovereign and His plan is going to come to pass regardless of through whom He chooses to manifest it.

With that said, let's get back to Moses. Moses had spent the previous forty years of his life living as a shepherd in the mountains of Midian. He was married to Zipporah, the gentile daughter of the Midian Priest, Jethro.

Prior to his time in Midian, Moses was the adopted son of Pharaoh's daughter which made him a prince in the royal court of the most powerful man on earth. As you most likely already know, while Moses was tending to the Hebrew slaves he witnessed one of the Egyptian masters beating his Hebrew brethren. Moses, being completely aware of his heritage, rose up and in a fit of rage killed the Egyptian guard. As you might imagine, this did not sit well with Pharaoh, and thus, his flight to Midian and his eventual marriage to Zipporah, the pagan princess of Midian. The rest, as they say, is history.

If you are like me, you must be thinking, "What an unlikely candidate for a prophet of God. Moses was a rebellious, most likely idolatrous, murderer, married to the pagan daughter of a heathen priest. Aren't God's prophets supposed to be perfect? This Moses dude was a mess. Who would have ever thought—but then again, no one expected the Messiah to be born in food trough either.

Did you know Jesus was born amongst the filthy, smelly mess of farm animals? Jesus was not born in the tidy manger that you see displayed in front of churches, or assembled under your Christmas tree. Jesus was laid in a dirty, smelly trough used to feed livestock. Have you ever smelled the inside of a barn? There were no sparkles, Christmas lights, or plush blankets; just dirt, hay, cow dung, and animal feed. That secret alone speaks miles about the heart of our Father.

Do not believe that Mary and Joseph were perfect either. When Mary and Joseph heard *"there was no room in the Inn,"* (Luke 2:7) I am quite certain their first thought was not, "Well . . . I guess we will just have to sleep in the barn tonight. God has a plan." No way. You will never get me to believe that. Mary must have been like, "Man, this sucks! Joseph, this was your idea. Find me someplace to sleep . . . *now!!!"*

Do you think they were not human? Have you forgotten that Mary was nine and one half months pregnant, hormonal, exhausted, most likely hungry and after a journey like that, undoubtedly well beyond cranky!? If you have ever lived amongst a pregnant woman, especially one so close to giving birth, you know I am right.

I know we have a tendency to put her on a pedestal, but be real for just a moment. Mary's water was on the verge of breaking. I am sure her feet were swollen. She had just traveled for God knows how long on the back of a donkey, which undoubtedly would have rattled the sciatic nerve of any pregnant woman; and to top it all off, then found out she had nowhere to stay upon arrival. Wouldn't you be pissed, as well? Think about how we react to a traffic jam while sitting comfortably in an air conditioned car. Joseph must have made a beeline for the first hiding spot he could find— with Mary's shoe rattling the door behind him. Personally, I must admit that I have lost my temper for much less.

As you progress in your relationship with God, however, you will undoubtedly discover that God has an incredible ability to turn lemons into lemonade, filthy rags into pure gold and incredibly, the inside of a barn into the birthing room of the Messiah. If you read *God Culture,* you will recall our discussion of Joseph, the son of Jacob, and how certain situations arise that are so vital to the plan of Almighty God that He has to remove you from one city, town, job etc . . . and place you into the exact location, situation or circumstance He needs you to be.

For the one being called, it is never pretty, usually comes as a total shock, and quite honestly, is scary as you know what. For Joseph, the son of Jacob, it was prison. (Genesis 39–40) For Isaiah, it was three years of public nakedness! (Isaiah 20:3) How do you think that felt? I write about that in my next book. For Mary, it was being homeless in Bethlehem (to fulfill the prophecy of Micah 5:2) and for Moses, it was the mountainous desert of Midian.

Do you think it was an accident or some random act of chance that Moses found his newly found abode directly at the foot of Mount Horeb, which was also known as, *"The Mountain of God?"* (Exodus 3:1) Incredibly, our holy Father, Yahweh, was simply biding His time. As you are about to discover, *"The secret of the Lord is with those who fear Him, and He will show them His covenant."* (Psalm 25:14) Although he had no idea at the time, and let that be an encouragement to all of you God lovers, the time of Moses' call had arrived.

God was no longer satisfied with Moses tending a flock of sheep in the Midianite desert. Jehovah had a plan for the would be mighty man of God. It was now time for him to tend a much greater flock. His newly appointed task would certainly require an infinitely more mature and patient man than the one who had fled the Egyptian desert forty years prior. The new "flock" was five hundred thousand strong.

No longer was Moses to hear the tranquil bleating of sheep in the wilderness of Midian. Moses ears were about to be consumed with the bleating complaints of five hundred thousand obnoxious Israeli slaves being led into the Egyptian desert to meet their Maker; and as Moses was about to find out, only two of them wanted to be there (Joshua and Caleb). Can you imagine? That sounds a lot like church on Sunday. How on earth has God not blotted out humanity? Are you still yet to realize how incredibly long-suffering our Father is?

With that said, Israel had a secondary problem. They had not heard Yahweh's voice in more than two hundred thirty years. They had no idea who He was—and neither did Moses! That was all about to change though. In the twinkling of an eye and in a flame of fire, God was about to make Himself known to a nation He had never left. God heard their cries all along. The eventual time of delivery had come. Welcome to the wilderness!

A Blaze of Glory

"Now Moses was tending the flock of Jethro his father-in-law, the priest of Midian. And he led the flock to the back of the desert, and came to Horeb, the mountain of God. And the Angel of the Lord appeared to him in a flame of fire from the midst of a bush. So he looked, and behold, the bush was burning with fire, but the bush was not consumed."

"Then Moses said, **'I will now turn aside** and see this great sight, why the bush does not burn.' So **when the Lord saw** that he turned aside to look, God called to him from the midst of the bush and said, 'Moses, Moses!'"

—Exodus 3:3–4

Upon first glance this may not seem all that unusual, but think about what just occurred. All too often we have a tendency to read the Bible as merely a book of stories rather than it being the thoughts and will of Almighty Jehovah. In this instance, Moses was simply going about his normal daily routine, just like you and me. It was the same old-same old, that had been occurring repeatedly for the prior forty years of time. Moses was tending his father-in-law's sheep; just like he did every day of his boring, uneventful new life in Midian.

Like every single one of us, I am sure Moses woke up that day believing he was going out for an ordinary stroll in the desert. In Moses' mind it was routine—wake up, eat breakfast, tend the sheep, go home, go to sleep, and do it all again tomorrow. On this historic day, however, things were radically different. Moses had no idea his life was about to be forever altered and quite honestly, neither did I on the fateful day that Yahweh grabbed hold of me either. As Moses is leading the flock to the back of the desert, something . . . or should I say, *Someone,* caught his eye. Check out the following revelation of God.

The "Burning" Bush

Let's use our imagination's for just a moment. Picture the following chain of events. As Moses is headed down the desert path he notices something strange out of the corner of his eye. It appears to be like some sort of fire but this fire is different. It is radiant. It is beautiful. Something is ablaze in the distance but Moses has not an inkling of what it is. It sort of looks like fire, but there is no crackling and popping emanating from the searing branches, nor does Moses see any smoke billowing into the atmosphere. Something very strange is going on. In fact, it is so odd that it causes Moses to deviate from the path he is on. Moses forgets all about the sheep and begins heading in the direction of Yahweh. Without ever realizing it, Moses is about to come face to face with almighty God!

What is interesting is the words used for "flame" and for "fire" when examining the original Hebrew text. The word translated as "fire" comes from the Hebrew word "esh," pronounced "aysh," and it means "ablaze." The word "flame" comes from the Hebrew word "lehaba," and it means a "blade," similar to the tongues of fire that rested upon the Apostles when they experienced the outpouring of the Holy Spirit. (Acts 2:3)

Therefore, keep in mind that the *"tongues of fire"* (Acts 2:3) that rested upon the disciples on the day of Pentecost was the manifestation, or otherwise stated, the glory of God (Greek word, *glossa*). It was not merely a chemical reaction causing the combustion of some sort of element combined with oxygen from the air.

Amazingly, the literal translation of "glossa" is "the tongue of a nation," or "language," and thus, when empowered by the glorious flaming "glossa" of almighty God, the disciples began to speak in languages that were completely unknown to them. Similarly, when Moses came face to face with the blazing lehaba, or "tongues of fire" at the burning bush, God too began to speak. Isn't that incredible? God's fire is undoubtedly above the ordinary. The fire of God can actually speak!

That, therefore, begs the question; what is it that Moses actually experienced on the *Mountain of God?* As Moses was walking down the path of Horeb, he noticed what appeared to be tongues of blazing fire radiating from the midst of a distant bush. Interestingly enough, the spontaneous combustion of dry dead bushes is somewhat common in the searing hot desert. Therefore, perhaps at first glance nothing seemed out of the ordinary. I know what you are thinking, but it is actually true; desert bushes occasionally, and of their own accord, burst into flames. Unfortunately, I know a bunch of people who believe a similar reaction will occur if they walk through the church door. Although spontaneous combustion is incredible in its own right, this was no extemporaneous event. God's timing in your life is never a random act of chance.

Often times in God culture, that which appears to be spontaneous to a man is actually a carefully laid out plan both created and implemented prior to the foundation of the world as we know it. God meeting Moses at the burning bush was certainly one such example. Just like the birth, death and resurrection of Jesus Christ, God's divine rendezvous with His Messianic archetype had been appointed from time everlasting.

Moses did not just encounter a fire at the burning bush. It was God manifest who awaited Moses at the end of the path, and, as a result, when Moses *"turned aside to look,"* he came face-to-face with the glory of God who was radiantly ablaze, just as He was when Jesus peeled away His earth suit on the Mount of Transfiguration. (Matthew 17:1–3) The sight Moses encountered was not merely a fiery, burning bush, it was the blazing glory of your Father, Jehovah.

Therefore, keep this incredibly important secret in mind. *Moses did not just stumble upon God, and neither will you.* God was in control of every event, circumstance, and, in fact, every step that Moses would ever take. It is not that God was micromanaging Moses. God was quite simply aware of every step that Moses would take throughout his entire life. Just like you and me, when Moses appointed time came to fruition, God met him exactly in the place He had foreordained. For Moses, it was the burning bush in the midst of *Horeb, the Mountain of God.* For you, it will be somewhere else. Although I have no idea where or how God will meet you, I can guarantee that He has you penciled somewhere into His divine appointment book.

God, however, was not forcing Moses to turn. Just like He does with us, God was prodding Moses along while patiently awaiting Moses return. Therefore, keep the following secret in mind as well. *God did not speak until Moses turned toward Him.* The secret to Exodus chapter three is that *God will only speak upon our repentance.*

Prior to our turning, God will prod us along the path of destiny. He will not actually speak, however, until we turn to face Him. Why do think the world believes we are crazy? If you are in Christ, how many times have you heard, "You mean God actually speaks to you?" Repentance is the secret to hearing God. The world does not believe it because they cannot hear Him. God's voice is deafened by sin. In repentance, the glory of God is revealed and our ears are unstopped. In repentance, God speaks. Therefore, take a closer look at what the scripture actually says:

*"Then Moses said, 'I will now turn aside and see this great sight, why the bush does not burn.' **So when the Lord saw** that he turned aside to look, **God called to him** from the midst of the bush and said, 'Moses, Moses!'"*
—Exodus 3:3–4

Once again, take note of the fact that God did not speak until Moses turned His way. The phrase "turn aside," however, does not do justice to Moses decision. "Turn aside" comes from the Hebrew word, "luz." It actually means, "to depart." Moses did not just turn aside and gaze down the path. He did not observe God from afar or even from a "safe" distance. Moses departed from the path he was on and headed directly down the path toward God. He did not stop until he reached his ultimate destination, the burning bush. In fact, he got so close that God commanded Moses to remove His shoes. Moses made it all the way to the holy ground of Jehovah. It was at that moment, and not one second before, that God began to speak—*"Moses, Moses . . ."*

I pray that you all get the revelation I am attempting to communicate. God works the same way in our own personal lives. Only now, *"God, who at various times and in various ways spoke in time past to the fathers by the prophets, **has in these last days spoken to us by His Son."*** (Hebrews 1:1–2) Therefore, through Jesus Christ anyone and everyone can enter His presence. In Christ, anyone and everyone can hear God's voice.

Think about why. In Christ, sin is no longer an issue. By the blood of Christ your sin has been rescinded. The second you make Jesus your Lord you can enter the presence of God and hear Him speak. In Christ, the barrier between God and man has been broken down. Jesus escorts us all the way to holy ground. However, it seems to take a wilderness experience to point us in the right direction, which is not Jerusalem, Mecca, New York or any city made with hands. The wilderness always points us to the cross.

Let's not take lightly what actually occurred in the life of Moses. Moses' departure from the path was an act of repentance. The word, "repent" means to turn one hundred eighty degrees from the path your life was on. Repentance is the only way out of the wilderness.

As Moses was strolling through Horeb, God caused a change in his life. When Moses turned toward God, he turned away from Midian. The burning bush was a crossroad for Moses. It was the point of singularity that every believer must encounter, but none is forced to choose.

With each subsequent meeting, the Spirit of Jehovah only intensified in His life. As you are about see, this type of encounter only happens in the wilderness. In the wilderness, Moses became so full of the Almighty that God radiated out of him. Later, as Moses descended from the wilderness of Sinai, His face shone like the sun. Because of the sinful Israelites before Him, Moses actually had to wear a veil. (Exodus 34:33–35) Just like God, they were unable to gaze upon his countenance. He had become a fore-shadowing of both the redeemed and the Redeemer. Moses became the temple of the living God.

With that in mind, what if Moses had responded to the burning bush the same way the modern-day Christian responds to the call of God. All too often, we attempt to encounter God from a distance. We catch a glimpse of God's glory out of the corner of our eye. Sometimes, we even turn to face Him. That, however, is all too often where our journey with God ends. We never make it to holy ground.

Let me give you an example of what I mean. I recently watched the movie *War Room.* I must say that this was one of the best Christian movies I have ever seen, but there is an applicable reason as to why I bring it up. I would venture to guess that nearly everyone watching the movie has the following thought enter their mind at some point during the viewing, "I should create my own war room." Although it is a noble thought, it is merely gazing at Jehovah from afar. How many of us will make it all the way to the holy ground of actually doing it?

Christianity is not simply about going to church on Sunday. It is about accomplishing the foreordained will of God and transforming every life we encounter from the path to hell to the glory of heaven. Therefore, with God remaining silent in our lives, we never head down the path that leads to glory. We remain distant, observing, but never really doing. Because we are yet to come face to face with God, we never actually hear His voice calling our names and directing our lives. We are, therefore, unable to fully accomplish His will.

As a result, the "Israelites" in our lives, who are enslaved by *"all that is in the world—the lust of the flesh, the lust of the eyes, and the pride of life,"* (1 John 2:16) never encounter their divinely appointed deliverer's who have been assigned to cry out to the Pharaoh's of today's world, *"Let my people go!"* (Exodus 9:1)

Jump In!

Consider God's direction to Joshua as the Israelite's were about to cross the Jordan River and enter the Promised Land. This too occurred in the wilderness.

> *"And the Lord said to Joshua, 'This day I will begin to exalt you in the sight of all Israel, that they may know that, as I was with Moses, so I will be with you. You shall command the priests who bear the ark of the covenant, saying, 'When you have come to the edge of the water of the Jordan, **you shall stand in the Jordan.'"***
> **—Joshua 3:7–8**

Once again, make a mental note that the Israeli Priests were not commanded to stand on the bank of the river. They were not instructed to merely observe God's Word. Learning the Word of God is simply not enough to fulfill your call. You must become a doer in God's kingdom.

> *"But be doers of the word, and not hearers only, **deceiving yourselves."***
> **—James 1:22**

Notice that accomplishing only half of the task is the equivalent of deception. God is not a half way God, He is an all in God. The cross would require nothing less. Imagine what eternity would be like if Jesus never left the Garden of Gethsemane. What if Jesus said, *"Nevertheless, not my will, but yours be done,"* (Luke 22:42) and failed to show up at the cross. Certainly no one would be able to argue against Jesus both knowing and understanding the will of the Father. The work of the cross, however, was not complete until the blood was shed. God's will for your life follows the same pattern. Your task is not complete until you actually *do* the Father's will.

God instructed the Priests bearing the Ark of the Covenant to step into the water. He commanded that they actually stand in the river. Although this may seem trivial, or perhaps even simple, keep in mind that the Jordan river had reached its flood stage. The raging current would have been on par with swimming in a flash flood. How is that for a wilderness experience? Jumping in was an act of incredible faith. I am one hundred percent sure that they fully expected to be swept away. Yet they stepped into the river anyway. Faith in action is always where the power of God resides. Watch what happens as the Priests obey our Lord.

> *"So it was, when the people set out from their camp to cross over the Jordan, with the priests bearing the ark of the covenant before the people, and as those who bore the ark came to the Jordan,* **and the feet of the priests** *who bore the ark* **dipped in the edge of the water** *(for the Jordan overflows all its banks during the whole time of harvest), that the waters which came down from upstream* **stood still, and rose in a heap** *very far away at Adam, the city that is beside Zaretan. So the waters that went down into the Sea of the Arabah, the Salt Sea, failed, and were cut off;* **and the people crossed over opposite Jericho.** *"*
> **—Joshua 3:14–16**

This incident is incredibly relevant to answering the call of God. Just like Moses, the Priests under Joshua's command had to get in the water before anything occurred. There was no manifestation of God as they stood at the bank of the river. They could have waited from now until doomsday, crying for the river to split both day and night and for the power of God to manifest while standing on the shore. They could have yelled at the river, commanded the river, taken authority over the river, claimed victory over the river, or used whatever religious techniques the pop culture false prophets of their day taught them to use. In truth, however, the river was not going to split until they actually stepped in. Until they did, the power of God remained dormant.

Amazingly, the second their little toes hit the water the power of God manifested, the Jordan split, and the entry way to the Promised Land broke open. Since God never changes, (Malachi 3:6) I have to believe this is still true today. Therefore, whatever doctrines we have implemented, argued over and allowed to divide Christianity into factions, only one concept remains true. Whether it is due to ignorance or rebellion, today's "believer" has simply refused to answer the call. We are yet to stand in the water. Therefore, not only does the Promised Land remain distant and inaccessible, unrighteousness dominates our darkened, sin-stained worldview as God is sidelined by humanism.

Jesus Had To …

Do not forget that even Jesus had to have a wilderness experience. Whether you like this or not, if Jesus had to, so do you. The wilderness is where God shapes your spiritual personality. The wilderness is where God divinely intervenes in your life and burns off the dross of the world. Therefore, let's take a look at the wilderness experience of our one and only Messiah. Let's follow Jesus into the wilderness.

*"Then Jesus, being **filled with the Holy Spirit**, returned from the Jordan and was led **by the Spirit** into the wilderness, being tempted for forty days by the devil."*

—**Luke 4:1–2**

And you think your wilderness experience is difficult? I am sure that you just read right past the pre-cross misery of Jesus Christ. "Oh, forty days of temptation ... how nice." Seriously, this is how we read the Bible. "Oh, Jesus sweat blood ... is that even possible? Let me check the medical journal," is how we discount the suffering of the one who saved us.

Do you realize that Jesus spent forty long days being tempted by Satan? Do you think that was fun? Do you understand how vicious Satan is? It was Satan who influenced men such as Adolph Hitler, Joseph Stalin, Charles Manson and whomever you may consider to be the most vile human beings to ever walk the blue planet. Most of us are afraid to face one second in the presence of evil. Jesus faced the author of *Helter Skelter* for forty straight days.

Let me break that down for you. Forty days equals 960 hours. 960 hours equals 57,600 minutes. 57,600 minutes equals 3,456,000 seconds. Do you still think this was easy? Have you ever noticed how long a minute is when you are miserable? The next time you feel ill, or even bored, think about your predicament increased by a factor of several thousand and lasting for 57,600 minutes. In fact, to get a real sense of the duration try counting to 3,456,000. That is how long Jesus had to face the constant torment of the most evil being in all of creation, without a speck of food or a drop of water, by the way.

Think about it, for forty days Jesus did not eat or drink, He was abandoned in the wilderness, but never once did He attempt to avoid the experience. In fact, Jesus embraced His dilemma. Even while in the midst of horrendous torment Jesus never shut down. He did not attempt to hide or even avoid Satan. He faced Satan headlong, courageously but carefully, while persistently wielding both the Word and authority of God. As you are about to discover, in the end He obliterated Satan.

Incredibly, through this experience we find the exact opposite of what most Christian's believe in regard to the wilderness. Most modern day Christian's believe their wilderness experience is an attack from Satan. Nothing can be further from the truth. Although you will most certainly encounter Satan in the wilderness, take note of who led Jesus into the abyss. It was not Satan, it was the Holy Spirit.

Therefore, this could not be an attack of Satan. It had to be an attack *on* Satan. Think about it. Satan was doing what he always does—tempting the flesh. In this instance, however, it was God on the attack. Contrary to what you may think, God was not attacking Jesus, just as He was not attacking Job during his time of great trial. God was using Satan to attack their sin, or to be more precise, and particularly in the case of Jesus Christ, God was attacking their potential for sin. The goal was to eradicate sin from their lives, but here is the vital secret; *He was using the devil to do it.*

Just like Adam, Jesus had a choice. The temptation could have never been real otherwise. Therefore, this was an act of purification. God was sanctifying His only begotten Son. The Father was obliterating Satan from the life of Jesus Christ and that is exactly what every wilderness experience is designed to do. Only upon His deliverance from the wilderness could Jesus face the much greater challenge of the cross. Therefore, make note of the following revelation.

First and foremost, and what I have found to be an incredible secret of the Father, is that *Jesus was not led into the wilderness until He was **first** filled with the Holy Spirit.* Read the above scripture again. It is true. Therefore, if you are yet to have your wilderness experience, perhaps you ought to check on your relationship with the Holy Spirit. Have you let Him in?

If you think about it, it makes perfect sense. The wilderness experience is not designed to destroy you. It is designed to perfect you. Therefore, the truth of God is that He will always equip you *before* sending you into the wilderness to be tempted and tried. How else could you pass the test? *"Apart from Him we can do nothing."* (John 15:5)

Secondly, the scripture is clear that this was not designed by the devil as an attempt to put an end to the Messiah. The wilderness experience is never the devil's design. It is not even his idea. The wilderness is always designed by God. The devil, as always, never had a chance at victory. He was being used by God. Therefore, according to the scripture, it was not the devil that led Jesus into the wilderness, it was the Holy Spirit.

The wilderness experience always has a divine purpose in your life. In the case of Jesus, He had to confront the same adversary and pass the same test that the original man, Adam, failed. In doing so, Jesus made it clear that *"the first man Adam became a living being, but the last Adam **became a life-giving spirit.**"* (1 Corinthians 15:45) By enduring the wilderness experience, Jesus, who in the flesh was one hundred percent human, proved Himself worthy to pay the redemption price for humanity. In doing so, He purchased our eternal lives.

Perhaps you are thinking that there must be a better way for God to accomplish His will. If so, check out the result of Jesus' time in the wilderness.

*"**Then** Jesus returned **in the power of the Spirit** to Galilee, and news of Him went out through all the surrounding region."*
—Luke 4:14

That is the purpose of the wilderness experience. The wilderness empowered Jesus for the task to come. The temptations were specifically designed for the divine task that Jesus alone could accomplish. The same holds true for you.

*"Blessed is the man who endures temptation; **for when he has been approved,** he will receive the crown of life which the Lord has promised to those who love Him."*

—James 1:12

In the wilderness, we discover the will of God for our lives. Therefore, only one question remains; what is the purpose of your individual wilderness experience? If you dare follow His will and are yet to have one, beware, it *is* coming.

With that said, it is time to get close to God. Begin praying. Learn the Word of God and begin worshipping His holy name. Invite the Holy Spirit to fill you and reconnect you to your Maker. You will need to be intimate with God to prosper in the wilderness. That takes time and it takes diligence. I know that you may not like hearing this, but the secret of the wilderness is that *we all must go.* God has a wilderness experience designed for everyone.

Thus, just like both Jesus and Moses, Christianity finds itself at a crossroad. The great I AM is calling—waiting to anoint the church with His holy fire. The question is, will Christianity turn aside to see God? In truth, only time will tell. I must, however, let you know that it all begins with you. Will you dip your feet into *"the rivers of living water?"* (John 7:38) Christianity always has and always will be propagated one believer at a time. In a world of mega churches and pop culture Christianity, that too has become a secret. Therefore, let's move on and discover the keys to unlocking the kingdom of heaven.

CHAPTER 3

Dreams and Imagination

(THE SECRET OF THE IMAGE)

Have you ever noticed that something seems to occur in adults that crushes our childhood dreams? I have often wondered why this happens. Perhaps it is the veracity of real world pressure that consumes our every waking moment while stalking the elusive American dream, or whatever your culture's most valued prize is.

For some reason, the worldly pursuits and desires of adulthood seem to suck the life and imagination right out of humanity. In the face of family responsibilities, the adolescent dreams of youth begin to seem immature and perhaps even childish. In the wake of responsibility, the prospect of failure becomes too harsh of a reality to face head on. To justify our escape, we proclaim to have grown up, and out, of our unattainable youthful fantasies. Therefore, as the bellow of greatness that exists inside of every human soul is quietly asphyxiated, we settle for the whispers of mediocrity. As ambition gives way to hopelessness, the devil smiles an eerie yet joyful grin. Another dream has died.

Is complacency really a necessity of maturity? I spent the better part of my youth dreaming of playing basketball against my childhood heroes. When I was not on the court I was imagining all the places I would go and the great things that I would accomplish in my life. To this very day, I still have so many dreams.

In fact, if you are reading this book series you are smack dab in the middle of one. It has been a dream of mine to have this series published and placed into the hands of every man, woman and child with whom God desires to communicate. The fact that you are reading this book is a testament to the greatness and glory of God. On my own, I am incapable of accomplishing such a monumental task. I didn't even *like* English class. What is even more exciting is that if *"God shows no partiality,"* (Romans 2:11 and Acts 10:34) and has caused my dreams to come true, He will do the same for you.

Something seems to go terribly wrong, however, as we age. It seems that the game of life has a way of beating the imagination out of us, thus causing us to abandon our hopes and dreams. I want you to know that settling for ordinary conventionalism is not God's will for your life. God has created you for greatness—a greatness that only *He* can define and *you* can fulfill. His idea of greatness is for you to accomplish the hopes and dreams He has implanted in your heart. Your dream, and the ability to fulfill it, is a unique gift fashioned only for you. You cannot fulfill someone else's destiny.

Therefore, I have one compelling question to ask you. Do you still have a dream? If you do not, I would strongly encourage you to look deep inside your heart and resurrect one. The kingdom of God is depending on it. *"Where there is no vision the people perish."* (Proverbs 29:18) Another translation of the Bible says it this way, *"Where there is no vision the people cast off restraint."* To understand why this is so important, I even dare to say urgent, let's spend a few minutes breaking down the meaning of this short but infinitely valuable piece of scripture. In it, you will find the secret to God culture.

Dare to Daydream

The word translated "vision," or "revelation," is the Hebrew word chazown, *khaw-zone.* No, not Calzone... that's a lump of bread, meat and cheese that makes you fat. Although I love Italian food, that is certainly not the topic of discussion here. The meaning of chazown is that of a dream, a revelation or a vision. Its context connotes a mental state of dreaming and not the actual night dreams that you have while in a R.E.M. state of sleep. Having a chazown is the equivalent of having vision for your life. Although God can and does speak to people through night dreams, which was how God warned Joseph the father of Jesus both to keep Mary after discovering she was pregnant and to go to Egypt to avoid the slaughter of the Messiah, when we have chazown God speaks to us through our *daydreams!* In God culture, spacing out is a heavenly exercise.

Unfortunately, adulthood breeds a misunderstanding that causes us to abandon a vital tool that God has implanted within each of us. Receiving vision and revelation from God requires the use of our imaginations. Apart from sexual fantasy's, many adults seem to lose the ability to visualize. We forget how to imagine.

The hole left in your dream's wake has caused humanity to build an entire industry around personal coaches reteaching this valuable childhood skill. For those unwilling to engage God culture, New Age Mysticism and every form of Satanic deception is more than willing to fill in the gaps. The abandonment of imagination has not just caused a lack of vision for our own lives, it has propagated a separation from the will of God.

Keep in mind that imagination and fantasy are two separate animals. Imagination, when used properly, is a powerful spiritual gift. Without it, we lose the ability to perceive God's will. *"Where there is no vision the people perish."* Living in a fantasy world, on the other hand, will always lead one down the road to perdition.

I would venture to guess that the most successful people you know are those with the greatest vision and imagination, even *if* they lack faith in God. Manifesting vision into reality is a spiritual law placed in motion by Yahweh. It is no different than the turning of the earth or the expansion of the universe. It is the essence of humanity and what separates human beings from every other class of primate. Therefore, it will work for anyone bold enough to implement and harness its power.

God has planted imagination within you as a tool for accomplishing His will. Do not get me wrong, I am not saying that you are imagining that God speaks to you. I *am* saying that God often times uses your imagination to communicate His greater will. The revelation, or vision, you receive from God is absolutely real and so are your dreams, in a visionary sense, when you pursue them. The use of your imagination, as well as, your subconscious mind is God's conduit for manifesting His supernatural revelation into the physical realm in which we reside.

Imagination, coupled with the prompting of the Holy Spirit, is what drives your body into physical action. You must use your God given authority and talent, which we have previously defined as the blessing of God, to bring God's will to pass. That is how dreams become reality. To avoid being misunderstood, I will demonstrate this to you shortly from the Word of God.

The second part of Proverbs 29:18 states that without this revelation, the people, in a collective sense, perish, which means are destroyed and can apply to both physical and spiritual death. In actuality, however, the true meaning of the Hebrew word translated as "perish" is not an instantaneous death. Its literal meaning is to "cast off restraint," which after careful study communicates that the people, culture or society begins the process of "loosening" and, thus, experiencing the long drawn out process of death caused by the effects of sin.

> *"But each one is tempted when he is drawn away by his own desires and enticed. Then, when desire has conceived, it gives birth to sin; and sin, when it is full-grown, brings forth death."*
> **—Romans 1:14–15**

In other words, they slowly drift away from the will of God. It is like the lug nuts loosening on one of the wheels of your automobile. At first, you do not even notice. In time, however, the wheel slowly begins to wobble, becoming progressively worse until all of a sudden it falls off and you find yourself in the middle of a car accident.

In terms of modern culture, can you see what is happening? Without ever realizing it, the wobble has become a wreck and we have woken up in Sodom and Gomorrah. I recently read that the once great city of New York has erected its first masturbation booth smack dab on the corner of Twenty Eighth Street and Fifth Avenue—and it is being applauded. Over one hundred shameless perverts visited the *Guy-Fi* booth on its first day of operation. Can you imagine the shame of exiting such a booth on a jam packed New York City street? What sort of person has the gaul to actually use a *Guy-Fi* booth? Although it has been revealed to be a publicity stunt by a sex shop, do you see how deplorable our culture has become? Sexual shame no longer exists and we are about to experience the hand of God as a result.

> *"Were they ashamed when they had committed abomination? No! They were not at all ashamed; **nor did they know how to blush.** Therefore*

they shall fall among those who fall; at the time I punish them, they shall be cast down," says the Lord."
—Jeremiah 6:15–16

America and the West need to take note. Not only is this the direction we are headed, we have apparently reached our destination. The "American Dream" has become the abandonment of God.

Child Abandonment

To illustrate our loosening, I would like you to consider something very serious. Cast off your political bent for just a moment and peer honestly into our nation's past. When did our modern culture begin to loosen, that is, to cast off restraint? If you are above the age of fifty, you must have noticed the "recent" change in both American and world cultures? If you are under fifty, you probably do not know the difference.

Therefore, I will enlighten you. The American process of loosening began with the social programs of the 1930's and began using steroids under the progressive ideology of the 1960's. Progressive liberalism has culminated in the years 2000 and beyond with the same hippy generation seizing control of the nation's political agenda, media and government, and thus the flow of information and propaganda.

Watching world news outside of America is an incredible experience. American public propaganda is mind boggling. With the cooperation of the media, the American government has stolen the entire nation. What was intended to be government of the people by the people has become control of the people by the government. The United States constitution was intended to grant control of the government to the people. With the onset of a plethora of amendments, including the unintended right to tax the people, the tables have been turned. The government now controls you. You are now subject to their every whim.

If you believe you are free, try not paying any one of the manifold taxes that have been imposed upon the public. They will take your property, your money and ultimately your freedom. In fact, just try putting a deck on your house without a variance. You will very quickly find out that true freedom, even over property that you allegedly own, is a mere pipe dream. With government imposed health insurance now classified by the United States Supreme Court as the latest and greatest tax, you are no longer even free to choose how to spend your own hard earned money. The IRS has already spent it for you. Resistance is futile. Pay the penalty. The death march of freedom has begun.

What was once the land of the free has been swallowed up by the IRS, media, and government "regulated" financial institutions. All have been solidified by government social intervention and a public revamping of the national educational system. They teach you how to think, how to act, how to vote and how to believe. Those in opposition are labeled as bigots to gather you back into the herd. The government sponsored intimidation has shackled the hearts, minds and freedom of the entire nation.

With the "Generation X'ers" having been fully indoctrinated the political and cultural shift has washed in like a flood. You have been enslaved by the system and morally inculcated to believe exactly what they want you to believe. Thus, as I stated in a previous writing, for the first time in American history gay marriage has the majority support of the public.

If the above realization came as a surprise, the following revelation will really open your blind eyes. America is not alone its quest for control. Western government's have covertly sought and seized control of the spirit, soul and body of your most precious asset—your children, whom they indoctrinate for no less than six hours per day, five days per week, nine months per year, through the most powerful government agency on the planet—the public educational system.

Do you think the NEA (National Education Association) is looking out for your children's best interest? The teacher's, in some ways . . . your kids? No way! Why else would they compel a teacher's strike when they do not get their way? Do you think that is for the kids? Have you ever heard of the NEA striking over the curriculum? Of course not. How do you think books like *Heather Has Two Mommy's,* or similar publication's make it into the nation's pubic educational system. It is always for the best interest of the organization. The NEA is a propaganda machine. They have two purposes, labor and propaganda. Everything else is smoke and mirrors.

The average parent, by the way, spends less than thirty minutes of quality time per day with their children. With that in mind, who would you say has more influence over your children, you or the government? If you do not know, ask them a few questions. Their answers may shock you.

Coup D'etat

Sadly, *"We the People"* not only allowed this to occur, we conspired with the godless through the use of the governments second greatest outlet for change—the institutions known as higher learning. Yes, I am referring to the College's and University's of our rapidly declining nation.

Many of you may get upset when I proclaim that our once dominant nation is currently in a global tailspin. Therefore, here are a few eye opening statistics to feast your eyes upon. According to *Ranking America,* the United States, who was once the world leader in education and development, now ranks fourteenth in overall education. We have skyrocketed to second, however, in global ignorance in regard to social issues such as teen pregnancy, unemployment rates, and voting patterns. America is thirty-third in internet download speeds and have fallen to a whopping twenty-fourth in literacy. I was shocked to see that we have fallen to seventy-fourth in girls going to grade school and eighty-fifth in boys going to grade school! We are seventeenth in educational performance and have slid to eleventh in fourth grade math. We are twenty-third in our PISA science score.

The great scientist Michio Kaku, Professor of Theoretical Physics at the City College of New York, recently stated that one hundred percent of his PhD students are from abroad. In fact, he also stated that if all the H1b visa workers in the United States went home, our creation of new industry would all but cease and our economy would utterly collapse.

My question is, what did we expect to happen when we ousted Yahweh? Did we think it would cause the nation to prosper? The result has been a progressively educated generation that has removed Yahweh from the public square, and you, or should I say we, being a part of the voting public, helped oust Him. Do you know how? The same propagandized public that has graduated from the radically progressive schools and University's have come to a near unanimous agreement regarding the deceptive constitutional interpretation known as the *Separation of Church and State*. Yes, the devil is still *"more cunning than any beast of the field which the Lord God had made."* (Genesis 3:1) The rest, as they say, is history. "Love the one your with" (Crosby, Still and Nash) replaced *"Love your neighbor as yourself,"* (Mark 12:31) and became the generation's new mantra.

Do not be fooled. These two visions may sound similar but they are diametrically opposed to one another. False love, otherwise known as lust, is now controlling world cultures. The command of God fosters respect, purity and justice. The pop cultural slogan of the 1960's is merely a licentious mask that transforms the true meaning of love into uncontrolled hedonistic lust. With God out of the way, immorality spills into society like the shattered tanks of the Valdez oil spill. The blackened coating of sin suffocates every soul in its path.

Please understand that the intention of this discussion is not to be a political commentary. This actually is a theological discussion. Unfortunately, or fortunately, depending upon your viewpoint, ideologies come crashing together when discussing the culture of Yahweh.

Any reference to "liberal" ideology is to denote the change in society as opposed to those desiring to conserve the "old way," for lack of a better term. The word "liberal," according to *dictionary.com,* means "favorable to progress or reform, as in political or religious affairs." Recently the term "progressive," obviously denoting progress, has become the synonymous norm.

In the Western world, the death of God Almighty, as some have deemed it, has been both a political and religious reform that has changed the entire thought process of the progressive nation and world in which we now live. Even the modern church has extinguished the power of the Almighty. Modern cultures are moving beyond the old ways of God and New Age Mysticism, or perhaps, even, worse, "the Religion of Peace" having adopted the murderous ways of Satan is filling the hole left in Yahweh's wake. Since the beginning of the public execution of Yahweh every generation has grown a bit looser, casting off a little more restraint, until our children are not even safe in their own homes, neighborhoods, and sadly enough, in their schools.

Sad But True

Over the past twenty-five years or so, we have seen something appalling begin to escalate. Namely, when you send your precious children, the most beloved objects of your affection, into the public schools of America, and many other countries for that matter, there is no guarantee they will come home alive.

If you do not believe that, just ask the elementary school parents in Amish country Pennsylvania, or the high school parents of Columbine High School in Colorado. Ask the parents of the students of Northern Illinois University or Virginia Technical University. How about the parents of the precious young children of Newtown, Connecticut? This is not just an American problem either. Internationally, Russia and France immediately come to mind as having experienced similar tragedies as well. I am sure there are many others.

I have three children of my own. If I did not have faith in God this would terrify me. Do you remember the good old days when the suicidal would only kill *themselves?* Nowadays, the suicidal "Me Generation" has become viciously homicidal. The new face of personal demonism has become insistent upon taking as many innocent people as possible with them. Through violence, greed, abortion, pornography, and the like, people from the baby boom generation on down have cast off all restraint. We have devalued the miracle of human life and thus, defined a new morality. In the name of progress, we have taught our children to kill.

Don't worry if you are a parent. The children you have so diligently sheltered and allowed the television to baby sit have been sufficiently indoctrinated by Hollywood, MTV and video games to efficiently spread the gospel of "progress." Unbeknownst to many, the media has also seized control of our nation and our world's imaginations. Their subliminal form of mind control does not discriminate and reaches to the four corners of the globe. I challenge you to uncover what your children find acceptable within the "new normal." As I stated earlier, you would be shocked to learn the thoughts and intents of their hearts.

The fruit of this defiled harvest is now being reaped and is manifesting itself in the cultural norm of "anything goes." Just ask the Supreme Court of the United States of America. Morality has been broken down along side the monument of the Ten Commandments. The laws of God have been replaced with the statue of Baphomet as the new symbol of freedom in America while Hollywood and the media flood our senses with Satan's lustful will on daily basis. Perhaps you yourself have become so desensitized that you barely even noticed the change. Wouldn't it be nice if the gospel of Jesus Christ was spread with the same voracity? Perhaps one day we will awaken from our cultural stupor. Pandora's box, however, has been opened. Can it ever be shut?

Dare to Dream

Does that mean there is no hope? Of course not. *"Now may **the God of hope** fill you with all joy and peace **in believing,** that you may **abound in hope** by the power of the Holy Spirit."* (Romans 15:13) There is still time to overcome our cultural nightmare. We must, however, recapture the imaginations of our people, young and old alike. We must point them back in the direction of God. The first step to solving any problem is recognizing that you have one.

Video games, movies, computers, media, music and as you now know, the educational system, has polluted the imaginations of the masses, not to mention the drug dealing politicians and doctors who prescribe anti-depressants and other mood altering drugs to every theologically illiterate soul that wanders through their office doors. I know several people, my wife included, that are perfectly healthy and to whom doctors have recommended anti-depressants, simply because they were not in a "happy" mood that day, or even during a particular season of life.

As a society we need to wake up. We are not supposed to be emotionally happy all the time. Problems, and having to deal with them, are completely normal. Seasons of sadness always have and always will be part of the human experience.

> *"To everything **there is a season,** a time for **every purpose** under heaven: a time to be born, a time to die; a time to plant and a time to pluck what is planted; a time to kill and a time to heal; a time to break down and a time to build up; **a time weep and a time to laugh; a time to mourn and a time to dance**…*
> —**Ecclesiastes 3:1–4**

Joy is not the absence of pain. Joy is the presence of the Holy Spirit who will guide and strengthen you through each and every situation. That includes when you are happy, sad, angry or glad, and everything else in between.

Altered States

Before you go crazy and accuse me of ignorance, I do realize that there are chemical imbalances that need to be dealt with. I also believe that God has given us the wisdom to use every resource, prescription drugs included, to resolve our problems. However, they are not for every situation or person and my belief is that they are a last resort and not a first; unless the patient is suicidal or potentially harmful to others.

Isn't it just like Satan to pervert God's goodness, especially with something as potentially miraculous as prescription drugs? Isn't that the only power he truly has? All he *can* do is pervert the gifts and blessings God has bestowed upon His people.

Therefore, in the name of clinical depression he uses the medical system to alter even the minds of the healthy. Why? For Satan to accomplish his will amongst mankind he needs you to abandon your God-given gift of imagination. He needs you to be sedated and in a state of mental apathy.

He uses drugs, both prescription and recreational, to keep you in a drug induced haze. Have you ever thought about the implied meaning of the word "recreation?" "Re-creation..." Recreation is an attempt to momentarily recreate the pleasures of life. As human beings we accomplish this by constructing a temporary fantasy through vacations, sporting events, games, drug and alcohol abuse, and now more than ever due to the internet, pornography.

Satan is well aware of the fact that once the mind altering, hallucinogenic, fog lifts, you will recognize his devices and begin to dream again. Therefore, through the use of substance abuse he attempts to re-create a new normal in your mind. Whether or not the drugs modifying your consciousness are recreational or prescription, and believe it or not, he will even use the endorphins released by your brain, when misused they promote one common and unified goal. Deep within your new altered state your motivation begins to wane and your dreams slowly slip into the blackout of unconsciousness. Unlike sobering up, however, in the perpetual hangover of addiction your dreams never come to. They simply flat line and die. Game over. You lose!

Media Twisted

Although Lucifer has perverted the gift of imagination from the time of the Garden of Eden, over the last fifty plus years he has intensified his efforts. He has influenced mankind to the point of actually changing our thought process. Technology and media have been huge factors in both the world's progress and Lucifer's hostile takeover of humanity. Many may disagree with me, but I would go as far as to place the young generation's addiction to video games, internet and smart phones in the same category as the drug addiction I described above. Lucifer has embarked upon a technological revolution—a coup d'état for the hearts and minds of mankind. When you consider the time wasted on the computer, video games, and as of late, chasing around imaginary creatures, he appears to be winning.

I am amazed by how isolated and socially inept many of our young people have become. Some never even look up from their not so smart phones when spoken to, or worse yet, crossing the street. South Korea is actually in the process of passing legislation requiring its citizen's to look up from their phones when crossing the street. Can you imagine? In my day we had a term for people with so little sense—stupid! You cannot be so judgmental, however, in the world's version of the new normal.

Incredibly, I have personally witnessed several young folks become startled when an unfamiliar adult says something as simple as "hello" to them. I suppose that is somewhat understandable given all the godless whacko's, pedophiles and rapists roaming the streets today, but c'mon, if you kept your eyes even slightly forward, hello would not be so terrifying. Human behavior is evolving before our very eyes and not for the betterment of the species.

World culture's have become utterly desensitized to sin. Violence and sexual immorality has become the norm. I will never forget watching an episode of the then hit show *Glee* with my then adolescent daughter. As the plot shifted from hotel room to hotel room, I was appalled to witness the glorification and encouragement of fornication, adultery and homosexuality contained within one episode, and most within a five minute span of time. It was as if Satan was firing an M-16 into our living room.

I was absolutely astounded to watch the incredibly cute and seemingly "shy" main character jump from bed to bed, promoting outright harlotry. My guess would be that she has no idea how the influence of her character is contributing to the degradation of society. She, along with the rest of society trying to *Keep Up With the Kardashian's,* is no doubt blinded by fame and money.

Keep in mind that the show was geared toward and based upon *High School* students! The only sexual sin(s), if I can still use that simple three letter word, not covered were bestiality and pedophilia. I suppose they were saving that for the following season. The unfortunate death via heroine overdose of one of the shows star's put an end to that, however. That alone is the tragic truth of our pop cultural progress.

Since Ellen Degeneres broke the gay barrier, nearly every new television show aired on primetime slots includes some form of homosexuality. What is most disturbing is that most young people do not even notice anything wrong. **"Not that there's anything wrong with it . . ."** **—Seinfeld** is considered progress and is both encouraged and applauded. Folks, there *is* something wrong with it. It is toebah!

While we are on the subject, college students no longer need to go to their local drug store to face the "embarrassment" of buying condoms either. In today's world, they simply sashay over to the student center. My daughter's college has a giant bowl filled with them on the first table you see—and they are free. They did not even put it away for parents day. To be fair, this is true of nearly every College and University in the country. Can it get any better to a testosterone crazed, virile young man who also has the cooperation of both the University and the young girls committed to such a higher form of "learning?"

The multicolored basket of fornication looks as inviting as a pillow-case full of Halloween candy. To a sexually revolutionized teen age guy, and sadly nowadays, to a teen age girl as well, its like "heaven"—until the break up occurs, or even worse, the hung over walk of shame from the guy's room back to the lady's dorm that occurs from the previous night's drunken black out. Excuse me, that is no longer true either. Today's walk of shame only needs to span the distance of three doors down. Guys and girls live on the same floor in the new normal. They have even taken away the fun and excitement of attempting to sneak into the lady's dorm. Can anyone really argue that the lack God has not caused the people loosen?

Hold on for just a moment. Just when you thought it was over the story gets far worse. My daughter's "school" also brought in a porn star to publicly celebrate her female "empowerment" and her taking "control" over her own body. Control? Really? Did they mention that the majority of porn stars are also drug addicted sex slaves that will never again have a fruitful sexual relationship. Of course not. That could damage the institution's satanically inspired progressive agenda. Just love the one your with and if you get pregnant kill the baby. That may sound harsh, but, yes, that is the modern message. It is the hard truth behind a woman's right to choose? The youth of the world have been completely anesthetized to sin. In their eyes, sin no longer exists, and, therefore, the killing of an innocent unborn child is not just okay, it is encouraged.

It is utterly astounding how in such a relatively short period of time we have strayed from the truth. Think about it, society tolerated the presence of God for approximately five thousand, nine hundred-sixty six years. It is only in the last fifty that we have purged the Lord from our culture. The expulsion of everything pure is the fruit of our labor.

The Word of God is very clear about what results when this occurs. *"As a man thinks in his heart, so he is."* (Proverbs 23:7) We are watching the culmination of this scripture play out before our very eyes. The media has conned the public into believing sin no longer exists and that God is hatred and not love. Christianity is purported to be nothing more than a platform for the homophobe and racist. If it feels good, do it. There is no right, wrong or absolute truth in the new normal and if God is truly loving and merciful He would never condemn one persons "love" for another.

Although it sounds both good and holy, this doctrine obliterates morality. It is as far from God, and as sinfully cunning, as Lucifer himself is. God is not condemning love. He is defining sin. As I recently stated, for the first time in world history the majority of the public is in favor of gay marriage. If you dissent from the opinion of the "tolerant" you are a bigot. Intimidation is the tactic and where do you think intimidation originated, in heaven or in hell? In today's new normal God is the bigot. Therefore, if you follow His ways, so are you.

My call to action is not for the hatred or persecution of homosexuals, nor any sinner for that matter. The gospel does not promote, nor condone the hatred of any sinner. In fact, it is quite the opposite. We must reintroduce the sinner to the love and righteousness of our creator. Because God's law has been effectively removed from society and the moral lines have not just been blurred, but vanquished, many believe God is dead—or if He is alive, He hates them. Do not fret over this. The true meaning of revival is "life from the dead." Revival is a resurrection from death to life. As former Washington Bullets basketball coach **Dick Motta** so aptly proclaimed, **"The opera isn't over until the fat lady sings."** Although that saying is highly offensive to the politically correct new normal, and although the "fat lady" may be warming up, she is yet to utter her first note.

With that said, we are beginning to see the fruit of immorality manifest en masse not only in America, but all over the world. Therefore, it is time for the people of God to turn up the intensity. Alcohol, drugs, sex, greed, violence and egocentric political leaders are destroying human lives from ages eight to eighty. They have become the new "god" of the people and have stolen their goals, dreams, and ambitions. If a man believes in his heart that he is Godless, worthless, a gangster, or even an assassin, he is. No wonder the youth of America are killing just for the thrill of it. Through their despondent and mournful eyes their Father has died.

As a nation and as individuals, we must learn to dream righteous dreams again. The American Dream was never to cheat or sleep your way to the top. When did it become, "If I want something I will just take it, regardless of who gets in my way?" The American Dream, as given to our forefathers, was the ability to love and worship God without interference. It was the right to own property and to defend it only if necessary. It was never to "*take* what is mine," it was to "*earn* what is mine." There is a cataclysmic difference between the two. One facilitates love, respect, integrity, and hard work. The former propagates hatred, selfishness, and crimes against humanity.

If you are a parent you must recapture your children's dreams. **Ernest Hemingway** stated, **"All thinking men are atheists."** Does that sound as idiotic to you as it does to me? No wonder he blew his own head off with a shotgun. Yet, he is revered among men. A suicidal madman, undoubtedly despondent over the self-induced death of God, is considered the ultimate cultural icon. This is an unprecedented tragedy. Earnest Hemingway cannot hold a candle to Jesus.

Contrary to what Ernest Hemingway may have thought, God *created* man to think. It is what separates us from every other being. Well . . . that and deposable thumbs. It is my opinion that not all thinking men are atheists, but that all thinking men contemplate the existence and will of God.

Rising Tides Lift all Ships

We must learn to recognize when imagination has run amuck and redirect the thoughts of our children's hearts and minds. This requires paying close attention to our children's lives while simultaneously teaching them to think critically. I would strongly encourage you to teach them to reject sin and not just to accept whatever they are being covertly force-fed by the media and modern world culture. This means spending time nurturing, teaching and loving. It also, by the way, means diligently teaching them the Word of God.

> *"Therefore you shall lay up these words of mine in your heart and in your soul, and bind them as a sign on your hand, and they shall be as frontlets between your eyes. **You shall teach them to your children,** speaking of them when you sit in your house, when you walk by the way, when you lie down, and when you rise up."*
> **—Deuteronomy 11:18–19**

As a leader in community or business, *"Let nothing be done through selfish ambition or conceit, but in lowliness of mind let each esteem others better than himself. Let each of you look out not only for his own interests, but also for the interests of others."* (Philippians 2:3–4).

The practice of love, caring and patience will not be in vain. In due time, and in a manner that is specific only to you, God will exalt you. You will begin to experience true success, not just monetary gain.

The state of our world depends upon this paradigm shift. As men and women of God it is imperative for us to impart a Godly dream back into the hearts and minds of our people. However, leading others down the path of righteousness is impossible if you yourself remain in total ignorance. You cannot share what you do not possess. Change begins in the mirror.

Imagine That

Did you know that God is a dreamer and that He has created *you* to be a dreamer as well? As I stated earlier, your imagination is a powerful gift from God. It is part of the image that you were created in. Image is the root word of imagination. You were created directly from the imagination of Yahweh. No other created being in heaven or on earth can make this claim. It is who we are and being created in His image is what separates us from every other animal or created being.

Unlike any other creature on earth, humanity was created with the ability to dream and to visualize. I would argue that imagination is without a doubt the most powerful gift that God has implanted within us. Through it, we determine the success or failure of our lives. With it, we decide and ultimately act upon doing good or evil. Entire nations have strayed and entire races of people have been brutally annihilated due to the imagination of the human heart and mind.

It is our dreams and imaginations that determine our futures. Every successful business, career, ministry, and even nation, was born in the imagination of a man before it ever became reality. So is every crime and act of hatred. Therefore, the question is, how will you use your imagination, or, if you have already matured as an adult, will you use it?

Many of you may question if and why God is a dreamer. I believe the reason is due to His creative nature. It is how He creates. Think back about our discussion in *God Culture* regarding the Book of Genesis and how God appointed everything before He manifested it. In other words, God foresees, or imagines, everything before He brings it to pass. Even, *"God, who gives life to the dead and **calls those things which do not exist as though they did,"*** uses His imagination. (Romans 4:17) What do you think that last highlighted phrase infers?

Think about the words that God spoke; *Let Us make man in our image, according to our likeness ... **Then** God saw everything that he had* *made . . .* (Genesis 1:27 and 31) These are words of foresight. Creation was not an afterthought until He had seen the finished product. God's words are visionary. They are words of (image)-ination.

In Mark 10:15, Jesus stated, *"Whoever does not receive the kingdom of God as a little child will by no means enter it."* This can only be accomplished in the imagination of our hearts. That is how children think. Why do you think it is so easy to convince a child that a fat man can fit down every chimney on the planet in a day? even if they do not have a chimney. A child sees life through the image of their dreams.

The secret is that *our faith will always follow the images we dwell upon.* As you might imagine, this can be either positive or negative. Are you an optimist or a pessimist? What has been filling your mind and your heart? Perhaps, you have quit dreaming altogether. Unlike so many adults, all children have dreams. It is not until they begin to mature that society beats those dreams out of them. We must become as children in this area of our thinking, and to be clear, I am not encouraging immaturity. I am espousing vision. If it is good enough for God to operate in this manner, it is certainly good enough for humanity as well. In the eyes of God, we are *all* children.

Seeing the Future

Think about prophecy for a moment. Prophecy is evidence that God is a dreamer. Isn't prophecy God revealing the imagination of His heart and His intention to bring it to pass before He ever does? God informed us of His dream to bring the Messiah into the world four thousand years prior to performing it. As amazing as this may seem to you, He even informed us of the fact that He would bring Him through the womb of a virgin girl. Now that takes imagination! Here is that revelation.

Let's go back in time to the Garden of Eden, over six thousand plus years ago. Imagine all of the beauty that surrounds you. You are relaxing in a plush green meadow. The fragrant smell of wildflowers is only surpassed by their florid opulence. A warm and yet somehow elegant breeze glazes your skin. The sound of running water commingling together with the luminescent surge of iridescence overwhelms your senses. You are basking in paradise—you are experiencing Eden.

All of a sudden you overhear a commotion in the garden. There is chaos amidst the innumerable fruit trees. Although terrified, you are drawn to it. As you move closer your fear intensifies, overwhelming the essence your being. Something has gone terribly wrong! You gaze upon His majesty but cannot peer into the fire of His blazing eyes. Although you turn away, you cannot help overhearing.

Suddenly you realize you are witnessing the point of origin. It had just happened. The fruit of sin had just been ingested and an angry and yet sorrowfully, merciful God illuminates the garden. He is speaking, rebuking and loving—at this very moment in history, the only living God of the universe is setting the dreams and imagination of His heart into motion.

His voice bellows in the face of Satan . . .

*"Because you have done this you are cursed more than all cattle, and more than every beast of the field; on your belly you shall go, and you shall eat dust all the days of your life. And I will put enmity between you and the woman, and between your seed and **her Seed;** He shall bruise your head, and you shall bruise His heel."*

—Genesis 3:14–15

Still Active

If you are like me, you were actually able to see that description of the cataclysmic event that that forever changed man's destiny. You should be encouraged by this. It is evidence that your imagination is still operable. Therefore, begin to use it once again. What would you like to accomplish with the rest of your life? It is God who has placed that dream within you. Let your imagination run free and go for it . . . but for now, let's go back to the garden.

By coupling the Word of God with your imagination you just witnessed history in the making. You must, however, comprehend one thing in order to understand the majestic plan of God. A woman does not have a seed. The seed originates from the man. His sperm joins with the woman's egg at the point of conception and creates a living human being. Yet, God uses the term "her Seed," capital "S."

God was showing the entire universe and clearly making known to every spiritually alive being in all of creation that He was about to defy physical law. A woman is about to give birth without ever "knowing" a man. The Seed of God had been planted. In the blink of an eye God envisioned coming to earth as a man, dying on the cross, and stamping out the power of sin and death.

It was all born in the thoughts and intents of God's heart. It is the fruit of His imagination. The only thing left to bring it to pass was the process of time. Your eternal life is the result of the dreams and imagination of Yahweh. By the way, and in case you are wondering, Satan is spiritually dead and to this day he is completely unable to perceive the truth. Thus, in vain he continues to defy the living God.

Life Partners

Let me show you how this amazing secret of Almighty God works. Unbeknownst to most, God couples *your* imagination with His in order to bring *His* will to pass. We will stay with the theme of the Messiah because Jesus was, and is, the end goal for mankind. I know many of you are seeking God to get your needs met, but please understand that in Christ they already have been. Although God deeply cares for your well being and has undoubtedly promised to fulfill all your needs, the ultimate goal of the cross is salvation, not worldly prosperity. Therefore, let's return to our fore-father Abraham and reexamine the incredible events of his life.

When God showed up in Abraham's life He did not just say, "Abram, get out of your country and away from your family and go to the land I am going to show you . . . I'll see you when you get there!" No. This would have never caused Abram to spring into action. It would have simply facilitated disobedience. Therefore, the first thing God did was capture the imagination of Abram. When you let Him, He will do the same thing for you. Take note of God's call to Abram.

> *"Now the Lord said to Abram, 'Get out of your country, from your family and from your father's house, to a land that I will show you. I will make you a great nation; I will bless you and make your name great; and you shall be a blessing. I will bless those who bless you, and I will curse him who curses you; and in you all the families of the earth shall be blessed.'"*
> **—Genesis 12:1–3**

Did you notice what God did? He immediately captured Abram's imagination by implanting a dream into his heart. He imparted a vision into Abram's spirit. Do not forget that Abram's wife Sarai was barren. She could not produce the most prized possession of the ancient world, a son. Knowing this, God grabbed hold of Abram and not only promises a child, not even a nation of children, but an entire world full of children. When God dreams, He dreams big. You should take note and follow suit.

Here is the lesson we must learn. Pay close attention because this is remarkable. When God peaked Abram's imagination with the promise of a world full of children, *"in you **all** the families of the earth shall be blessed,"* Abram did not shy away from it. He simply took hold of the dream, packed up his family and embarked upon a journey to pursue the promise. Abram believed God just like a child believes his father. He had a childlike imagination, which produced childlike faith. I believe this is the preeminent reason that God chose Abram over every other human alive at the time.

What could have possibly been going through Abram's mind at that point? Of course this is speculation, but I would venture to guess that it is fairly accurate. Abram is imagining, "Wow! I wonder what it will be like when God makes me a great nation. I can picture all my children laughing and playing, sitting on my lap and looking into my eyes. Now as they have grown up and they are multiplying, the whole land is full of my people. We are a great nation, healthy, prosperous, powerful and happy—a great and mighty nation."

Do not scoff at the possibility of Abram's imagination. You go through the same process every time you buy a lottery ticket. The difference between you and Abram is that you do not really believe you can win. Therefore, after you have played the mental game, you abandon the dream of new houses, cars etc . . .

Why not just go for it? If that is the dream, go for it. Forget about the limitation's. God has none. Just imagine what you could accomplish if you remain diligent and apply the same hope and imagination to the pursuit of God as you do money. Nothing would be impossible. *"Jesus said to him, 'If you can believe, all things are possible to him who believes.'"* (Mark 9:23) Did you notice the word, "if?" That one simple word determines your future.

Abram must have heard the laughter, seen the joy, perhaps even the tears and pain of parenthood and it became real to him—so real that he could reach out and touch it. That is exactly what he did. *"He did not waver at the promise of God through unbelief, but was strengthened in faith, giving glory to God, and being fully convinced that what He had promised He was also able to perform."* (Romans 4:20–21)

Therefore, he reached into the spiritual realm of the Almighty and grabbed hold of both the dream and the promise of God. But what if you are unaware of God's dream for your life? It is simple, and it is also why the Word of God is so important to your spiritual life. If you are unaware of God's dream, simply open the Bible and begin to read. It will connect you to God's heart and in time you will undoubtedly comprehend His will. Although, Abram did not have a Bible, (it was yet to be written, which is also why God physically appeared to Abram) that is exactly what he did. He believed God. Therefore, the plan of God became so real to him that he uprooted his family and went on a quest in pursuit of his Father. It all began with a vision, born of God and captured by his imagination.

Rough Times Ahead

Do you think this was easy for Abram? Do you honestly believe everything went smoothly all the time? I think not. Without a doubt Abram was criticized and I dare say, even persecuted. Can you hear the voice of his father? "Are you crazy Abram? Have you gone completely mad!? You are going to do what based upon what? You are going to leave us and all that we have provided for you because of some man-made dream in your mind? Because of some imaginary "god" that you *think* spoke to you. Boy, you have been in the sun too long! Go take a rest and think about what you are doing"—but it was too late. Abram was already gone. He *had* been in the Son too long. He was caught up in the dream and fully persuaded. God had captured his soul.

Do not be deceived. The journey was not without trouble. Along the way, his wife was captured, his nephew was kidnapped, he and his servant's had to fight an army, his family split up and wound up in Sodom and Gomorrah, and he even had an affair with his wife's hand maid that produced an illegitimate child—and that is the abridged version of events! From the point of view of most, Abram's life was a disaster. However, within every trial the Lord pulled him through by making use of his imagination.

> "After these things the word of the Lord came to Abram **in a vision,** saying, 'Do not be afraid, Abram. I am your shield, your exceedingly great reward.' But Abram said, 'Lord God,

what will you give me, seeing I go childless, and the heir of my house is Eliezer of Damascus?' Then Abram said, 'Look, You have given me no offspring; indeed one born in my house is my heir!'"

"And behold, the word of the Lord came to him, saying, 'This one shall not be your heir, but one who shall come **from your own body** *shall be your heir.'* **Then He brought him outside and said, 'Look now toward heaven, and count the stars if you are able to number them.'** *And He said to him, 'So shall your descendants be.'* **And he believed the Lord . . ."**

—Genesis 15:1–6

One Flesh

Before I address the vision, let me clarify the phrase, *"But one who shall come from* ***your own body*** *shall be your heir."* I am about to show you an incredible secret. As you may or may not know, at this point in time Abraham already had a son. His name was Ishmael. He was born as the result of a demented plan dreamed up by Abram's wife Sarai to provide the son God promised. Because she was barren, she convinced Abram (although it was not very difficult) to follow the custom of the time and sleep with their maid Hagar in order to provide the son they so desperately desired. Although this was a common practice by the ancients, it certainly was not God's plan, and as you will see, it was way beyond His will. Unfortunately, Sarai's plan "worked." Hagar conceived and Ishmael was born. Thus, the illegitimate son I just mentioned.

God, however, never intended for Ishmael to be the forefather of the Messiah prophesied from Genesis chapter three. In fact, God never actually intended Ishmael at all. As you will see shortly, He knew what would occur, but God never ordained the birth of Ishmael, and thus, his descendant's, who have become the Arab nation's of the world and for the most part entirely Muslim, continue to oppose the living God to this day. Ishmael was the result of imagination run amuck on the part of Sarai, Abram's wife. Therefore, when speaking of the heir of the Messiah, Ishmael was never the intended target. God only intended for Isaac to be born through the miraculous promise He made to Abram so many years ago.

Yet Ishmael still came from Abram's body, right? In God's eyes, the answer is no. If you are wondering why, it goes all the way back to God's creation of Adam and Eve. Remember, when God created humanity, He first created Adam. Later, God decided that it was *"not good that man should be alone"* and, therefore, He created Eve. But where did Eve come from?

"And the Lord God caused a deep sleep to fall on Adam, and he slept; ***and He took one of his ribs,*** *and closed up the flesh in its place. Then the rib which the Lord God* ***had taken from man*** *He made into a woman, and He brought her to the man."*

—Genesis 2:21–22

Let's now piece this together. In the beginning God created Adam. There was no Eve. It was not until God decided that Adam should not be the only member of the human species that He fashioned Eve from Adam's body. In other words, Eve was originally one with Adam. She was physically a part of him. After the separation, however, Adam's body had become divided. What was once one is now two.

If you read Genesis chapter one closely, you will discover that in the beginning God created humanity (Adam) both *"male and female."* (Genesis 1:27) Adam was one being. The evidence of this lies in the fact that the biological material for Eve did not come from the dust of the ground as Adam's did. It came from Adam's body. This is important. Eve was not created in the same manner as Adam. This is intentional on God's part, and illustrates that God originally created one being, not two. In the beginning, God created humanity to be "one flesh."

Once divided, however, this was no longer true. It was a deviation from the original state of Adam at creation. I am not implying that it was a deviation from God's original plan, just from Adam's original state. Division is humanity's altered state. Let that sink in for a moment. Division is always problematic.

It is also the reason that a woman is intended to be submissive to her husband. Adam was given life directly from the breath of God. Eve was not. As I stated earlier, she was fashioned from the body of Adam. That gives Adam the higher place of authority, and also, by the way, the greater responsibility for the fall of man.

As you continue to progress in God culture you will discover that God never leaves anything incomplete and humanity was certainly no exception. It is not that Eve was an afterthought. God does not have afterthoughts. God knew exactly how the universe would unfold from the moment of creation. Thus, He made Adam *"male and female"* in Genesis 1:27. With that in mind, consider the manifold wisdom of God. How did He solve the problem? What was the solution to both reunite Adam and provide him (us) with a companion? *"Therefore a man shall **leave his father and mother** and **be joined to his wife,** and they shall become **one flesh.**"* (Genesis 2:24)

Through the covenant of marriage (which includes sexual intercourse) God has re-instituted the origin of creation as the two being one body. Therefore, when Abram had a child outside of the marriage covenant, God considered that child illegitimate. Ishmael was not a product of the covenant body of Abram, and, therefore, could not qualify as the forefather to the heir of the throne of God.

Redemption could only be accomplished by a child born out of the marriage covenant between Abram and Sarai who were "one flesh" in the eyes of God, just as Adam and Eve were "one flesh" in the Garden of Eden—and just as you and your spouse are "one flesh" to this very day. That is why adultery, premarital sex and homosexuality are all sin. There is no marriage covenant associated with either. Therefore, the forefather of the Messiah had to come from a child produced through, "one flesh," Abram and Sarai. Anything else would be the product of unrighteousness. The Messiah had to be a child of the "one flesh" covenant.

Do you still believe God lacks imagination? How about foresight? God had solved the Messiah problem right from the beginning while at the same time addressing why salvation is non-existent in Islam. The covenant of salvation was to be born through Sarai as she was Abram's only true "one flesh" partner. Take a bow Yahweh! You are truly unmatched in all the universe.

I Can Only Imagine

With that objection out of the way, let's now get back to the commingling of wills between God and Abram. It is imperative to realize that the promise to Abram did not immediately come to pass. Neither will God's promise to you, certainly not in its fullness. If you believe the promise has already been fulfilled in your life then you need to go outside and look up at the stars. Try to number them because you are not dreaming big enough. I do not care how much you already have or have not achieved. There is more. So go outside, look up, and put on your imagination.

That is exactly how God kept Abram in pursuit of the promise. When things did not appear to be going Abram's way in the natural, he always had that supernatural picture which was born in his imagination to fall back on. It is what kept him going. Without it, Abram would have failed to achieve the fullness of what God had for him. So will you if you do not operate in the same manner. God has given you a "now" picture to accomplish a "forever" plan. It *is* that big! Without "the dream" it will never come to pass.

Double Vision

We cannot leave this subject without my showing just how active the imagination of Abram was. With the inspiration of God, Abram was able to dream dreams that were absolutely unheard of at the time, and they produced foresight. They produced what we call, "prophecy."

Let's fast-forward to the event which caused the greatest trial in the life of Abram, who is now known as Abraham. I will show you that without the use of His imagination, which produced vision, he would have loosened and deviated from the true will of God. In other words, without imagination it would have been impossible for Abraham to obey God.

> *"Now it came to pass after these things that God tested Abraham, and said to him, 'Abraham!' And he said, 'Here I am.' Then He said to him, 'Take now your son, your only son Isaac, whom you love, and go to the land of Moriah, and offer him there as a burnt offering on one of the mountains of which I shall tell you.' So Abraham rose early in the morning and saddled his donkey ..."*
> **—Genesis 22:1–3**

I want you to notice that God did not implant anything in Abraham at this point except the death of his son. As we learned in *God Culture,* this was the ultimate goal of the Lord with respect to the redemption of mankind. However, under the inspiration of the Almighty, Abraham created his own version of events and here is the truly amazing part, which also happens to be a tremendous *Secret of the Father*. **The vision Abraham created was the exact vision God had for the redemption of mankind,** only on a smaller scale. This is exactly what occurs in the heart of every man when we follow God intimately. The secret of vision is that *your will begins to line up with God's will.*

Before this occurs you have nothing but a pipe dream. Prayers go unanswered primarily because they are outside the will of God. "God, please let me hit the lottery so I can buy a mansion and a yacht" is nothing more than an Elmer Fudd fantasy. There is no salvation in it. God inspired vision, on the other hand, produces an alignment with the will of God. Once this occurs, nothing is impossible. Why would God call you to perform His will and then refuse to equip you to do it? The answer is, He would not. That makes no sense at all. Therefore, when you dwell in God's will nothing *becomes* impossible.

As you are about to see, the incredible use of imagination was required in order for Abraham to pass this immensely difficult test. Imagination transformed into Godly vision is what gave him the strength, and as you will see, God was never left out of the vision. In fact, God, along with His power, might, mercy and goodness was always the central figure of it. When you line up your vision with the plan of God this is exactly what will occur in you, as well.

> *"Then on the third day Abraham lifted his eyes and saw the place afar off. And Abraham said to his young men, 'Stay here with the donkey; the lad and I will go yonder and worship, **and we will come back to you.**'"* (Keep this phrase in mind for a moment.)
>
> *"So Abraham took the wood of the burnt offering ... he took the fire in his hand ... he took the knife, and the two of them went together. But Isaac spoke to Abraham his father and said, 'My father! Look the fire and the wood, but where is the lamb for the burnt offering? And Abraham said, 'My son, God will provide for Himself the lamb for a burnt offering.'"*
>
> **—Genesis 22:4–8**

We have already seen the end of the story and know that is exactly what God did. He provided a Lamb. The point is, however, that Abraham had to use his imagination and his ability to envision in order to obey this command. He never let go of the stars in heaven. He never let go of becoming a great nation. Imagination coupled with the will of God transformed into faith. When intermingled with the process of time, this is now twenty-five years later, it brought Abraham all the way to this incredible point:

> *"By faith Abraham when he was tested, offered up Isaac, and he who had received the promises offered up his only begotten son, of whom it was said, 'In Isaac your seed shall be called,'* **concluding that God was able to raise him up, even from the dead ..."**
> **—Hebrews 11:17–18**

Wow! Do you find that as amazing as I do? No wonder Abram said to his servants, *"The lad and I will go yonder and worship,* **and we will come back to you.'"** Abraham had already concluded that God *"who cannot lie"* (Titus 1:2) was going to raise Isaac from the dead. How else could he become the father of many nations? He used his incredible gift of imagination to produce a vision that lined up exactly with the plan, dreams and goals of Almighty God. Abraham did not know about the crucifixion. In fact, at this point in history crucifixion did not even exist. I am also certain that Abraham had never seen anyone resurrected before, since that is not exactly a common occurrence either.

God had given Abraham the authority and the ability to dream. He has also administered the same anointing upon all who dare to enter the secret of God culture and operate His way. Therefore, as outlandish as it may have seemed to anyone involved, including Abraham himself, there was absolutely no risk of failure. In fact, it is even greater than that. Abraham now viewed following God's command as an act of worship.

Have you ever consider why? The answer reveals to us a vital and integral secret to participating in God culture. The secret is that *Abraham's dream was interfused with God's dream.* Therefore, it could not fail.

Consider this as compared to modern day Christianity's "Godly" dreams. Abraham never asked God for money. It is true that God blessed him and made him wealthy, but Abraham was not asking nor believing God for money. He was believing God for a son. In fact, the money never satisfied Abraham. *"But Abram said, "Lord God, what will You give me, **seeing I go childless,** and the heir of my house is Eliezer of Damascus?"* (Genesis 15:2)

Think about this statement, Abraham had already been blessed by God. Abraham was incredibly wealthy and yet he is still proclaiming, *"What will you give me?"* By our standards, Abraham had everything a man could want—including a child. Do not forget about Ishmael. Abraham, however, had a different goal in mind and money was never a part of it. The secret to God culture is that *it is never about the money.* This is a message that the modern-day church must pick up on. The money, if you are fortunate enough to be blessed in this manner, is intended merely to serve people.

> *"And you shall remember the Lord your God, for it is he who gives you the power to get wealth, **that He may establish His covenant . . ."***
> **—Deuteronomy 8:18**

Have you forgotten about the plight of the *Rich Young Ruler?* (Mark 10:17–27 and Matthew 19:16–22) Twisting the intention of the blessing into a self-aggrandizing act of greed is a satanic perversion of the will of God. In the end, no one wins.

Abraham used his incredible imagination to manifest God's exact plan for redemption. All of God's plans are in regard to redemption. Therefore, Abraham believed God was going to raise Isaac from the dead. The two of them working together produced the salvation of the entire human race! Amazingly, the same visionary power of God that was available to Abraham is still available to the believer in Jesus Christ today.

Do you want to change your life? How about your cities, towns or even the world? It must begin in you. It must start with the dreams and imaginations of your heart. As you progress, you will quickly find that God is still in there.

Dark Shadows

Unfortunately, there is a flip side to imagination. As I stated earlier, we are seeing the dark side of imagination manifest itself within the world on a daily basis. Therefore, before we leave this chapter I must show you the result of imagination run amuck. Let's go back to Genesis and visit the tower of Babel.

> "Now the whole earth had one language and one speech. (This demonstrates the power of unity) *And it came to pass, as they journeyed from the east, that they found a plain in the land of Shinar, and they dwelt there. Then they said to one another, 'Come, let us make bricks and bake them thoroughly.' They had brick for stone and they had asphalt for mortar. And they said, 'Come let us build ourselves a city, and a tower whose top is in the heavens;* **let us make a name for ourselves,** *lest we be scattered abroad over the face of the whole earth.'"*
>
> "But the Lord came down to see the city and the tower which **the sons of men had built.** *And the Lord said, 'Indeed the people are one and they all have one language, and this is what they* **begin** *to do; now nothing that they propose to do will be withheld from them. Come, let Us go down and confuse their* language, *that they may not understand one another's speech.' So the Lord scattered them abroad from there over the face of all the earth, and they ceased building the city.*
>
> **—Genesis 11:1–8**

The power of unity is quite obvious in this passage. There is even immense power in ungodly unity which is clearly illustrated here. We see this at work all over the world today, displayed in gang violence, organized crime, and perhaps in the greatest demonstration the modern world has ever known, radical Islam. Do you think it is a coincidence that all this violence has cropped up in the face of the most divided church in history? You may not like this, but the Islamic Caliphate is being revived. The end time implications are inevitable and according to scores of biblical prophecy, the antichrist will rise from somewhere out of the territory occupied by the Caliphate.

That, however, is not the purpose of this message. The origin of the power contained within the unity of the people was embodied by their imagination. If you think about current events all over the world, we are still seeing this occur today. It was imagination that led to the magnificent vision of building a city so majestic that its tower would reach into the heavens—and reach heaven it certainly did! It got God's attention in a big way. Do you think it is possible that we have gotten God's attention again? Do not underestimate Yahweh's propensity to intervene.

What is particularly interesting, however, is God's response to their plan. The Lord stated, and you can reread it if you find it necessary, that the city had already been built, but then reiterates, "this is what they *begin* to do."

Modern Day Babel-onians

Think about what our current society has begun to do? Just like the ancient Babel-onians, we have attempted to make a name for ourselves and leave God out of it, as well. From God's point of view it may already be finished. Perhaps the damage is already done. We have our own version of the tower and unlike Babel, when they were knocked down we rebuilt them. Although they are majestic, one has to wonder if that was God's will.

God knows all too well that a society cannot repair itself and that it will continue on its current path of destruction until God has no choice but to put an end to it. Rebuilding the towers did not heal America. The towers were not the problem. The human heart is the problem. New York City, for example, is a haven for sin. This is exactly what occurred in Babel. When reading the Book of Revelation, there is no doubt that we are once more headed down the same path.

If you read on a bit further in the Genesis account you will find that after the Lord scattered the people's speech they ceased building the city, which confirms it had not been physically completed. In all practicality, before it was too late the Lord put an end to their evil plans.

Perhaps this is the plight of not just our society's and world culture's, but the modern church if we do not lay aside our own plans and get on board with Yahweh's. It was not long after the third century, perhaps even earlier, that the church's focus shifted from the pursuit of God to the pursuit of power. Is denominationalism how God has scattered *the church's* speech? History confirms what "Christianity" had begun to do, and how much evil even a scattered church was able to perpetuate in its pursuit of political power and earthly gain. There is a reason it was called the *Dark Ages.* To this day, we are still feeling the effects.

If you consider the abject spiritual poverty contained within the division of the modern church, perhaps we should be thanking God for scattering the church's speech. How can we bring a message of hope to the lost when the messengers cannot even agree on what the message is? When putting it that way, perhaps denominationalism is God's will after all. Although we have experienced some of the fallout, only God knows what may have happened if He allowed such misguided unity to remain. Do you still think you are smarter and wiser than God?

Additionally, we must stop giving the devil so much credit. He does not have the foresight to accomplish such a global task as denomination-alism. His power is pale in comparison to the King's. God, on the other hand, does possess such foresight *and* He has the power to bring it to pass. Everything God does has purpose. There is a reason behind every thought in the Word of God.

"As for you, you meant evil against me, but God meant it for good . . ."
—Genesis 5:20

To take this one step further, does the Lord need to "scatter" we Americans, or whatever your nationality is? Perhaps it is the rest of the world being scattered and through immigration they are landing at our doorstep. If that is the case, do you really think we have the power to stop it?

The scattering of the Babel-onians, who later became the infamous Babylonians, was a form of judgment. In case you have not noticed, they no longer exist on this nor any other planet. They have been eradicated by the judgment of Yahweh. What makes the world's nations believe we can escape the same fate if we continue down the ungodly path we are currently on?

One Way Street

So what's the point? The truth is that once the city of Babel had been conceived in the imagination of the people *and* they achieved unity in the vision, in the eyes of God it was already complete. It was just a matter of manifesting their dream in the form of bricks and mortar.

The problem, however, was that their plan could only produce evil. Why? Because of the statement, *Let us make a **name for ourselves**.*" (Genesis 11:4) Think honestly, isn't this a problem within our modern church, and world, for that matter? Hasn't *"let us make a name for ourselves"* polluted the leaders both in the pulpits and in the pews? I will answer for you by saying, no wonder God has caused such division. Prideful unity of the flesh would be the death of the church.

The church was never intended to be an outlet for political activism, nor a social club using the Word of God as a means of earthly gain. Do not get me wrong, I am all for the monetary blessing, but only when God doles it out as a means for accomplishing His will. Otherwise it is not a blessing at all. *"The blessing of the Lord makes one rich, and He adds no sorrow with it."* (Proverbs 10:22)

The purpose of the body of Christ is to gather the lost to salvation. Providing relief to the needy and alleviating the pain of those who suffer is the introduction to our Lord. It is the means to God's end. The modern day political activist Reverend, taking the name of Christ in vain by dividing the masses and neglecting the message of salvation, is an exercise in futility. It is laboring in vain. No political leader can save the lost. The church is in need of electing only one King, Jesus Christ of Nazareth.

Somewhere along the line, however, the body of Christ transformed its ideology from "death of self" to *"let us make a name for ourself,"* and has become concerned mainly with their own reputation and public opinion. In the business world a good reputation is everything. The problem, however, is that we are not discussing the world's business. We are discussing our Father's business. The body of Christ needs to be about *the Father's* business only. Jesus is an offense to those in the world of business. It has been my experience that the beloved of the world have utterly abandoned the gospel, even if they reside in the pulpit.

In fact, scripture specifically warns, *"Adulterers and adulteresses! Do you not know that **friendship with the world is enmity with God?** Whoever therefore **wants to be a friend of the world makes himself an enemy of God.**"* (James 4:4) It is not that we intentionally offend. Offense is merely the fallout of confronting sin with the truth. Making a name for oneself inevitably forces one to compromise the truth and places that particular person, or body, in direct opposition to God. Jesus purposely *"made*

Himself of no reputation." (Philippians 2:7) Whether we like it or not, *"of no reputation"* is to be the church's earthly plight.

The Hebrew word translated as "name" is **"Shem,"** pronounced oddly enough, *"shame."* It means a memorial based upon individuality. Denomination, as well as, those using the Word of God for worldly gain, immediately comes to mind when I read that. In other words, whether consciously, or unconsciously, the intention is to exalt one's self above God, which even if done unintentionally leaves God out of it. That sounds very familiar in today's world and now it is time to fully go there.

Intents of the Heart

We can build all sorts of towers, cities, towns, schools, businesses, churches, etc . . . if our intention is to leave God out of it, He will never bless us and society will continue to degrade. Condoning sin, as well as, picking and choosing what stays in and what is to be purged from church doctrine is to leave God out of it. The Word of God is to be the church's doctrine. Period, the end! I cannot say this any clearer.

Degradation of the human condition is the only possible outcome of such heretical behavior. In fact, degrade is too soft a word. If we continue in the present direction we are going we will be judged and eventually destroyed. We have seen this occur throughout history. God will obliterate the problem.

> *"Then the Lord saw the wickedness of man was great in the earth, and that **every intent** of the **thoughts of his heart** was **only** evil continually. And the Lord was sorry that He had made man on the earth, and He was grieved in His heart . . ."*
> **—Genesis 6:5–6**

These were the days of Noah and the end was the destruction of mankind by flood. My question to you is; what was the root of their problem? The answer is clear as day. It was their corrupt imaginations. *"Every **intent** of the **thoughts** of his heart..."* Notice that the scripture delineates the thoughts and intent of man's heart. In other words, man's imagination had run amuck.

Are we headed down the same path? God does not change. (Malachi 3:6) It is my opinion that we are already there. If we do not repent as a nation God will execute judgment. Read about such cities as Sodom and Gomorrah, Nineveh, Philistia, Babylon etc... Consider past empires. God will bring judgment upon the disobedient. No one nation can escape, regardless of its earthly glory. Compared to heaven, the greatest empires of all time are mere cesspools of filth and shame. Because God is merciful, however, He always sends a messenger to call for repentance first. Keep in mind that destruction does not bring joy to our Father, life does.

The truth of Noah's day was the same as the days of Babel, just as it was with Sodom and Gomorrah and every other city and nation God has ever judged, including Israel. The people had loosened. They had cast off restraint and they used their imaginations to do it. Sadly, we are seeing this same cancer manifesting in our own cities, towns and country. The further it goes the more scattered we become. Although God has promised not to *flood* the earth again, He *will* destroy it by fire. The Book of Revelation is clear.

How many of your family and friends are you willing to lose? If God ended it tomorrow, what would happen? Where would your family and friends go? Therefore, let's "tighten" the people and reconnect with heaven. In so doing we have absolutely nothing to lose and everything to gain, namely, the Almighty creator of the universe, Yahweh the King of all kings.

The Audacity of Hope

In conclusion, you will find dreams, visions, and imagination in use all over the Word of God. The purpose is to change your life and the rapid unraveling of society. Do you want to get yourself and your children off Prozac, Ritalin and Valium? Are you fed up in your addiction, regardless of what it is? Then open up the Word of God which will change the thoughts, intents and imagination of your heart. It will instill hope and real change.

Together, let's begin tapping into the dream of God. He will impart true Life into your spirit. That is what the Word of God does. It changes your life by changing the way you think. It lines up *your* thoughts with God's thoughts. It affixes your imagination to God's imagination and manifests the supernatural thoughts and intents of *God's* heart into the natural realm. *"Now we have the mind of Christ,"* (1 Corinthians 2:16) thus, causing the will of God to come to pass in our lives. My friend, Yahweh is our only hope. Not only will your life change "now," but the Lord God Almighty will imagine you right into the golden streets of "forever." I look forward to seeing you there.

CHAPTER 4

Reaping What You Have Sown

(THE SECRET OF THE SYSTEM)

*"**While the earth remains,** seedtime and harvest, cold and heat, winter and summer, and day and night shall not cease."*

—Genesis 8:22

Our next secret appears to be contained in nothing more than a harmless little four word phrase, *"While the earth remains . . ."* As you have no doubt heard, things are not always as they appear. According to these four seemingly innocent sounding words, which most of us read right past, as long as the third planet from the sun remains the abode of we upwardly mobile and capacious brained bi-pedal creatures, (that simply means upright and big-brained) you must operate within the bounds of the law that follows the phrase, *"While the earth remains..."* There is just no getting around it. Therefore, in order to prosper in the kingdom of God you must gain an understanding of how it functions and learn how to work within the rules of what you are about to read.

Take careful note of what the actual law contains; *"While the earth remains, 1) seedtime and harvest, 2) cold and heat, 3) winter and summer, and 4) day and night shall not cease."* (Genesis 8:22) In other words, God created a rocky, rotating, primarily liquid covered planet, tilted at exactly 23.4 degrees, that just happens to orbit the perfect sized yellow dwarf star. The slightly off kilter whirling of this perfectly engineered not so modern marvel is the cause of day and night, as well as, the four seasons. The not so coincidental tilting of earth's axis causes just the right temperature shifts to allow the vegetation responsible for the earth's oxygen rich atmosphere to progress from seed, to fruit, to harvest, while simultaneously doubling as the basis for all known food sources.

Therefore, as long as the earth remains humanity's present tense abode, the physical attributes of our uniquely suitable for carbon based life chunk of floating rock that is hurling toward infinity at roughly 373 miles per second, while simultaneously spinning at nearly 1000 miles per hour, (roughly 1600 kilometers per hour) is not going to change. Yes, that is what Genesis 8:22 actually states!

If the earth were even slightly different in the engineering of its make up, the temperature shifts would be too severe to sustain life. Day and night, as well as, Frankie Valli's four seasons, is what allows the earth to heat and cool in just the right manner to sustain our thriving existence. 93,000,000 miles also happens to be the perfect distance from the sun to allow for our sustenance, as well.

If we were any closer, the life sustaining miracle compound known as H2O (water) would vaporize. If we were farther from the sun it would freeze. Had the earth been created ever so slightly outside of the "sweet spot" in which we currently reside, sustaining physical life would be impossible.

As if that were not enough, if kinetic energy (energy that a body possesses by virtue of being in motion) did not break the hydrogen bond, water would not convert to a gas, thus preventing the water cycle from occurring. The incredible God breathed water molecule contains a positive charge on one side and a negative charge on the other, giving it the amazing ability to both attract other water molecules while simultaneously sticking to them. They miraculously respond to one another as tiny polarized magnets of life. Without this amazing ability, clouds could not form in the sky, raindrops could not coalesce, and thus, the miracle known as precipitation that so many of us so desperately despise would be non-existent. With all that said, the above head spinning overload of information most certainly begs the following question; could all of this be coincidence or some random act of chance?

Pause and think before you answer; God's incredibly viscous life giving water molecule contains even more amazing ability's. If water were not one of the only known compounds, and by far the most plentiful, to lose density when freezing, ice could not float and insulate the water underneath. If this were not so, the oceans of the world would freeze solid from the bottom up, thus killing all the marine life contained within while simultaneously ceasing the operation of the water cycle. Our perfectly engineered sun would then dehydrate all known life, thus polishing off God's "grand experiment" in one fell swoop.

Incredibly, and against all odds, the density of water actually increases until it reaches four degrees celsius—that's forty degrees Fahrenheit to all my fellow Americans. If you really want to be precise about it, and just in case you may be wondering, four degrees celsius, a.k.a. forty degrees fahrenheit, is the equivalent of 277.594 degrees Kelvin. I told you I was a bit odd. Many of you have probably never even heard of the Kelvin scale.

From that point forward, water's density begins to decrease, thus increasing its volume by nine percent, and voila, the ice cube floats to the top. Had Yahweh overlooked even one "minor" detail, and trust me there are a multitude of others, all life on planet earth would cease to exist. In fact, it would have prevented life altogether.

Therefore, keep in mind that perception is not always reality. As chaotic and random as things may sometimes appear, God is perfect. There is always order in the chaos. Can you believe all of that information is contained in the phrase, *"While the earth remains?"* Yes, the Bible is that amazing!

Therefore, if you truly have the desire to live within the kingdom of God you cannot disregard Genesis 8:22. I find it interesting that no one denies that cold and heat will always be a part of the earth's function, as well as, winter and summer, and day and night. In our minds they are a given.

Why, then, do we ignore seedtime and harvest? Seedtime and harvest was number one on God's primary list of earthly functions. It is every bit as much a part of the earth's function as the prior three physical laws, yet we never regard it as an integral process of life. The law of sowing and reaping, also known as seedtime and harvest, is God's method of operation upon planet earth in both a physical and spiritual sense. Perhaps unbeknownst to you up until now, whether consciously or unconsciously, it is how we humans function as well.

Smoke and Mirrors

In recent years, the law of sowing and reaping has become largely connotative with obtaining money and financial success. Although that is true, I am not only going to suggest, my intention is to reveal to you that *everything you do* falls under the law of sowing and reaping. It is the source of your success and it may also be the cause of your troubles and failures. That, my friend, is a secret that must be revealed to function within the kingdom of God. Sowing and reaping is a law that is in constant motion. You cannot start it and you cannot stop it. Therefore, without ever having realized it, the situation that you have found yourself to be in is a direct result of every decision you have ever made, whether good or bad.

Perhaps you have not noticed, but in recent times Christian people have fallen in love with blaming every negative situation that occurs in their lives on the devil. Although Lucifer is quite influential, it is *we* who empower him. As you will soon discover, he has no power on his own. Very little of your trouble is actually a result of Satanic influence. You are not under constant demonic attack. Neither Satan, nor any of his detestable little minions, are omnipresent, omnipotent nor omniscient. The devil wishes he had that type of power, but I can assure you that he does not. God *does,* however, and if you would empower God the same way you naively empower Lucifer, your life would be forever altered—to the positive.

Therefore, Satan must deceive you into believing he has power, even over God. In truth, it is merely an illusion. It is nothing but smoke and mirrors—a cheap parlor trick. He does not know your thoughts. He only knows what you tell him. Therefore, watch your mouth. Be careful with the words you speak. He is listening to exactly *what* you say and how and when you say it.

To be successful in the kingdom of God, we must come to the realization of the following secret. *Lucifer has not been controlling our lives.* In most cases, we have been experiencing a law that has been enacted for the good of mankind—but a law is a law. If you cherish it, you will reap all the goodness God has to offer. If you abuse it, you will reap the corrupted results of chaos. In most cases, therefore, the devil is not the source of your trouble. *You are!* You have been empowering the devil by sowing mixed or perhaps even corrupt seed and you are experiencing a defiled harvest as a result. (Deuteronomy 22:9)

Over Ruled

Allow me to be perfectly blunt with you. If you eat cheeseburgers and french fries, or bacon and eggs every day, you drink and smoke, and you weigh three hundred-fifty pounds while never exercising, your heart attack or stroke was not a Satanic attack on your body. You have simply reaped what you have sown.

> *"Do not be deceived, God is not mocked; for whatever a man sows, that he will also reap. He who sows **to the flesh** will **of the flesh** reap corruption."*
> **—Galatians 6:7–8**

Your lack of discipline and self-control is what made you sick. According to the same scripture, if you were expecting a different result you have been deceived. You have been making a mockery of God. Being *healthy* in that situation would be miraculous.

Are you wondering why God considers this to be a mockery against Him and why He feels so strongly about it? After all, God expresses a genuine rebuke in regard to treating Him in jest. The answer is quite simple once you have removed any preconceived notions. The reason you are making a mockery of God is because you believe you can overrule His law of seedtime and harvest. In other words, you are placing yourself in a position of power and authority above Him. You actually believe you can sow corruption and reap life. According to the Word of God that is not just impossible, it is borderline blasphemous.

The Ultimate Goal

I must, however, preface my next point with the following scripture: *"Though now you do not see Him* (Jesus), *yet believing, you rejoice with joy* *inexpressible and full of glory, receiving **the end** of your faith—**the salvation of your souls.***" (1 Peter 1:8–9)

I bring this up for the following reason. As previously stated, we all too often associate sowing and reaping solely with money and positive or negative events that occur in our lives. As I also mentioned earlier, everything you do, every day of your life, is under the law of sowing and reaping—and not just the things you *intend* to sow. You cannot impede this law and you cannot override it. We sow continuously, all day, every day, and as a result, we reap a continual harvest every day of our lives.

The ultimate goal of Yahweh's message is to convey that just like everything else God has implemented on the earth, seedtime and harvest is all about salvation. That is the real meaning of 1 Peter 1:8–9, that we just read. The end of our faith, or stated another way, the primary objective of our faith, is obtaining the necessary power to receive the salvation of our souls. I don't know about you, but that is my ultimate goal for everyone I know—and even for those I do not know.

With that in mind, the beginning of our faith, which is our first and primary seed, must be Jesus Christ? According to scripture, without Jesus Christ, faith leading to salvation, also known in Christian circles as "saving faith," is nonexistent. "***But before faith*** (Jesus Christ) ***came, we were kept under guard by the law …***" (Galatians 3:23) Without faith you cannot be saved. So without Christ, who *"is the author and finisher of our faith"* (Hebrews 12:2), there is no salvation.

That makes Jesus both the beginning and the end of our faith and our salvation. Every other experience is simply life and the day to day actions we need to pursue in order to live it. What we accomplish in life is, therefore, determined by what we sow on a daily basis. From that perspective, which is the heavenly perspective of Jesus Christ crucified, the harvest we should truly be sowing seed for is salvation—salvation for yourself, your family, your friends, and anyone else God puts in your path.

In eternity everything else is irrelevant. Everything material will be separated by death, the New Heaven, the New Earth and the Lake of Fire. Therefore, every seed in between now and the day you "go home" should somehow be for the purpose of attaining the ultimate goal—the salvation of someone's soul.

Contrary to modern doctrine, the kingdom of God is not about making your life comfortable. There will be plenty of time for that in heaven. In fact, we will have all of eternity to celebrate and make merry. The current mission, however, is about saving those around you. It is about overcoming the wiles of the devil and being transformed into the image of our loving Creator. (Romans 12:2 and 21) I hope that makes sense. That is what it means to be God minded. Therefore, let's dive back in and begin to gain understanding.

Growing a Bumper Crop

As I mentioned earlier, according to Genesis 8:22, *"while the earth remains,"* God has implemented the following physical laws. Therefore, they must remain in force until at a minimum God destroys the earth in its totality, recreates it by fire, or in truth and according to Revelation 21, He does both. Unbeknownst to most, a "New Heaven" denotes that the "New Earth" will be in a new universe—one that has not been corrupted by sin. Incredibly, the New Heaven that gives birth to God's holy and everlasting city, the New Jerusalem has no night. It also *"has no sun, nor moon, for the Lamb of God is its light."* (Revelation 22)

The redeemed universe is devoid of darkness, both physically and spiritually. It appears to operate according to a completely new set of physical laws, as well. Its radiance is derived solely from the essence of almighty God. Therefore, it is perfect. It does not even need the sun, moon or stars to provide light upon the earth. Jesus, the holy and eternal Lamb of God is its everlasting light. Until that time, however, *"seedtime and harvest, cold and heat, winter and summer, and day and night shall not cease."*

If all of the other laws simply happen, why do think seedtime and harvest would be any different? Keep in mind what is illustrated by day and night, winter and summer, and cold and heat. God's physical laws are going to operate whether we obey them or not. We cannot pray them out of existence. When winter comes it is time to put on a coat. If you do not you will freeze. Therefore, what we really need to grasp is how to function properly within the latitude of seedtime and harvest. It is here by default. Since we can neither pray it away nor change its complexion, wouldn't you agree we should learn how to use it? To get a better picture of this vital truth, let's observe Jesus' description of seedtime and harvest.

> *"The kingdom of God is **as if** a man should scatter seed on the ground, and should sleep by night and rise by day, and the seed should sprout and grow, **he himself does not know how.** For the earth yields crops **by itself**, first the blade, then the head, after that the full grain in the head. But when the grain ripens, immediately he puts in the sickle, because the harvest has come."*
> —**Mark 4:26–29**

As you grow in your relationship with Jesus you will find that He quite often used natural illustrations to convey heavenly principles. He was a master at engaging humanity at each individual's level of comprehension and life experience. Once again, Jesus uses the phrase "kingdom of God" to contrast God's method of operation with the natural kingdom, or ways, of man.

Since God's ways are intended to be our ways as well, the phrase "kingdom of God" is a clear representation that humanity's method of operation within God's "kingdom" is through the process of sowing and reaping. Take note that Jesus states, *"he (the person sowing) himself does not know how"* it grows, but nevertheless it does. Unfortunately, most do not understand that there is a process involved that does not allow us to proceed from seed directly to harvest. Apart from the miraculous, instant gratification is non-existent in the kingdom of God.

As I mentioned in a previous writing, I love Mixed Martial Arts (MMA), in particular, the Ultimate Fighting Championship (UFC). Most novices to the sport have no idea that your gut reaction when caught in a submission attempt is nearly always the wrong response. As an example, when someone grabs hold of your arm to attempt an arm bar, the first reaction is to try to quickly rip your arm out of your opponents grasp. The problem is that panic, and even a lack of patience, only tightens the grip and nearly always causes one to either "tap out" or have your arm broken. The correct response is to patiently shift your position to counteract the move of your opponent.

Unfortunately, many of us live our lives constantly trying to rip our lives out of trouble while never shifting our position. Refusal to face the issues we have created only tighten's the grip of the enemy. Most problems will not simply go away. Without making an adjustment to the seed we are sowing, we will perpetually reap the same defiled harvest.

The problem is that patience in a painful situation can be quite uncomfortable, and for many, may even seem to be unbearable. With every situation life has to offer, whether it be perceived to be positive or negative, patience is a virtue. We must take our time in transforming the seeds we have sown into the harvest we truly desire. This always requires time, diligence, and patience.

Therefore, you must sow your seed, tend to your seed, and wait until it matures to reap your harvest. You cannot change this principle—ever. It is impossible for any man to do so. However, God can and from time to time He does. He overrides the physical laws of the universe and that is when and how we experience miracles. Outside of God's overriding power, however, you must sow and reap.

Allow me to provide for you an illustration of *God* sowing and reaping. Even God operates in accordance with this principle and this will also demonstrate what is truly important to your heavenly Father. When Satan stole the heart of mankind in the Garden of Eden it presented a twofold problem between God and man. God's problem was that man became ineligible for heaven because of sin, which does not and cannot exist in heaven. Congruently, man's problem was also that he became ineligible for heaven because of sin, which does not and cannot exist in heaven.

Yes, you read that correctly, both God and man had the same dilemma. So what to do? Why not just declare a "do over" and start again? Certainly God could have. After all, He is God. God can do whatever He pleases, can't He?

Although I am certain that God could have blown the world to smithereens and started over, declaring a "do over" would *not* please Him. God knew exactly what was going to happen in the Garden of Eden and He acted accordingly both before and after the event. Yahweh was not surprised when Adam rebelled. He did not get scared. He certainly was not shaking in His boots over Satan's ridiculous attempt to overthrow Him. God can speak a single word and instantaneously vaporize Satan. I would be willing to wager that God could eradicate him with a mere thought. So why doesn't He?

The Harvest

It is simple. God *uses* Satan to accomplish His will. When God created Adam, He gave him dominion over the earth. Dominion incorporated the authority for Adam to do as he pleased. Included in dominion was the power and ability to choose between right and wrong. If God were to enter into the situation and through an act of jurisprudence override Adam's choice, it would mean that He did not really give Adam dominion, authority *or* the ability to choose. In other words, what God said and what God did would have been two different things. Freewill would have been merely an illusion. Do you realize that what you are asking God to do is more descriptive of Satan's ways than God's?

God chose to create mankind out of His love— *"God is love"* (1 John 4:8) and He created mankind to love *Him*. Love, however, requires freewill. If you were created to love God by force, that would not be love at all. It would be compulsion. Compulsion is an act of force. There is no love or compassion in force unless it is for the purpose of avoiding personal injury. Of course I would push someone out of the way of a moving vehicle. I would not, however, push someone through the door of the church building. For authenticity's sake, that must be done by personal choice. Once again, the force humanity is asking God to exercise, the rescinding of freewill, describes the intention of Lucifer, not Yahweh. Love *requires* choice.

Satan's role is to test that love which causes you to choose between good and evil. As a result, you have the choice to love and the choice not to love. You also have the choice to obey whom you love and the choice to disobey whom you love. These two choices are one of Satan's primary tactics. He uses it as a means to bully his way into our lives. Think about how many crimes have been committed as a result of love perverted. The jail cells of history have overflowed with crimes of passion. God, having absolute control and authority over every situation, however, had a better way. Yahweh would not declare a "do over."

> *"Now the Lord had said to Abram, 'Get out of your country, from your family, and from your father's house, to a land that I will show you. I will make you a great nation; I will bless you and make your name great; and you shall be a blessing . . . in you all of the families of the earth shall be blessed.'"*
>
> **—Genesis 12:1–3**

Why is the Lord moving Abram in the above scripture? Remember, at this point in human history God had lost mankind to sin. Mankind is separate from God and cannot be reunited with God on his own. To this day, all men have inherited sin, and thus, have been separated from our Maker. Without a Savior, there is no means of reunification. Without Christ, who is our advocate with the Father, we are all condemned to hell.

> *"Now it came to pass after these things that God tested Abram ... Then He said, 'Take now your son, your only son Isaac, **whom you love**, and go to the land of Moriah and offer him there as a burnt offering...'And Abraham stretched out his hand and took the knife to slay his son ... But the Angel of the Lord called to him from heaven ... And He said, 'Do not lay your hand on the lad ... for now I know that you fear* (love and revere) *God, **since you have not withheld your son, your only son, from me.***'"*
> —**Genesis 22:1–10**

In this section of scripture, we find two incredible acts of sowing and one immense harvest. First of all, God was sowing a Seed. God needed to bring the Messiah into the world in a legal manner, which we have previously learned means both through the womb of a woman and *"in the likeness of sinful flesh."* (Romans 8:3) Nothing else, and no manner of ritual would suffice.

In other words, God's Messianic Seed had to be at minimum equal to the man, Adam, who perpetrated mankind's original sin. As a result, *"it is not possible that the blood of bulls and goats could take away sins."* (Hebrews 10:4) Why? It was Adam, a man, who sinned. Therefore, God's covenant partner Abraham was not asked to offer a bull or a goat to Yahweh. God asked for Abraham's miraculous son Isaac, whom he loved. (Genesis 22:2)

Abraham, knowing full well what God was asking and being completely obedient to his Lord, therefore, did not bring a bull or a goat on the journey to Mount Moriah. He understood the command of God, and, thus, offered up his son, Isaac. Isaac was a foreshadowing of Jesus Christ.

Therefore, God could not, and would not, accept anything less than obedience to His will from Abraham. It had to be Isaac.

In truth, however, God was merely testing Abraham's heart. From God's perspective, the sacrifice had been made the second Abraham said, "yes" to God, saddled up his donkey, got the boy and headed to Mount Moriah. It is similar to our earlier discussion of Babel. Once the intent had been fixed in the people's hearts, God considered the deed to be done. Brick and mortar is merely a manifestation of the intent to build. The same holds true of Abraham's intent to sacrifice Isaac. Once He fixed it in his heart, and proved it by raising the knife, God considered the deed to be done. Therefore, God put a stop to Abraham's sacrifice of imperfection and planted the perfect seed of the Messiah to be harvested in the century's to come. The Messianic harvest sown into the nation of Israel had begun.

Consider the following; because of Adam's disobedience leading to sin, a human sacrifice *"without deformation,"* (Leviticus 21:18) became necessary to fulfill the law. Since *"all have sinned and fall short of the glory of God,"* (Romans 3:23) only one man could ever qualify to fulfill the ultimate sacrifice for sin. It was not Isaac, nor was it any other human being who has ever lived. Only one "man" could ever qualify. His name is Jesus Christ and He is *"the only begotten Son of the Father."* (John 3:16)

Therefore, God released Isaac, caught the Ram in the thicket, and implemented the foreshadowing of salvation with its ultimate fulfillment coming from the sacrifice of the true Lamb of God, Jesus Christ. In Christ alone lies the secret of eternal life. Therefore, God declares:

> *"Their sins and their lawless deeds I will remember no more. Now where there is remission of these, **there is no longer an offering for sin**. Therefore, brethren, having boldness to enter the Holiest by the blood of Jesus, **by a new and living way** which He consecrated for us, **through**

*the veil, that is, **His flesh** ... and having a High Priest over the house of God, let us draw near with a true heart in full assurance of faith ...*"
—Hebrews 10:17–22

Seeds of the Flesh

Think about it this way, since it was a human being (Adam) who originally sinned, another human being—a living, breathing, human being, with real emotions, his own will, and the same bent toward temptation, had to serve as the sacrifice. Therefore, God chose the family of Abraham, Isaac in particular, who was also born of a miracle, as His seed to usher in the Messiah. Do you see the resemblance? Incredibly, the Messiah, Jesus Christ, was a Seed sown by God with the intent of reaping the harvest of salvation.

Pay attention to what follows. This is where it gets truly amazing. Unbeknownst to Abraham at the time, he was also sowing a seed. Do you remember where I stated that everything we do is an act of sowing, even if we are unaware of our actions? When Abraham willingly offered Isaac to God, he planted *the same* seed as the Almighty. That is right, and yes, that *is* amazing! Through obedience to God, and perhaps without ever realizing it, Abraham planted Messiah Seed.

Look again at God's response to Abraham and allow me to interject a little paraphrase into Genesis 22 that you may understand. God said, "Since you have not withheld your only son, whom you love—since you have sown him to Me as a seed, I will not withhold My only Son, whom I love. I will sow Him as a Seed, as well."

Abrahams "seed" of loving God more than is own son reaped a harvest of all those who will *"call upon the name of the Lord"* throughout eternity. In return, God loved mankind more than *His* own Son, as well. In fact, and contrary to what the atheists of the world believe, God loved mankind even *more* than Himself. *"God so loved **the world** that He gave His only begotten Son,"* (John 3:16) who happens to be Yahweh *"the Word."* (John 1:1)

We will talk more about the somewhat confusing issue of God's oneness in a later chapter. That, however, is what sowing and reaping is all about to God. If you read *God Culture,* you have learned that by definition, equality is how covenant partners behave. Thus, the miracle of Jesus Christ, *"who, being **in the form of God,** did not consider it robbery to be equal with God,"* (Philippians 2:6) and whom also came *"in **the likeness** of sinful flesh."* (Romans 8:3) Jesus Christ is the contractual consideration that equates both God and man. That, my friends, is absolutely amazing!

Thus, salvation can only exist by the covenant God made with Abraham. Jesus is simply the final fulfillment thereof. (Matthew 5:17 and Romans 10:4) In terms of sowing and reaping, all of the blessings and harvests are designed to keep you doing His will. Although the blessing of God may include prosperity, material wealth is not the goal of the covenant. The covenant of God is for one purpose alone, the salvation of the human soul.

Therefore, we have just discovered a vital *Secret of the Father.* From God's perspective *Abraham and Isaac were seeds in the kingdom of God.* Christ was "the blade," the cross was "the head," the resurrection was "the full grain in the head, or first fruit" and all those redeemed to heaven are God's harvest. Praise God! As a result, God has put in the sickle and begun to reap!

The Secret of the Lord

Now that you see the big picture from God's point of view, let's learn how to practically sow into our own everyday lives. Unbeknownst to many, God is very concerned about both you and your family. Psalm 25:12 states the following:

"Who is the man that fears the Lord? Him He (God) *shall teach in the way He chooses. He himself **shall dwell in prosperity**, and his descendants* (literally seed) ***shall inherit the earth**. The secret of the Lord is with those who fear Him, **and He will show them His covenant.** "*

Did you know that in Romans 16:25, Paul refers to Christ as a mystery revealed to those of us in these last days. Read the last sentence of Psalm 25:12 again. *"The **secret** of the Lord is with those who fear Him, and **He will show them His covenant.**"* Since the Old Covenant had already been revealed and the line of the Messiah was to be through King David of the tribe of Judah, I believe the Lord was referring to the New Covenant in this reference, which is Christ, and is a mystery, or secret, to those who do not believe.

However, just like Abraham, at some level God revealed the secret to David. I am not sure in what capacity, but he continually prophesied in regard to Jesus. We also read that the Godly man's descendants or "seed" shall be prosperous and will inherit the earth. We do not need to conform to worldly pressures to experience prosperity. God is all sufficient.

Take some time to read Revelation 21–22. You will find this Psalm to be true. Heaven, our eternal dwelling place, will be on a recreated earth reserved for the heirs of salvation. We *will* inherit the earth, but you must first sow the following seed:

First and foremost, before you can expect any measure of success in the area of sowing and reaping you must receive the Seed of Christ into your life. You must be fertile soil and that means you must begin by sowing, or implanting, the Word of God firmly into your heart. You *must* read and learn your Bible. The Word is where everything in creation begins. That includes your own spiritual life.

> *"In the beginning was the Word, the Word was with God and the Word was God . . . and the Word became flesh and dwelt among us . . ."*
>
> **—John 1:1 and 14**

Jesus and the Word of God are one. We also read earlier the phrase, *"Before faith came,"* referring to Jesus. You must sow the Word into your heart to reap a Godly harvest. If you have children you must sow it into their hearts. If they are grown and no longer under your influence, continually sow the seed of prayer. It worked for my parents and it will also work for you. If, and it is your choice, you obey this principle you can expect the following harvest:

> *"I have been young and now I am old; yet **I have not seen the righteous forsaken**, nor **his descendants** (seed) **begging bread.** He (the righteous man) is ever merciful, and lends (which is sowing seed), and his descendants (his seed) are blessed (empowered by God to prosper)."*
>
> **—Psalm 37:25–26**

A Time to Sow

In order to proceed, let us discuss a few different types of seed. Please understand, these are not the only seeds you can sow but I feel these are essential. You may have others that are equally important and powerful. I am not so arrogant as to believe that I know everything. The day I stop learning is the day I die and I am quite sure we will continue learning throughout eternity.

First and foremost, prayer is a seed. I list this first because I feel that apart from receiving Christ as your Lord and Savior, it is most important. Prayer is what keeps you connected to God. Every Christian must pray. When you get others to pray the "prayer of agreement," (Matthew 18:19) meaning all those involved are in agreement with each other and God's Word, it creates unity, which ushers in the Spirit of God and His resurrection power.

Secondly, your "words" are a seed. Watch what you say. Matthew 12:37 says *"for by your words you will be justified, and by your words you will be condemned."* We must be conscious of what comes out of our mouths.

I once heard a story about a man who was continually putting down his wife. One day his Pastor showed up at his front door and said, "Let's go for a ride." When the man got in the car he noticed that his Pastor had a pillow next to him, a big goose down pillow, the kind you sleep on. When they got on the highway, the Pastor, who had previously sliced open the pillow, held it out the window at about fifty-five miles per hour, shaking feathers all over the highway. He then pulled the car over, turned to his shocked passenger and commanded, "Now get out and pick up every last feather!"

His alarmed excursionist peered back at him incredulously and responded, "That's impossible! There is no way I can pick up all those feathers." His Pastor looked him straight in the eye and declared, "Neither can you take back a single word you have said to and about your wife. The damage is already done. Now go home and apologize to your Father's daughter."

Your words are like little spiritual packets sent into eternity. They are powerful and you cannot get them back. What you *continually* say and think about *will* at some point come to pass. Note the following passage from the Book of Job:

> *"For my sighing comes before I eat, and my groaning's pour out like water. For **the thing I greatly feared has come upon me, and what I dreaded has happened to me.**"*
>
> **—Job 3:25**

A careful study of the Book of Job reveals that the safety and salvation of his children was the primary fear in his life. In fact, he became so obsessed with it that he sacrificed to the Lord every single day on behalf of his children in the hope that they would one day find the Lord.

On the surface it sounds holy, but unfortunately, it revealed his lack of trust in Jehovah. Keep in mind that I am not referring to Job's love or his faithfulness toward God. Apart from Jesus Christ, Job's love and faithfulness toward God is unmatched in all of scripture. Job was, however, continually sowing the seed of fear. I understand that there is a time to pray, but there is also a time to believe. Living in constant fear is to bow before the spirit of fear and that always yields the same result—a defiled harvest. Despite Job's incredible loyalty to God, his misguided efforts ultimately came to fruition as he reaped the loss of his precious children. Satan, with the permission of God, by the way, stole them from right under his nose. Job's sowing of mixed seed reaped a defiled harvest. We will discuss this in more detail shortly.

How many of us have the same fear? How many of us live in the same daily torment? How many of us completely lack any trust in our heavenly Father? Are you aware that you are sowing the seed of unbelief? Your actions are diametrically opposed to faith? Under such conditions, a defiled harvest is the only possible outcome.

If this is you, I would encourage you to open the Word of God and get to know God. Trust that God loves your children as much—no, in actuality, even more than you do. Set your thoughts and your words upon the one and only living God who has declared that *"everyone who calls upon the name of the Lord **will** be saved."* (Romans 10:13)

Oops!

As a child I loved the sport of basketball. As I stated earlier, I have always had an active imagination. When I was six or seven years old my father erected a basketball hoop in front of my house. In retrospect, I must have driven my neighbors crazy. For the next twelve years I was out there every day, from the time I came home from school until it got too dark to play. I would even play in the dark.

When most thought I was alone, just practicing moves and shooting around, I was not. In my imagination I was in the Boston Garden or the Philadelphia Spectrum. I was playing against Dr. J, Larry Bird and Magic Johnson. As a result, I became pretty darn good, but there is a reason I am telling you this story. For some reason, still unbeknownst to me, I would always pretend I was playing with, or recovering from, some sort of injury. Usually it would be coming off a major knee injury.

In the introduction to *God Culture*, I have previously discussed the injury that stalled my Division I basketball career. What I did not disclose is that I tore my ACL sophomore year of College, and blew out the other knee in my thirties.

Most of you will most likely discard that as coincidence. I beg to differ. I believe I have reaped the defiled harvest of the corrupt seed that I had sown for so many years of my early life. I have reaped both the spiritual seed of my thoughts and I have undoubtedly reaped the harvest of the physical strain that so many years of athletics had placed upon my body. It is all good though. *"And we know that **all things** work together for good to those who love God, to those who are the **called according to His purpose."*** (Romans 8:28) I understand that it got me to the point of being able to share these experiences with you through the power of this discourse.

Mind Control

Thirdly, and right on cue, your thoughts are also a seed. You must learn to control them. Interestingly enough, you can control your thoughts by *using* your mouth. Your mouth has the ability to overrule your thoughts.

Try this little exercise that I learned from the great Preacher Kenneth Copeland. Begin by counting to yourself from ten back to one. When you get to around five, say your name out loud. Take careful note of what happened to your counting. You will find that it has stopped.

Likewise, when you begin having negative thoughts, begin speaking the Word of God over your thoughts. Not only will the negative thoughts stop, but you will change both your thought and your word seed. This will undoubtedly change your harvest.

Remember, every accomplishment in your life will begin with the seed of a thought or an idea. But beware, as stated earlier, you cannot shut down the law of sowing and reaping. It will remain active just as the change of seasons remains active. Therefore, you must pay attention to the thoughts you are sowing. Every sin will begin in your thoughts, but thankfully, so will every act of righteousness.

Acting Out

Fourthly, your actions are a seed. Everything you do affects someone, somewhere, sometime. The effect of your actions may not be immediate. In fact, it could be years before you feel it, but *"there is nothing covered that will not be revealed, nor hidden that will not be known."* (Luke 12:2)

That is quite scary if you give some actual thought to it. Even if we escape the consequence of our actions in this present life, the Lord is watching. All will be revealed upon our appearance before Him. That alone should keep a man in line. It is also the reason a society falls apart when God is erased.

Do not fear this, however. When you make Jesus Christ your Lord you escape judgment. Your sins are erased. Therefore, you no longer need to fear the consequence of your sin. You become a new creation, sinless and one with Yahweh. Your new-found image causes you to begin seeking what is right, while simultaneously, the Holy Spirit brings all unrighteousness to the forefront of your attention, thus allowing the opportunity for repentance.

How do you change your actions? It is simple, go back to seed one. Begin with prayer. Prayer will help you change your thoughts, which will allow you to change your confession. Your new-found words will solidify your thoughts and lead to repentance which will cause you to change your actions. It is all interrelated.

A Physical Connection

Finally, your money is a seed. A portion of your funds should go to establishing the Kingdom of God. *"It is He who gives you the power to get wealth that He may establish His covenant."* (Deuteronomy 8:18)

Did you know that the only material thing you can give God is money? Whether it be cash, jewelry, stocks, bonds, etc . . . by supporting the ministry, the poor, and the less fortunate, it is the only thing you can give back to Him that can be physically touched. It is also what we hold on to the tightest.

Do not be fooled. God does not need, nor even want, your money. Money has no value to God. It is simply a medium of exchange. He does, however, want your heart. He also does not want you in idolatry. Many people trust their money more than they trust God. As we discussed in *Yahweh Revealed,* this was the case with the rich young ruler and that is idolatry. Therefore, I would encourage you to use your money as the medium of exchange that it is. Exchange the physical for the spiritual. Serve God with your money. Although you could never buy Him, you can demonstrate your love for Him by letting go of the idol you hold onto the tightest.

Do not worry. God is just. When you sow something material you will reap something material. *"Give, and it will be given to you, good measure, pressed down, shaken together, and running over will be placed into your* *bosom. **For with the same measure you use it will be measured back to you.***" (Luke 6:38) If you give a little, you will reap a little. If you give abundantly, you will reap abundantly. If you give of yourself spiritually and materially, you will reap everlasting life.

What's the Mix Up?

This leads us to a very important point which brings us back to the loss Job experienced in his life. Leviticus 19:19 states the following: *"You shall not sow your field with mixed seed"* and Deuteronomy 22:9 states, *"You shall not sow your vineyard with different kinds of seed, **lest the yield of the seed** which you have sown and the fruit of your vineyard **be defiled."***

Without realizing it, we continuously mix our seed. This is why we all too often reap a defiled harvest. We repeatedly say one thing and do another. We confess the Word of God around our church friends and are embarrassed to confess the Word around our secular friends. We apply situational ethics at work, or even when it is just easier to do. All of this leads to a defiled harvest.

Sowing mixed seed is where our primary battle resides concerning sowing and reaping. It determines the difference between success and failure and it is difficult to overcome. You must be full of the Word to overcome it. *"Out of the abundance* (overflow, NIV) *of the heart, the mouth speaks."* (Matthew 12:34) If you want to know what is in your heart, listen to the first words out of your mouth when you are under pressure. That is your overflow. At times I have found this to be horrifying. It is, however, an unparalleled means of discovering what lies beneath the surface of your own heart.

Therefore, if you want to change what is coming from your heart, your actions, thoughts, or anything about your life, you must change the seed you are sowing. You must replace what is in your heart. This can only be done by filling yourself with God's Word. It is not difficult, but it requires time, patience, and most of all, diligence. You will need to turn off the television and fight your old habits, but remember, **"the victory always resides beyond the battle"** —**Me** Lol!

Origin of the Species

At this point, it is imperative to recognize that no two seeds are alike. Some require more time to come to harvest while others require more water, better soil, or more or less light. You must get to know *your* situation. You must learn to sow intentionally. Otherwise, you may not recognize what has grown or you may attempt reap before your fruit ripens. In either case, you will cut off God's abundance. You may gather, but not to the fullest.

There is no magic formula for recognizing this. The only way to learn is by spending time in God's presence. Therefore, when in doubt, just keep sowing. This usually entails remaining in prayer and in the Word of God. To be effective, you must make the time to do this. Do not make excuses. Anyone willing can pursue the presence of the Lord. The question is, will you?

Allow me to illustrate the sowing of "good seed" into "good ground." Let's say, hypothetically, that your leg hurts. You have been to numerous doctors and none can find anything wrong, but still, your leg hurts. The first thing you must do is unsheathe your Sword, which is your Bible.

In addition to the Spirit of God, your Bible is a book full of spiritual seeds. What we need to find in this example is some "healing seed." So we turn to Isaiah 53:5, for example, and we find our seed.

*"But He was wounded for our transgressions, He was bruised for our iniquities, the chastisement for our peace was upon Him, **and by His stripes we are healed.**"*

So what do we do with it? First we need to sow it by reading it over and over until it becomes firmly implanted in our heart. At the same time, begin to pray it by confessing it out loud—regardless of who is listening. The seed has been sown.

At this point, do we just walk away and wait for it to grow? Of course not. We must tend to it. We must continue to confess it regardless of the circumstance. Every time you feel a pain, every time you have a negative thought, no matter what you are doing, or who you are around, continue confessing God's Word.

In addition, you will need to pull the weeds growing around it from time to time. Weeds choke the roots, as well as, steal the essential nutrients required for abundant growth. These are the negative thoughts that come to mind. They are the negative words coming from your mouth which contradict the Word of God. Do not just pull the head off the weed either. You must get it by the roots or it will simply grow back.

Now this is important. A farmer does not just use water. They need something to boost the crop. This process requires fertilizer. If you are looking for a "bumper crop" you need to mix some *Miracle Grow* with your water. This is simple, but it requires immediate action.

Find someone sick or injured, either physically or emotionally. They are not hard to find. Churches, hospitals, and even your own family and friend groups are full of them. Begin praying for that person or people. Begin teaching them. If you are trusting God for finances begin helping those in need. If you are believing God for healing, head to the hospital. There are plenty of people to pray for. Use whatever resources and abilities God has blessed you with.

Now you are beginning to enter a different realm. You are beginning to connect with Luke 6:38 and you are entering the realm of faith. While you are doing this something strange begins to happen. You begin to believe what you are praying for, particularly when you see other people being delivered by the power of God through your prayers.

Beware when this begins to happen. You will have a tendency to ask, "Why haven't I been healed?" Do not give attention to this thought. It is a weed. Spray it some spiritual *Round Up* (The Word of God) and kill it by the root.

In the Spirit you have become unstoppable. It is now simply a matter of your harvest coming to fruition. Jesus said, *"Whatever things you ask in prayer, believing, you will receive."* (Matthew 21:22) I am no genius but I *do* know that "whatever" means whatever, and since your newfound lifestyle is based in and upon obeying the Word of God, you are in the will of God. Therefore, anything is possible.

The last thing you must do is take a stand. That means to hold on to what you *know* is the truth. God's Word is truth. *It* says you are healed. *It* says you are prosperous. *It* says you are whatever God wills you to be. Period, the end! God has final authority and His Word is the last word. Now forget about all the naysayers who are calling you crazy. Close your mouth to negativity and begin expecting.

Begin your stand by thanking Him in advance for your healing or whatever it is you are believing for. You must make it real. The late **Kenneth Hagin** said, **"If you are willing to stand forever, you will not have to stand very long."** That is a little known truth and undoubtedly one powerful secret of the Father. God always honors faith.

Don't Make a Mockery

In conclusion, let's complete this vital secret. Do you remember our earlier discussion, *"Do not be deceived, God is not mocked, whatever a man sows that shall he also reap. For he who sows to the flesh, will of the flesh reap corruption, but he who sows to the Spirit, will of the Spirit reap everlasting life?"* (Galatians 6:7–8)

If you believe you can sow one thing and reap another you are deceived. Even worse, you are mocking God. Do you believe you can overrule His law? That cannot be done and you must continuously, on a daily basis, check yourself for deception. Most never come to the realization that the most dangerous thing about being deceived is that you do not know when you are; otherwise you would not be. The only way to discover your own deception is by peering intently into the Word of God. It will always reveal the truth.

Therefore, do not hesitate. Begin by consciously sowing the Word of God into your life right now. It takes practice and you will make mistakes, but God and His Word are a discerner *of the thoughts and intents of the heart."* (Hebrews 4:12) God will honor your intent. He will honor your seed and what you purposely sow into the now will reap a harvest that spans all the way into forever!

—— CHAPTER 5 ——

Greater Works

(THE SECRET OF THE RESURRECTION)

In light of who Jesus is and what He was able to accomplish while walking the blue planet, I am compelled to believe that apart from salvation, the following one sentence passage is the most astounding promise in all of scripture. In John 14:12, Jesus makes the following proclamation, *"The works that I do, **you will do even greater.**"*

Why is this so amazing? For a brief moment, consider what Jesus did while roaming the blue planet. In addition to teaching and preaching, He healed the sick, opened the eyes of the blind, caused the lame to walk, and incredibly, even raised the dead back to life. He then made the seemingly implausible assertion that His disciples would possess the capability to perform even greater miracles than *He* did while adorning an earth-suit. That is an outrageous statement! How is that humanly possible?

I must admit that for a long time this seemed outlandish to me. Deep inside my spirit, however, I also knew that God *"can do exceeding abundantly beyond all we can ask or think."* (Ephesians 3:20) Therefore, I never closed my spirit to the possibilities of what this may entail. After all, the meaning of the above scripture is that if we can even contemplate a particular action, God can not only bring it to pass, He can achieve something even greater.

Yet, it was always the issue of raising the dead that tormented my thinking. Quite honestly, it even hindered my faith. I have heard stories about the dead being raised, but have never seen nor even known anyone who has actually experienced it. Have you? Therefore, in reality it seemed like a fable to me. I would venture to guess that many of you feel the same way.

Unveiled

Early one morning I was at a prayer meeting with several fellow believers. I have to be honest with you; I did not want to go to the meeting that fateful morning. There were even several hindrances to our getting there, yet my wife and I persisted and went to the meeting anyway.

It began as nothing unusual. After about thirty minutes or so, however, it began to heat up. The Lord's people began to become more fervent in spirit. We knew the presence of the Lord was beginning to manifest, yet nothing unusual was happening. There were no physical manifestations or anything like that.

When one particular woman began to pray, God immediately spoke to my heart. It was not an audible voice, but a revelation. It was the unveiling of a mystery that had haunted my thoughts and encumbered my faith for years. It lasted for only a millisecond of time, but in that instant the

Lord implanted the following revelation within me. It was as if He simply flipped a switch or if my spirit and mind was a computer, He downloaded a file that contained our next Secret of the Father. My eyes were instantly opened. I could now see clearly.

When the room quieted down the Lord had me share the above scriptures and precede them with the following question; what is the greatest miracle the Lord can provide? After a brief period of silence and without realizing where the Lord was leading, the participants began to name several of the needs in their lives, all of which are significant, but none of which are essential to salvation leading to eternal life. I then shared the following truth.

The greatest miracle the Lord can provide for any individual is the salvation of their soul. Think about it, every other miracle that can be conferred upon humanity is merely temporary. If you are sick and God heals your body, it is temporary. Eventually you will die. If you are in need of finances and God bestows them upon you, it is temporary. Eventually you will need more money or you will die leaving your wealth to your heirs. Whatever miracle God provides for you, you will eventually be separated from it through death. There is only one exception—the salvation of your immortal spirit and soul.

Salvation is eternal. It will cause you to live an eternity in heaven with the Almighty and all those who have been saved. Scripture declares, *"The things we can see are temporal, but the invisible things, which we cannot see are eternal."* (2 Corinthians 4:18)

That means if any problem or situation has manifested itself in your life, and if it has gotten to the point where you can actually *experience it,* it is temporary and subject to being changed. It does not matter whether it is positive or negative. That is good news.

The invisible things, however, which are the things of the Spirit, such as the Word of God, salvation, and the promises of God, are unchanging. They are eternal. That is even better news. The truth that your destiny can be changed from hell to heaven, and that it can be secured for all of eternity is the essence of the gospel of Jesus Christ.

Dead on Arrival

While you are pondering this revelation, I would like to submit the following. First allow me to lay the foundation of this concept with the following preface. As a church, or as a "body," and I am referring to all believers and not the institution, building, or particular denomination, we spend an awful lot of time praying for revival without really considering what our petition really entails.

In modern Christianity, revival simply means church growth in the form of putting some additional fanny's in the seats. With our limited view of eternity, we seem to measure success primarily by the number of members in the congregation. To a certain degree it is, but the direction I am leading you is of infinitely greater value. Think about it, what would you consider to be more successful, a church of five thousand apathetic, or perhaps, even, unsaved congregants, or a church of one hundred on fire, born again, Bible thumping believers whose hearts are set upon gathering the lost to eternity? Keep in mind that outward appearance is irrelevant. The Master of the universe was born amongst livestock.

As incredible as it may seem, Jesus changed the world with a misfit congregation numbering a mere twelve. *"Jesus answered them, 'Did I not choose you, the twelve, and one of you is a devil?'"* (John 6:70) I guess that makes the true number eleven. Apparently, Judas' heart was black from its origin. It appears that his primary motivation for "discipleship" was to rob from the money box. (John 12:6)

Do not forget, however, that Judas was meticulously hand picked from eternity past. Our Savior's primary mission of death had to be manifest. Our Father, therefore, carefully chose a man whom He knew would go through with the betrayal. That job was not for the faint of heart. That makes Judas a rather important player, does it not? When viewed from eternity, the purpose of both Jesus and Judas become clear as crystal. The rest of Jesus' disciples, numbering in the hundreds, by the way, *"went away"* (John 6:67) when He began to discuss the hard truth.

From that perspective, not a whole lot has changed in the church over the last two thousand years or so. Many of today's "disciples" are in it merely for the money. *"But since they have no root, they last only a short time. When trouble or persecution comes because of the word, they quickly fall away."* (Matthew 13:21, NIV) Not even the seventy-two that Jesus sent out ahead of the twelve were willing to stay when Jesus truly began to get truly radical.

> **"From that time many of His disciples went back and walked with Him no more.** Then Jesus said to the twelve, 'Do you also want to go away?' But Simon Peter answered Him, 'Lord, to whom shall we go? You have the words of eternal life.'"**
>
> **—John 6:66–68**

While entreating the Lord for revival, most people never consider the following truth. In order to revive something, or someone, it, or they, must have already been dead. That is what it means to revive. The prefix "re" means, "again" and the root "vive," means "to live." That means in order to experience revival you must bring something, or someone *back* to life.

Traditionally, there are two types of spiritual revival. You can revive "backslidden" Christians who have ceased to live the Christian life; or you can revive those born dead on arrival, meaning those who have never accepted Christ and remain separate from God. The latter, believe it or not, describes the majority of today's "Christians." They are still D.O.A. They have never made a conscious decision to follow Christ. Much of the body simply join a church, flaunt the name, but reject the life. In order to be revived, however, one must be "born again." (John 3:3–5)

In truth, we are all born spiritually dead. That is the effect of original sin. Spiritually speaking, we are all subject to a stillborn birth. Because everything in the natural realm is subject to death and decay, otherwise known as entropy, we are all D.O.A.—Dead on Arrival! The only thing that varies is the date of our decomposition.

Therefore, true revival means to raise a dead individual and/or church back to life, or, to fill it with newly born disciples of Christ, who are actually spiritually alive for the first time since being separated from their Maker by birth. That is the definition of true revival. True revival is not participating in some week long tent meeting in which only Christian people show up. As disciples of Jesus Christ, we must follow His lead by going into the wastelands of civilization to liberate the lost from the fiery depths of what has become hell on earth. That is not an easy task and it is not for the faint of heart. Whoever started the rumor that Christian's are wimpy has undoubtedly never met one. Continuos battle with the adversary is the most difficult task on earth. Unlike your worldly career, retirement only commences upon your last breath.

Alive in Christ

With that in mind, here is the next secret. Take note of the following revelation. Every time we preach the gospel under the divine influence or inspiration of the Holy Spirit, and a man or woman is convicted of their sin to the point of repentance, thus, receiving Jesus Christ as their Lord and Savior, that person becomes "born again." "Born again" is not a religious term, nor is it a religion, denomination or church group. "Born again" is a description of what happens to your spirit upon the acceptance of Jesus Christ into your heart. To become "born again," means you have been birthed for a second time. The first is into the natural realm of the physical universe. The second is into the heavenly Kingdom of our Father, otherwise known as the Spirit.

"Jesus answered and said to him, 'Most assuredly, I say to you, **unless one is born again,** *he cannot see the kingdom of God.'*

Nicodemus said to Him, 'How can a man be born when he is old? Can he enter a second time into his mother's womb and be born?'

Jesus answered, 'Most assuredly, I say to you, unless one is born of water **and the Spirit,** *he cannot enter the kingdom of God. That which is born of the flesh is flesh, and that which is born of the Spirit is spirit.'"*

—John 3:3–6

Once this occurs, your spirit, which was born dead due to original sin and separated from God, is reconnected to Yahweh, transformed into His image, and revived to eternal life. This new life, or revival, joins us together with God through the same power that raised Jesus Christ from the dead. **"In Him was life,** *and the life was the light of men."* (John 1:4) In fact, Jesus specifically stated, **"I am the resurrection** *and the life. He who believes in Me, though he may die, he shall live. And whoever lives and believes in Me shall never die."* (John 11:25–26) Because Jesus and Yahweh are one and the same, Jesus is the resurrection. Jesus is the manifest power of God. Without Him, we simply await our date with the Lake of Fire.

The first birth, which in reality is the conception of your natural being, delivers you into the universal realm of the cosmos. It culminates in your physical birth. Physical birth, however, only completes half of the heavenly requirement for eternal life. The second is a Spiritual revival that reconnects you to humanity's life source, Yahweh, and transforms you back into His eternal image.

To illustrate this, take a second look at the conversation Jesus had with a secret disciple known as Nicodemus. Nicodemus happened to be a member of the Sanhedrin, a council of Jewish leaders, and as amazing as it might seem, he was not only a follower of the Lord Jesus Christ, Nicodemus was also a Pharisee.

> *"Nicodemus said unto Him, 'How can a man be born when he is old? Can he enter the second time into his mother's womb, and be born?'*
>
> *Jesus answered, 'Most assuredly, I say unto you, except a man* **be born of water and of the Spirit,** *he cannot enter into the kingdom of God.'*
>
> **—John 3:4–5**

As many mistakenly believe, this is not a reference to baptism. The "water" being referred to is amniotic fluid. When a woman gives birth there is a flow, or "breaking of water" that accompanies the birth of the child into the natural world in which we live. That is the first, or water birth.

The second birth is of the Spirit of Yahweh. The new birth was garnered through our acceptance of the life, death and resurrection of Jesus Christ. His sacrifice liberates us from the effects of the law and, thus, reunites us to Yahweh. As a result, we become "born again," and are reconnected to the life giving power of the Almighty. The secret is that *the result is permanent.* It is everlasting life. You are no longer subject to spiritual death.

Therefore, when making disciples we are accomplishing exactly what Jesus claimed we would accomplish. That is the secret of greater works! Eternal life far outweigh's the healing's, miracles and even the raising of the dead that Jesus referred to in His statement. The work accomplished in the believer is permanent. Death has been defeated.

Do you realize that a man could not be born again until *after* the resurrection of Jesus Christ? Have you ever considered why? Jesus had not yet sent the Helper, the Holy Spirit, whose purpose is to fill your spirit and reconnect you to Yahweh. The Holy Spirit is the glue that binds us to the Lord. He is our conduit between the super and the natural.

1 Corinthians 6:17 states, *"But he who is **joined** to the Lord is **one spirit** with Him."* The Greek word translated "joined" is, "kollaó." It means, "to glue, to glue together, to cement, and to fasten together." In Christ, the

believer in Yahweh actually becomes bound to the Lord. Just like *Gorilla Glue* binds two objects together, thus creating an unbreakable bond, through the power of the Holy Spirit, the believer and Yahweh become one.

Accomplishing such a task requires the power of God that works in *us*. Incredibly, it is the same power of God that works through Jesus. I must make that clear. It is not our power, it is God's power. Therefore, Jesus said to His followers, *"It is the Father who does the works."* (John 14:10) It is the same with us. As amazing as this is, you are still not quite seeing the whole picture.

You are Mine!

Apart from the death and resurrection, let's expand on why the true work of the body of Christ is even greater than that of Jesus when He walked the earth. Do not forget that what I am about to disclose is intended to be the primary function of the church. Eternity seems to have taken a backseat to the self-centeredness of today's pop culture Christian. As previously revealed, Christianity is not, and never has been, about the comfort of the individual. It is not about the beautiful building or even the sense of community one feels as part of a local church. Those are all benefits of Christianity but it is not, never has been, nor ever will be, the central purpose of the crucifixion.

The death and resurrection of Jesus Christ is all about the eternal future of the collective whole of humanity. If that requires pain or at the very least, the discomfort of the individual, so be it. Didn't Jesus, the individual, die for the collective whole of humanity? In fact, Caiaphas, the High Priest at the time of Jesus crucifixion, unknowingly prophesied by making the statement, *"It is expedient for us that one man should die for the people, and not that the whole nation should perish."* (John 11:50)

Do you think Jesus' death was comfortable? In fact, I would argue that Jesus' life was anything but comfortable, as well. He was constantly on the move, continuously harassed, persecuted, taken advantage of, over-exerted, tortured and eventually murdered. Yes, Jesus was murdered. On top of everything, He lived every day of His life knowing His ultimate fate. Can you imagine the stress? particularly as His eventuality drew near?

If you have studied the Bible, you have undoubtedly recognized the same fate being experienced by the early church throughout the Book of Acts. Somewhere along the line, however, the individual members of the body rejected the work of the disciple and the church stopped functioning. God's true promise is not a life without pain. It is a life in His eternal presence, which also means He will not abandon us while we face the trials and tribulations of genuine discipleship.

> *"But now, thus says the Lord, who created you, O Jacob, and He who formed you, O Israel: 'Fear not, for **I have redeemed you;** I have called you by your name; **you are Mine.** When you pass **through** the waters, I will be with you; and **through** the rivers, they shall not overflow you. When you walk **through** the fire, you shall not be burned, nor shall the flame scorch you."*
>
> **—Isaiah 43:1–2**

I believe this is one of the most beautiful promises in all of scripture. I turn to it for guidance and comfort with every trial of life. I would encourage you to memorize it, know it, and turn to it, as well. Most, however, never recognize Isaiah 43 as being a Messianic chapter. Isaiah 43 is a description of the redeeming work of Jesus Christ. The Hebrew word used for "redeem," is the word *"gaal,"* pronounced, *gaw-al.* It actually means, "to become your kin," and/or "to act as your kinsman redeemer." It is a reference to Jesus being manifest in flesh and blood in fulfillment of Leviticus chapter twenty-five. Isaiah 43:1 read in Hebrew actually states, *"Fear not, for I have **become your kin**; I have called you by your name; **you are Mine."***

I do not know about you, but I find that to be absolutely incredible and quite a bit more than just encouraging. Isaiah 43 sets my heart ablaze!

With that in mind, take some time to read the whole of Isaiah 43. The Book of Isaiah has been nicknamed, "the gospel of the Old Testament," and rightly so. Therefore, take some time to look at it from the point of view of Jesus Christ, your Kinsman Redeemer. With such incredible knowledge you will never see God, nor the Old Testament, the same way again.

However, nowhere does the scripture say we will avoid the troubles of life. The promise, which I consider to be a guarantee, is that we belong to Him, and, therefore, while we are going *through,* and not around the troubles of life, the Lord will be with us. *"He will not leave you nor forsake you"* (Deuteronomy 31:6) all the days of your life.

The trials of life are inevitable, but once you realize that you have been redeemed, which means our Father has repurchased us through the blood of Jesus Christ, and once you realize that you belong to God and not the devil, the issues of life become not just bearable, they become joyous. The devil never became your kin! Mohammed, Buddha, nor whomever you have turned to, never became your kin. Only Jesus did!

Therefore, Christ alone has the power to save. Keep in mind that I did not say life would be easy. Unbeknownst to most, joy does not mean that you will feel happy all the time. Pharrell Williams chart busting song is not the key to happiness. Christ alone holds the key. (Matthew 16:19) Joy means you can experience peace in the midst of suffering. Joy in the midst of pain is where miracles, signs and wonders begin to manifest. God's power, which ultimately results in deliverance, is available when we *need* it, not just when we desire it.

Soul Catchers

With that said, let's return to our revelation. Do you remember when Jesus raised Lazarus from the dead? As great a miracle as that was, it was merely temporary. Lazarus would eventually die again. He was not, and could not, be "born again" until *after* Jesus was crucified, died, resurrected, ascended, seated at the right hand of the Father, and subsequently having sent the Holy Spirit to lead, guide, penetrate and bind humanity to our Maker. Only then could God create a brand new connection in us.

It was not until this work was "finished" that a man could even accept the sacrifice of Jesus Christ and be born again into the miracle of eternal life. Consider what the Word of God says about the resurrection of Christ. *"For whom He foreknew* (that's us)*, He also predestined to be conformed to the image of His Son, that He* (Jesus) *might be **the firstborn** among **many brethren.***" (Romans 8:29)

Jesus' restoration to His former place of glory and oneness with Yahweh was the first "new birth" in history. It was the first permanent spiritual reconnection to the Father. Even Jesus' mortal life was temporary. The *"firstborn among many brethren"* is Jesus' eternal state of being. *"When you make His soul an offering for sin"* (Isaiah 53:10) it becomes yours, as well.

Therefore, each time we touch even one soul through the power of the Holy Spirit, that spirit is reborn, or, in keeping with the topic of discussion, revived; only this time *they will never die!* That is the secret of greater works. When a man gets born again he or she passes from death to life. In Christ, we become eternally resurrected to the union of the Father. In other words, we are restored back to the image of God in which we were initially created, in unity with the Spirit and in oneness with Jehovah.

Through the resurrection power of Yahweh, we, the followers and disciples of Jesus Christ raise the lost into the everlasting bliss of eternity. Jesus, while on earth raised them back into the natural. The church, while we remain on earth, to the supernatural. Now do you understand our purpose? Can you now comprehend the greater work? When viewing the church's function in this brand new light, why did I ever doubt Jesus?

Do not get me wrong, I am not saying that you cannot, or will not, receive physical miracles, meaning those manifested in the natural realm.

Many will. What I *am* saying, is that the spiritual miracles are infinitely greater and of significantly greater importance due to the truth of their eternal consequence.

Here is what is even more amazing. Since you and I can now comprehend this eternal miracle and biblical truth, God has something even greater than we can even ask or think. I have no idea what that could possibly be. Until it is revealed by the Spirit of Yahweh, I cannot think of it, nor can I imagine it, but I know that God has already accomplished it. His Word says so.

There is none like Jesus, the Lord of all lords and the King of all kings. So put that arrow in your forever quiver and begin to accomplish the *Greater Works* of the body of Jesus Christ.

It is time to reveal another secret.

——— CHAPTER 6 ———

A Mystery Revealed

(THE SECRET OF HIS PRESENCE)

I love mysteries. Whether they are movies, television shows, novels or solving some mystery of life, I get a charge out of the not knowing. I enjoy the seeking. The enigmatic construction of the puzzle and the fabrication of the mystery revealed absolutely thrills me. This may sound strange, but one of the things I love most about Yahweh is the mystery that He is. I love the challenge of unmasking His essence. In effect, peeling away the layers of who He is, and how and why He does, or does not do, what He does.

As I continue to discover the excellence of His majesty and the pinnacle of His wonder, I cannot help but fall more deeply in love with and develop an even greater reverence for our almighty King. In addition to His incredible wonder, He also happens to be the most loving of Father's. He has been the motivation of my adult life and both the incentive and reward for writing this book series. *"The Lord is my portion, says my soul, therefore I will hope in Him."* (Lamentations 3:24)

What you are reading is quite simply a compilation of some of the mysteries that I have *begun* to unravel. I would never claim to have solved the mystery of God. No one consisting of flesh and blood will ever be able to make that claim. The Lord is great beyond measure. He is infinite. Our minds cannot even conceive of the vastness encompassing the nature of our holy God. That does not mean, however, that he will not let us in on a few secrets from time to time.

> *"Ask, and it will be given to you; seek, and you will find; knock, and it will be opened to you.*
>
> **—Matthew 7:7**

> **"The secret of the Lord** *is with those who fear Him, and He will show them His covenant."*
>
> **—Psalm 25:14**

What an incredible set of promises! Therefore, sit back and relax. It is time to discover another one of the endless *Secrets of the Father*.

Personality

Many people question whether it is possible to know God personally. Islam, for example, does not believe in a personal God. They do not believe that Allah interacts in the personal affairs of men. They believe Allah is all powerful and that he is the creator of heaven and earth. They believe he will empower them for war (if he wills for them to win). They also believe he will judge the deeds of men.

He is not personal, however. You cannot know him, love him and interact with him. Since a scale is the single determining factor in your salvation, he certainly does not reciprocate humanity's love for him. Conversely, when you consider the proactive sacrifice of Jesus Christ versus the callus, deadness of a scale, doesn't that put the love of Yahweh on a vastly higher plane? Which would you prefer determine your eternity, a living, loving, merciful God, willing to die for those He loves, or a merciless, loveless, dead, scale? Look deep within yourself before you answer. Between Islam and Christianity, those are the choices.

How about those involved in the Eastern religions of Hinduism or Buddhism, for example, and the numerous New Age religions that believe God is merely some etherial energy source and that "the universe" answers your prayers? Is their version of god personal? Can a human being have a relationship with an enigmatic energy source? How about with the more than 1000 Hindu gods?

Most importantly, however, what do *you* believe and why? Do you believe God is personal? What is your idea of God based upon? Is it merely an opinion, or perhaps, even worse, the judgment of another? Is it based upon emotion or misunderstanding? Have you looked into the foundation of truth by carefully examining, the Bible, the Qu'ran or the various texts available to humanity?

After having studied various religions, and while simultaneously experiencing Yahweh's goodness and His presence, I certainly believe He is personal. Unlike the Qu'ran and the vast array of other religious books, the Bible seems to agree. Therefore, have a look at the following scripture and we will discuss this markedly relevant issue.

Secrets

> *"The secret things belong to the Lord our God, but **those things which are revealed** belong **to us** and to **our children forever**, that we may do all the words of this law."*
>
> **—Deuteronomy 29:29**

What a fascinating piece of scripture. Perhaps you never before knew that God keeps secrets. I am delighted to inform you that He most certainly does and that His secrets are personal. Have you ever considered why? We will discuss that shortly.

Amazingly, once He reveals His secrets, they belong to us and to our children for the remainder of time. That means God is never going to rescind them. They are part of His Word and they are irrevocable. Do you remember 2 Corinthians 4:18, *"the things which are seen are temporal, but the things we cannot see are eternal,"* from the previous chapter? Because God's secrets are hidden in Him, they are eternal. According to scripture, that means they are not subject to change. The Bible is incredible in its consistency throughout. That, therefore, leaves us with several questions. What are these secrets; and why has God hidden them? Wouldn't it be easier to just get it out in the open and tell everybody everything?

We will spend the rest of this chapter exploring some of the secrets and mysteries of Yahweh, at least as much as He has been willing to reveal to me. There are some things hidden which quite simply have not been revealed—at least not yet! God refers to them in His Word as both secrets and mysteries.

Do not forget that *everything* belongs to God. It is only at *His* discretion that His secrets are to be revealed. They are intended to accomplish *His* purpose and, therefore, He releases them when He deems the time not just to be appropriate, but perfect. With that in mind, there is no time like the present. Let's delve into some of the hidden mysteries of El Shaddai.

No Escape

I would like to begin this discussion by exploring Psalm 139. It is a testament to the goodness and the power of our Father. Take note of the following:

> "O Lord, you have searched me and known me. (That one sentence lays to rest whether or not God is personal.) You know my sitting down and my rising up; you understand my thought afar off. You comprehend my path and my lying down, and are acquainted with all my ways. For there is not a word on my tongue, but behold, O Lord, you know it altogether. You have hedged me behind and before, and laid your hand upon me. Such knowledge is wonderful to me; it is high, I cannot attain it."
>
> "Where can I go from your Spirit?"
>
> "Or where can I flee from Your presence? If I ascend into heaven, you are there; if I make my bed in hell, behold, you are there. If I take the wings of the morning, and dwell in the uttermost parts of the sea, even there your hand shall lead me, and your right hand shall hold me . . ."
>
> "For you formed my inward parts; you covered me in my mother's womb. I will praise you, for I am fearfully and wonderfully made; and that my soul knows very well. My frame was not hidden from you when I was made in **secret,** and skillfully wrought in the lowest parts of the earth. Your eyes saw my substance being yet unformed, and in your book they all were

written, the days fashioned for me, when as yet there were none of them."

—Psalm 139:1–16

What a beautiful revelation. First of all, I want you to know and understand that Yahweh, your Father, is personal beyond any shadow of doubt. He knows you. He always has and in eternity, He always will. He knows everything about you—your every thought, your every word—even before they cross your mind or your lips. He has surrounded you and hedged you in, and there He waits—lovingly, and ever so patiently for an invitation into your life. He wants you to know Him as intimately as the author of this Psalm, King David, knew Him. He wants to protect you and deliver you from the giants in your life, just as he delivered Goliath into the hand of the mighty David, a mere shepherd boy turned king.

What I find utterly fascinating is the fact that Yahweh knew you before you were even formed in your mother's womb. He fashioned you and designed you before your conception. He formed your shape, size, personality and your spirit. He then "lifted a few specks of clay" from the lowest depths of the earth and formed you from fifty-nine of the earth's elements. He *"chose you in Christ before the foundation of the world."* (Ephesians 1:4) He is ever present, all knowing and all powerful. He is forever existent in the past, present and future. What a wonderful and incomprehensible mystery. He is totally and completely free!

You cannot escape His presence. He knows what will happen every second of every day "now" and "forever." He has always known it. Not only has He appointed it, He authored it. How wonderful and comforting it is to know that His power and glory unceasingly surrounds and protects you. He has guarded your future in the secret place of His presence from the beginning of eternity, and there He waits for you to turn to Him and to take hold of the mystery which is your life in Christ. In Christ, your destiny patiently awaits its fulfillment.

Trust Me

"The Lord is my light and my salvation; whom shall I fear? The Lord is the strength of my life; of whom shall I be afraid? When the wicked come against me to eat up my flesh, my enemies and foes, they stumbled and fell. Though an army may encamp against me, my heart shall not fear; though war may rise against me, in this I will be confident."

*"One thing I have desired of the Lord, that will I seek: That I may dwell in the house of the Lord all the days of my life, to behold the beauty of the Lord, and to inquire in His temple. For in the time of trouble **He shall hide me** in His pavilion; **in the secret place** of His tabernacle He shall hide me; He shall set me high upon a rock."*

—Psalm 27:1–5

I noticed something change in my life when I truly began to desire the Lord. A very close friend of mine and I began to wake up early and seek the Lord together in daily prayer. Incredibly, the Lord began speaking to us from day one. That, however, is not what surprised us. We were expecting that. What we did not anticipate was the incredible speed in which He began to intercede on our behalf. That was amazing. It was as if He were there the whole time—and He was. Jehovah was patiently awaiting our return.

It was right about this time that the Lord had led me to quit my job and begin my own financial planning practice. There was a group of us who were planning to leave on April first of the year. Our greatest worry and fear was how we were going to bring our clients with us and how diligently our previous employer would fight to keep them.

We were not intending to do anything which would violate our previous contract. Our attorney had interpreted that for certain product lines our contract allowed us to contact our clients upon our leaving. However, it could certainly have been challenged and we were fairly certain that we would be met with a great deal of resistance, and perhaps, even be tied up in court for a time. Our previous employer had very deep pockets compared to ours. Although we were confident that we would win the war, the battles could be financially crippling.

On our flight home from visiting and negotiating with our new Broker Dealer, approximately eight months prior to our leaving, my brother and I were discussing the situation and the various possibilities, as well as, our preparedness to handle the oncoming possibility of hardship. To be quite honest, I did not feel prepared to handle what may come. However, the situation at our current employer had become so unbearable that I had no doubt that change was my only recourse.

After our conversation ended I closed my eyes. Within seconds the Lord said to me, "January second! That's the date that I want you to leave."

So I said, "Okay Lord. You do realize that's three months prior to the rest of the team?"

Of course He knew. Therefore, I immediately turned to my brother and said, "I'm leaving January second."

He looked at me a bit stunned at first and replied, "I think that's a great idea."

So that is what I did. I became the test case.

Back to our morning prayer . . . My friend and I had been praying that we would learn how to walk in the Lord daily. We all know the *"Our Father,"* and how Jesus taught us to pray, *"Give us **this day** our **daily** bread . . ."* This had become so real to us that we began to no longer worry about tomorrow. *"Sufficient for the day is its own trouble"* (Matthew 6:34) is how we began to live our lives. You would be amazed how stress relieving this concept is. I must tell you that living your life in this manner is a beautiful thing. **"Prayer does not change God, but it changes him who prays."—Soren Kierkegaard**

That, by the way, is one incredible *Secret of the Father.* How often are our prayers an attempt to change God? God does not change. (Malachi 3:6) No wonder so many of them go unanswered.

Leaving our worry behind, however, does not mean that we are to become irresponsible. I believe in planning for the future and I believe the Bible agrees. *"A good man leaves an inheritance to his children's children..."* (Proverbs 13:22) However, we had progressed way beyond the point of worrying about it. In fact, I still do not worry about the future. Let me rephrase that. I now have the weaponry to battle worrying about my future. I have complete and total trust that the Lord has my best interest in mind. His Word says so. If that is the case and I am diligently following His lead, what do I have to worry about?

> *"For I know the thoughts that I think toward you, says the Lord, thoughts of peace and not of evil,* ***to give you a future and a hope."***
> **—Jeremiah 29:11**

That, pretty much, settles it..

This Means War

One evening as I was visiting with a client the phone rang. On the other end was a representative of my previous employer. What transpired did not surprise me in terms of what he said. The Lord's response and ensuing action, however, was truly awe inspiring.

The gentleman on the other end of the line began to slander, mislead and tell a plethora of lies concerning my current situation, of which he had not a clue. In fact, I had never met the gentleman on the other end of the phone. When I got into my car to drive home, I began to discuss with the Lord what my response to stop these lies should be. He had begun calling all my clients in an attempt to win them over by spreading his malicious deceit. I did not mind the competition. He certainly had the right to compete for the business. Just be honest about it and let the best man win.

Once again, the Lord began to speak and I must tell you that His response was shocking, to say the least. I grew up having been taught to fight. My natural inclination is to stand up for myself. Perhaps you are the same way. The Lord said to me, however, "Do not do a thing. I'll fight your battle."

At first, this made no sense to me at all. It made me feel incredibly uncomfortable and in all honesty, extremely vulnerable. The Lord was asking me to turn complete control over to Him. Folks, the financial future of my family and perhaps, even, my entire lineage was on the line. When your future is at stake this is easy to give lip service to but quite difficult to actually do.

Thank God for the morning prayer. Without it I would have never submitted. Trust me when I tell you that at this point I did not get it. The secret of obedience, by the way, *is submitting to God* (or anyone with authority over you) *when you do not want to submit.* Obedience is not obedience when you are on board with the plan. That is agreement and the two concepts are radically opposed to one another.

I was not in agreement with the Lord at the time, but I was spiritually astute enough to realize that He is infinitely more intelligent and powerful than I am. Therefore, it was time to *get* on board. I also realized how much God loves me and that He has my best interest in mind. Therefore, I submitted to Him and obeyed. I must stress how important these two concepts are to prospering in the kingdom of God. It is also true in regard to parenting, by the way.

In time, however, I began to understand another secret. *The Lord loves my competitors as much as He loves me.* Understanding this truth could save the world a whole lot of bloodshed. Therefore, it was really none of my business. It was between him and God. So I submitted to letting go and letting God deal with the problem.

I must tell you that God did fight for me. From that point forward the gentleman's impetuous lies were met with nothing but anger and disbelief on the part of my clients. Their response to me was, "Doesn't this guy realize that we have known you for ten years and have never even met him." That evening I learned first hand that slander does not make one look good in the eyes of others. Needless to say, I lost none of them.

Incredibly, the next day I received phone call from my brother to inform me that my previous employer had decided not to pursue me. It turns out that at the same time I had resigned, my previous boss accepted a position in the field of, and get this, client retention! How ironic is that? That is certainly no coincidence and I still get a chuckle out it. God has an amazing sense of humor.

Since he was just learning his new role, but I am sure would have had it figured out in three months, they had decided that I was not worth the trouble. I had acted quickly enough in moving my clients, and besides, we knew all their weaknesses. There was a reason I had left. I knew too much and was not a big enough fish to open up a can of worms on their behalf.

How about that January second departure date? Does the Lord know all or what? I would encourage you to make note of just how important it is to follow the Lord's instruction, immediately, and without question. You must, however, confirm that it is His voice, even if it requires perceived pain. That is accomplished by knowing the Word of God.

"So then faith comes by hearing, and hearing by the word of God."
—Romans 10:17

Victory is Mine!

This is not all that occurred. The story gets even better. My wife and I had been prepared to spend several months without income. We quickly became aware that this was definitely not the Lord's intention. In the third week of January when our checking account began to run low we received a check in the mail that was supposed to come in mid-February. Meanwhile my new broker dealer had decided to pay out an office transition fee to help ease the pain.

My wife, who belongs to a fellowship group, who for fun, and to keep the meetings interesting and exciting, contribute two hundred dollars per month. Each meeting they have a drawing and give one person a pile of cash. She won the drawing.

By the way, this is not gambling. It is more of a deferred savings plan. Every person must win before anyone can win a second time. It is good clean fun and no one loses. You can even request to be the winner if some sort of need arises in your life.

Additionally, my previous employer, as a result of some previous business, sent me a check and two weeks later another. Both were completely unexpected as well. Because I obeyed the Lord, He provided an abundance of funds to meet my family's personal and business needs during our period of transition.

My point is not to brag about how much the Lord loves me or to dupe you into believing some sort of prosperity doctrine where God, as if He were *I dream of Jeannie* in a bottle, responds to the right magic words. The point is that God is all sufficient. Given the circumstance, He would have done the same for you. My aim is to illustrate the faithfulness of our holy Father and the truth of the Word of God. Just like Psalm 27 stated, the Lord had set me high upon a rock. My enemies stumbled and fell and He brought me into the secret place of His tabernacle. The glory belongs to Him and no other.

Because I was willing to enter His gates and trust Him, He delivered me in my time of trouble. When we draw near to God, He draws near to us. (James 4:8) I love what **Zig Ziglar** said about Yahweh, **"When you turn to God you discover He has been facing you all the time."** I am amazed at how true that statement is. When we trust and obey Him, He has our backs. *"The God of Israel will be your rear guard."* (Isaiah 52:12)

By the way, those two elements work hand in hand. You must trust God in order to obey Him. Particularly, when it is something you do not quite understand. This can only be accomplished by nurturing your relationship with your Father. You must obey Him in the small things before you will be obedient in those matters that become truly life changing.

To us, our futures are a mystery needing to be played out. To God, the curtain has already been drawn. I would encourage you to be excited about this. Your days are no secret to God. When you walk with Him you cannot escape His presence. Therefore, enter the mystery of tomorrow with boldness and confidence. Although you may stumble, He will not let you fall. God is always present.

Polaroid Picture Show

With that in mind, let's get back to Psalm 139. Science is only now discovering the mystery that David already knew so many centuries ago, that the human body is awesome and wonderfully made. The complexity and the skillfulness required to fashion a human being is simply astonishing. It is light years beyond what could be accomplished naturally, even by the standards of the most modern theory of evolution.

We are actually beginning to see the mysteries of God revealed before our very eyes. The Psalm speaks of being formed in secret, and of David being covered by his mother's womb. In David's day, the secrets of the womb were inexplicably hidden from the eyes of man. The thought of peering into the womb was unfathomable in ancient times.

Recently, a friend of mine went with his wife for an ultra sound of their prenatal child. Not only did they leave knowing the sex of the baby, they departed with a detailed three dimensional picture of their yet to be born infant. Were you aware, by the way, that in some Asian cultures, Korean in particular, that the nine months in the womb are counted toward your age? You are actually twenty-one and one half month's old on your first birthday, assuming you were born full term. Perhaps the rest of the world should adopt this system, thus letting the rest of the world know that a baby is most certainly alive in the womb.

Anyway, they could see the eyes, nose, fingers, toes, lips, etc... It was as if they simply snapped a Polaroid photo of the child. The wisdom of the Lord manifested through scientific breakthroughs has allowed us to peel away the walls of the womb and peer into yesterday's secret mysteries of prenatal development.

However, there remains a multitude of secrets that our eyes still cannot see. There are more than can ever be counted. The Lord knows all and He sees all. He will reveal them as needed.

I must, however, let you know the following secret. *The mysteries of the Lord must be conceptualized in the Spirit to be understood.* The natural man cannot comprehend the things of God, no matter how educated he may be. It is these mysteries that we will primarily deal with from this point on.

I Have a Secret

Do you realize that sharing secrets reveals intimacy? Therefore, do not just be encouraged when the Lord shares something deep with you; be excited! He considers you to be His personal confidant. Think about it, you do not share secrets with those whom you mistrust. Secrets are reserved only for your closest friends and allies.

Do you still believe God is impersonal? The sharing of secrets denotes only the closest of relationships with the one to whom you bear your soul.

That is the essence of the Father when we long to know Him and when we diligently pursue Him. Intimacy is His nature. By His *"still small voice"* (1 Kings 19:12) the Lord desires to whisper in your ear and bear His soul to you. In fact, that is exactly what He did. He bore Jesus Christ for you. His desire is to be so intimate with you that He penetrates your spirit and soul. He wants to consume your thoughts and be the object of your affection. When He is, He will give you the keys to the kingdom of God.

With that in mind, let's take a look at another immensely powerful secret that the Lord wants to reveal to you. Psalm 91 is one of my favorite Psalms in the Bible. What I love most is its applicability to our modern world. If there is one thing we all need in this day and age, it is protection from the Lord. The world is a harsh place. A casual perusal of the daily news quickly reveals that the world is becoming more evil by the day. As believers in Jesus Christ, we need not fear. Apart from those honored with martyrdom, we have a secret place with God that contains our preservation. Therefore, let's probe into Psalm 91 and catch a glimpse of the timelessness of the Ancient of days. Behold, another secret is at hand.

Shadows of Illumination

> *"He who dwells **in the secret place** of the Most High shall abide **under the shadow** of the Almighty. I will say of the Lord, 'He is my refuge and my fortress, my God, in Him I will trust.'"*
> **—Psalm 91:1–2**

Psalm 91 makes it perfectly clear that God has a secret place. If one dwells in that place he, or she, will abide under the shadow of Almighty God. I do not need to tell you that being in the shadow of God is a desirable place to be. It is not like being in the shadow of your brother, sister, colleague, or parent, where you may actually be overshadowed. The Lord never over-shadows a man.

When you submit to God and dwell in the secret place of His Word, worship, and prayer, His love causes you to shine. *"Therefore humble your-selves under the mighty hand of God, that He may exalt you in due time."* (1 Peter 5:6) Look at this incredible scripture from the book of Acts, which reveals just how mighty the shadow of the Lord is.

> *"And through the hands of the apostles many signs and wonders were done among the people. And they were all with one accord in Solomon's Porch. Yet none of the rest dared join them, but the people esteemed them highly. And believers were increasingly added to the Lord, multitudes of both men and women, so that they brought the sick out into the streets and laid them on beds and couches,* **that at least the shadow of Peter passing by might fall on some of them.** *Also a multitude gathered from the surrounding cities to Jerusalem, bringing sick people and those who were tormented by unclean spirits,* **and they were all healed."**
> **—Acts 5:12–16**

In this amazing piece of scripture we actually see people being healed by the shadow of Peter as he passes along the road! To those who do not understand the mystery of God and have never dwelt in the secret place of the most High, nor abided under the shadow of the Almighty, this sounds like a fable. This, however, is no tall tale. This is a revelation of the shadow of God.

In the natural realm, it may have been Peter's physical embodiment that was obstructing the photons contained within the sun's rays and causing a physical matting of sunlight; in other words, a shadow. In truth, however, the shadow of God had manifested itself and lit up the spiritual darkness. His *"light is the life of men."* (John 1:4) Therefore, anyone and everyone who dared enter the glorious light of God's shadow were instantly healed. This is still true today. God has not changed. The secret shadow of Almighty God is the glory of God. It is a physical manifestation of the highest order. Therefore, the shadow of God is miraculous. Anyone bold enough to enter in is blasted with resurrection power.

It is important to note, however, that not just anyone's shadow had this incredible effect. This manifestation of power is reserved only for those willing to dwell in the secret place of the Most High. Peter spent so much time in the presence of God that the Almighty began to physically manifest in Peter. Yahweh became part of Peter's essence. They had become one. We see this same sort of manifestation in the life of the Apostle Paul, as well.

*"Now God worked **unusual miracles** by the hands of Paul, so that even **handkerchiefs or aprons** were brought **from his body** to the sick, and the diseases **left them and evil spirits went out of them.**"*
—Acts 19:11–12

When you spend as much time abiding under the shadow of the Almighty as Paul, and when you spend as much time dwelling in the secret place of the most High as Peter, the physical world around you is affected, and not with the death that sin manifests. It becomes illuminated with Light—with Life. Even your flesh is affected, or should I say, infected, in the shadow of God, and once again, not with some hellish disease produced by sin. In the presence of God you become infected with Life—the "Capital L," life that only the Spirit of the Holy One can produce. Check out this incident regarding the bones of the great Old Testament prophet, Elisha.

*"Then Elisha died, and they buried him. And the raiding bands from Moab invaded the land in the spring of the year. So it was, as they were burying a man, that suddenly they spied a band of raiders; and they put the man in the tomb of Elisha; and when the man was let down **and touched the bones** of Elisha, **he revived** and stood on his feet."*
—2 Kings 13:20–21

Can you imagine the shock they must have experienced? I can imagine God doubling over with laughter while watching this incident. I bet He found it to be hilarious. Incredibly, even though Elisha was dead—even though his spirit had left the building, the residual life of God was still contained in his bones. That is the resurrection power the Word of God speaks of. Death cannot thwart God. The same power of God that raised Jesus from the dead and the same power that will resurrect your mortal flesh upon Christ's return, remained in Elisha's bones long after his demise.

Elisha, just like the Apostle's Peter and Paul, had become one with God. This permeation of the Holy Spirit is known in Christian circles as the anointing. To anoint means, "To rub on or to pour all over." Therefore, the anointing of the Holy Spirit is God on, and perhaps, even, as we see with the bones of Elisha, *in* physical flesh. It is the Spirit of God working on and through mankind. It is found in the shadow of the Almighty and it is where miracles, signs, and wonders manifest in the lives of mortal men. Amazingly, not even death can separate a man from God's life giving Spirit.

> *"Do you not know that you are the temple of the living God, and that the Spirit of God dwells in you?"*
> **—1 Corinthians 3:16**

> *"For I am persuaded that neither death nor life, nor angels nor principalities nor powers, nor things present nor things to come, nor height nor depth, nor any other created thing, shall be able to separate us from the love of God which is in Christ Jesus our Lord."*
> **—Romans 8:38–39**

When viewed from that perspective the account of Elisha's bones makes perfect sense. When you are one with God, His Spirit begins to manifest in the natural realm where both you and I dwell. God begins pouring out of your sweat glands like *"rivers of living water."* (John 7:38) In addition to miracles, signs and wonders, salvation reigns supreme. *"And believers were increasingly added to the Lord."* (Acts 5:14) That is the purpose of the mystery. The intent of the hidden secrets of Yahweh is to preserve and impart the miracle of salvation.

Hanging Around

Unfortunately we read the following tragic phrase within the same miraculous account. *"Yet none of the rest dared join them."* (Acts 5:13) I believe this describes the majority of today's so called "believers" in Yahweh. We like to play religious games with God. We love our revival meetings and coming to the altar to be prayed for. Many only think about the Lord on Sunday and believe going to church is the key to heaven. "I'm no preacher," prohibits us from *"daring to join them."*

Let's not even dare talk about our liturgy or other ritualistic forms of worship. God forbid we are to change the order of worship. We show up every Sunday but never fully commit to Christ. Therefore, we never get to the place of dwelling and abiding. We never dare to join those willing to commit to God. There is a difference between dwelling and abiding. In order to abide you must first dwell. I love the quote I recently heard from **Frances Chan,** the author of the amazing book *Crazy Love* and several others. He said, **"God wants all or nothing. The thought of a person calling themselves a 'Christian' without being a devoted follower of Christ is absurd."** Unfortunately, far too many modern day Christian's fall into this tragic category.

Therefore, we, the church, rarely if ever enter *"the secret place of the Most High."* As a result, the miracle working power of God that changes everything in our lives remains dormant. In its wake, the blind ignorance of the world declares the death of Almighty God. "The church," overshadowed by modern science and worldly "wisdom" begins a slow descent into obscurity and tragically, even, irrelevance. Irrelevant, unfortunately, is the altered state of the modern believer who has more faith in Charles Darwin's theory of evolution than the miraculous history of creation portrayed in the Book of Genesis.

There is, however, an answer to this eternal tragedy. We do not need to accept Lucifer's "final solution" and the holocaust of human souls about to enter the Lake of Fire. The secret to changing the world lies in our willingness *to begin dwelling in the presence of our Father.* In Christ, the invitation has been sent. The door of His presence is wide open awaiting your reentry.

The word "dwell," as used in Psalm 91, actually means to "hang around." It is like being at a party and after all the guests leave just you and the host, perhaps along with a few good friends, dwell in fellowship for a time. If they are close friends you may dwell for hours. This dwelling time is essential in developing your relationship with God. It is vital to your learning to abide under the shadow of the Almighty.

Remember, when you dwell somewhere you hang around for a little while and then leave. However, when you abide somewhere you remain in that place indefinitely. It is where you live. When you do momentarily leave it is always the place to which you return. It becomes your place of belonging—your home. That is when and where the visible power of God manifests.

However, you can never abide without first dwelling. It is the time spent in the secret place where you get to know your Father. With that in mind, check out this "dwelling" revelation from Exodus 33 regarding the warrior Joshua, who succeeded the mighty prophet Moses.

*"And it came to pass, when Moses entered the tabernacle that the pillar of cloud descended **and stood** at the door of the tabernacle, **and the Lord talked with Moses.** All the people saw the pillar of cloud **standing** at the tabernacle door, and all the people rose and worshipped, each man in his tent door. So the Lord spoke to Moses face to face, as a man speaks to his friend. And he (Moses) would return to the camp, **but his servant***

Joshua the son of Nun, a young man, did not depart from the tabernacle."

—**Exodus 33:9–12**

Incredibly, Joshua was not only witness to this incredible relationship between God and Moses, he actually participated in it. It is amazing that the *"pillar of cloud"* which also is a manifestation of God, and, therefore, is the glory of God, is described as *"standing at the tent door."* I must conclude from this that there was some sort of visible form either to, or inside, the cloud. It was not just a tornado shaped pillar that we know from the movie *The Ten Commandments,* nor was it a puff of smoke. According to scripture, the cloud was *standing* in front of, and *speaking* to Moses.

It is as if God, being veiled by the cloud of His glory, was standing face to face with Moses. As you will see shortly, that is exactly what was occurring. God would veil Himself in the cloud to prevent instantaneous judgment from coming upon a sinful humanity. He would speak face to face, and friend to friend, with His servant and confidant Moses. That in itself is an incredible secret regarding the personal nature of Yahweh, and Joshua, who would later succeed Moses, would dwell in the tent after the meeting was over. As a result, God did not leave. Apparently, God would hang out with Joshua long after the meeting had ended.

I have heard other religions claim that you cannot interact with God on a personal level. To them, a relationship with God is a mystery. This scripture, along with various others we have examined, clearly refutes that doctrine. God was Moses' personal friend, as well as, his Savior, God and Deliverer. Joshua, in his pursuit of this same level of relationship, would remain in the tabernacle basking in the presence of the Lord after Moses' departure. God not only allowed it, He enjoyed it. In the end, He honored it. It was God's desire to have both Moses and Joshua dwell in His presence and to this very day it is God's desire for you to dwell in the mystery of His presence, as well. In the end, God blessed Joshua. If you are willing to commit in the same manner the Lord will bless you as well.

No Favorites

Therefore, let's have a look at the outcome. Did God pursue the same level of relationship with Joshua? or was this special friendship reserved just for Moses? Let's jump ahead forty years or so, just after the death of Moses and witness the appointment of Joshua as leader of the nation of Israel. God makes the following statement to Joshua:

> *"No man shall be able to stand before you all the days of your life; **as I was with Moses, so I will be with you.** I will not leave you nor forsake you. Be strong and of good courage.'"*
> **—Joshua 1:5–6**

If this is true, we must answer the question; how *was* God with Moses? How did He treat him? This is important to note. God just stated He was going to treat Joshua the same way. Here is the answer, *"The Lord spoke to Moses **face to face, as a man speaks to his friend."***

There is an incident in the Book of Numbers, where Moses' brother Aaron and sister Miriam become jealous of Moses regarding His relationship with God. In rebuking them, make a note of how God describes His relationship with His friend Moses.

> *"Then the Lord came down in the pillar of cloud **and stood** in the door of the tabernacle, and called Aaron and Miriam. And they both went forward. Then He said, "Hear now My words: If there is a prophet among you, I, the Lord, make Myself known to him in a vision; I speak to him in a dream. **Not so with My servant Moses;** he is faithful in all My house. **I speak with him face to face, even plainly, and not in dark sayings;** and he sees **the form of the Lord."***
> **—Numbers 12:8**

This is absolutely incredible! To all of you reading this who have the mistaken belief that it is not possible to have a relationship with God, can it really get any more personal than Face to face and Friend to friend? Also note that God is not some ambiguous energy source flowing aimlessly throughout the ether. God has a form. It is not "the universe" that answers your prayer as so many New Age believers in "who knows what" claim. "Ascended Masters" is nothing more than witchcraft. They are fallen angels. It is the one and only holy God of the universe whose name is Yahweh that answers your prayers. He is the only one worthy of worship and praise. Although we are at present unable to gaze upon His countenance, God is a living, loving, Father who desperately seeks an intimate relationship with His most valued possession, humanity—and that means you.

It was not a mistake or a random act of choice that God transferred Moses' office to Joshua. He was not playing favorites. *"God is no respecter of persons."* (Acts 10:34) That means He has no favorites. We are all God's favorite and He shows partiality to no one. The question is, therefore, is He *your* favorite?

If we are going to be completely accurate in regard to this event, God technically did not transfer His relationship from Moses to Joshua at all. He did not have to. The relationship was already in place. Joshua made sure of it. Because Joshua persevered in the presence of God, God chose to allow Joshua to abide permanently in His presence and lead the people, just as Moses did. He will do the same for you when you make the same decision and show the same commitment as Joshua. You too can abide in the *"shadow of the Almighty."*

Seek and You Will Find

I was recently at a youth convention with about two hundred young people. About forty of them were from our congregation. After a long day in the presence of God I retired back to my room with the intention of getting a good night's rest. Within five minutes, or so, I heard a knock at my door. Seven young men from our congregation had been discussing the status of the youth group and needed some counsel.

After about three hours, it is now two in the morning, we had settled upon several key issues that had been bothering them. Their primary concern was that they felt our youth Pastor had been favoring several of the kids. Here is what they overlooked, however. The perceived favorites of the Pastor had continually sought his presence and counsel, and thus, had developed a deeper relationship with him. So I asked, "Is it that he *likes* them better or does he *know* them better?" Once framed within the proper perspective the consensus agreed that he simply knew them better. So I stated, "If you would like that same relationship with him then you must pursue it as well." Problem solved. Finally, I can get some sleep.

Isn't it exactly the same with God? It was not that God liked Joshua more than Caleb or any other Israelite. As I just revealed to you, He does not have any favorites. Joshua simply took the time to pursue and dwell in the presence of God. God is always available. The question is, are you? Will you pursue a relationship with your Father?

While you are considering this, keep in mind that God's choosing of Joshua had nothing to do with the fact that God knew Joshua better than the rest of his brethren. *"He knows our frame,"* (Psalm 103:14) all of us. Therefore, listen carefully to the following immensely profound, but incredibly simple precept. The secret of why Joshua was chosen was not that God knew Joshua. *It was that Joshua knew God!*

Therefore, God knew that when He spoke Joshua would listen— even when it seemed outrageous. I do not believe that even Caleb would have marched around Jericho for a week and made war by blowing a few Shofar's. Joshua knew God's voice. He knew God's character, His integrity and His ability to perform outlandish miracles. Therefore, whatever God said, Joshua was willing to do. How about you? Do you know God? When you do life has no limits.

Therefore, *"draw near to God and He will draw near to you."* (James 4:8) Just to make sure that I drive the above point home I would like you to notice that scripturally speaking, and that is of utmost importance, *you* must make the first move. "And," is a consequential word. *"Draw near to God **and** He will draw near to you."*

As you move toward God, He moves and meets you somewhere in the middle. Only His middle is front and center, right in your face, the millisecond you turn. His presence is immediate. He is not constrained by space or time, and, therefore, distance is irrelevant to Yahweh. That, in itself, is a profound mystery. The secret of the presence of God is found in *your willingness to seek and pursue Him.* When you desire to dwell in His presence He invites you to live in His everlasting abode.

Therefore, we must learn how to dwell and abide. How do we do that? It is not as if you can just knock on His door is it? Actually, that is exactly how it is. *"Ask, and it will be given to you; seek, and you will find; **knock, and it will be opened to you.** For **everyone** who asks receives, and he who seeks finds, and to him who knocks it will be opened."* (Matthew 7:7–8)

I want you to notice the certainty of the language used in this scripture. Four times we see the phrase "it will" or "you will." Three times we see an all-inclusive phrase such as "everyone," "he who," or "to him." God is giving you proof positive that if you seek after Him you will find Him. If you pursue Him, you will catch up to Him, and right there, in that place, whoever you are and wherever you may be at the time, He will embrace you with loving, wide open arms.

You do not need to dress up, clean up, or wait until you can approach Him in whatever form of religiosity you have been deceived into believing. Just knock. He will answer the door. He is always home.

Once He does, you will learn the secret of abiding in His presence. It is a mystery that "the world" can never solve. It is like having children. It must be experienced to be understood.

However, *you* can now see it because the door of the Lord has been opened to you. Your eyes have been loosed. He has invited you into His marvelous light and you have accepted Him by stepping into His illuminating shadow. The presence of God is the secret to both giving and receiving "agape" love.

> *"Or what man is there among you who, if his son asks for bread will give him a stone? Or if he asks for a fish, will give him a serpent? If you then being evil know how to give good gifts to your children, how much more will your Father who is in heaven give good things **to those who ask Him!**"*
>
> **—Matthew 7:9–11**

The Golden Rule

Here is the secret to revealing the mystery of God. Incredibly, it has not been kept secret at all. It is visibly out in the open and in plain sight for every man, woman and child to experience.

> *"Therefore, whatever you want men to do to you, **do also to them,** for this is the Law and the Prophets."*
>
> **—Matthew 7:12**

The secret to abiding in God's presence is *brotherly love*. The only way to abide in the presence of God is to manifest the "agape," which is the unconditional love of God, amongst all whom you meet. No matter, and this is the difficult part, what they do to you. "No matter what they do to you," is what separates the men from the boys in the kingdom of God. It determines the quakers from the fakers—the OG's from the No G's.

"In this the children of God and the children of the devil are manifest." (1 John: 3:10) Once again, pay close attention. You are about to find out

who you really belong to, regardless of what you may have heretofore thought. If you find out you belong to the wrong "father," do not panic. Simply repent, accept Christ, and move forward. I promise Yahweh will not deny you.

> *"Whoever does not practice righteousness* (that which is right with God, not man) *is not of God, nor is he who **does not love his brother*** (referring to all men, not just your biological siblings). *For this is the message that you heard from the beginning, **that we should love one another.***"
>
> **—1 John 3:11**

> *"Beloved, **let us love one another,** for love is of God; and **everyone who loves** is born of God and knows God. He who **does not love** does not know God, for God is love."*
>
> **—1 John 4:7–8**

> *"If someone says, 'I love God' and hates his brother **he is a liar;** for he who does not love his brother whom he has seen, how can he love God whom he has not seen? And this commandment we have from Him: that he who loves God **must** love his brother also."*
>
> **—1 John 4: 20–21**

Since it appears that no one else in our politically correct culture is willing to stand up for the truth, I will be the one to do so. Based upon the teachings of both the Qu'ran and the Sunnah, Islam is precluded from being a religion imparted by Yahweh. The teachings of Mohammed are not, and cannot, be from the Father. His outright belligerence and imperialist motives in doctrines such as, "Slay them where you find them," is as far from the commandment of brotherly love as hell is from heaven.

52.7% of the Qu'ran is dedicated to threats and hatred of the infidel and promotes some form of violence against humanity. A mere 2% promotes good will toward man. It contains 164 verses that promote violent jihad against the infidel. Only three verses command humanity to love Allah and a mere two verses are about how Allah loves a believer. There are 25 verses about how Allah does not love Kafirs (non-Muslims). There are zero verses stating that Allah loves the sinner, and there are also no verses containing the universal love for all by either Allah or the believers in Islam. The agape love of Yahweh is non-existent in both Allah and his revelation to humanity, the Qu'ran.

Because I want you to realize that I am not just picking on Islam, also included in the category of teachings that cannot be from Yahweh are those within the religion of Christianity, or any religion for that matter, preaching homophobic doctrines of hatred and racism, blowing up abortion clinics, and burning the Qu'ran just to torment the "enemy." It is utter abandonment from the truth. As people of the cross, no human being is our enemy. *"For we do not wrestle against flesh and blood, but against principalities, against powers, against the rulers of the darkness of this age, against spiritual hosts of wickedness in the heavenly places."* (Ephesians 6:12) Sin, and the spirits behind it, is our only enemy.

Therefore, we must be able to make the following distinction which unfortunately, has become a secret. *Obliterating sin is Godly. Destroying another human being is tragic.* In order to obey the command of God we must be able to distinguish between these two truths. If God wants a human being, or any group of human beings, removed from planet earth it is *His* job to do it. For the most part, He either uses other nation's, not individuals, or some form of natural disaster (i.e. fire and brimstone, floods, etc . . .) to do it. As for the individual, *"thou shall not murder."* (Exodus 20:13)

Love is not optional whether you like the person and/or their religion, or not. *"Love thy neighbor as thyself"* (Mark 12:31) is a command that must be extended *to all*. It is in man's perception that love runs amuck. We mistake love for physical attraction. We mistake love for like, or the excitement of being around someone who makes us feel good.

This is not love. It is not even sensual love, let alone the agape love of God. You do not have to like me in order to love me. In fact, to enter the kingdom of God it is imperative that we love those whom we do not like. That is where you will find agape love within yourself. It is also where you will find the presence of God.

> *"But if you love those who love you, what credit is that to you? For even sinners love those who love them. And if you do good to those who do good to you, what credit is that to you? For even sinners do the same. And if you lend to those from whom you expect to receive back, what credit is that to you? For even sinners lend to sinners to receive as much back."*
>
> *"But love your enemies, do good and lend, **expecting nothing in return;** and your reward will be great, and you will be sons of the Most High. For He is kind to the unthankful and evil. Therefore, be merciful, just as your Father also is merciful."*
>
> **—Luke 6: 32–36**

That, right there, is the description, definition, and application of agape love. It is the golden rule. Make no mistake, it is not just difficult, it is impossible to fulfill without the Spirit of Christ dwelling in, and being an intimate part of a man's spirit. The inability and unwillingness to enter into the mystery of Christ is the reason we have so many wars, conflicts, murders, evil acts, etc... manifest in the world today. The lion's share of it is in the name of religion. It is a simple matter of the lack of righteousness on the part of mankind.

Man wants to be identified with, but independent of God. We want to carry His name, call upon Him for help, but only if it is right with us, whatever our deceived and twisted view of the truth may be. We have refused to do what is right with God, according to His Word and His ways, and as a result, we are reaping the harvest of chaos.

Now you know the secret mystery to the kingdom of God. *"Whatever you want men to do to you, do also to them."* (Matthew 7:12a) If you want people to do good to you, do good to them. If you want them to do evil to you, do evil to them. If you want them to kill you, kill them. It is your choice.

One Way Street

Jesus goes on to make the statement, *"This is the Law and the Prophets."* (Matthew 7:12b) He was referring to the Pentateuch and the writings of the prophets which constitute the majority of what Christianity refers to as the Old Testament. In other words, Jesus was saying, "If you truly, in truth and deed, not just in word, love your neighbor as yourself, you fulfill the entire Word and will of God."

That is what leads you into eternity. The acceptance of Christ as your Savior rescues you from the loveless evil of "now" and translates you into the loving beauty of "forever." Compare that to the teachings of the Qu'ran. Compare it to the teachings of Hinduism, or any other religion. The fulfillment of the Law and the Prophets can only be found in Christ.

> *"Therefore, I now rejoice in my sufferings for you, and fill up in my flesh what is lacking in the afflictions of Christ, for the sake of His body, which is the church* (the people not the buildings and/or organizations), *of whom I became a minister according to the stewardship from God which was given to me **for you,** to fulfill the Word of God, **the mystery** which has been hidden from ages and from generations, but now **has been revealed** to His saints."*

> *"To them God willed to make known what are the riches of the glory **of this mystery** among the Gentiles: **which is Christ in you**, the hope of glory. Him (Jesus) we preach, **warning every man** and **teaching every man** in all wisdom."*
> **—Colossians 1:24–28**

Jesus Christ and His presence within you is the ultimate mystery revealed. Your life in Christ is the secret to eternity. The mystery of Jesus has been revealed for the purpose of saving the entire human race. If you have just read this, you have been duly warned. Those who are wise will heed this warning, obey the Word and the will of God, accept Christ, and be transformed into forever. The fool will extinguish his lamp (see Matthew 25).

Most folks never come to the realization that it is not God who will send you to hell. You will send yourself to hell by the choices you make. *"See, I have set before you today, life and death, good and evil . . . blessing and curse . . . **therefore choose** life that both you and your descendants may live."* (Deuteronomy 30:15 and 19)

Heaven or hell, life or death, blessing or curse, is your choice. The Word of God contains countless mysteries, but one reign's supreme. The mystery of God's presence is *Christ in you*. Becoming one with Him is your only hope of glory. Therefore, unlock the secret of eternal life by choosing Christ. He will save your soul and escort you into the glory of "forever!"

CHAPTER 7 ---

The Process of Time

(THE SECRET OF GOD'S CHISEL)

Several days ago, as I was anxiously awaiting the time to tick away on my microwave oven I came to an epiphany. It was one of those eye opening moments as my grievous impatience deceived me into believing that two minutes is way too long for any man, woman, or child to wait for the leftovers of last night's dinner to coalesce into the glory of the previous evenings satisfaction of my most primal instinct—hunger. Translation . . . it simply could not heat up fast enough. Thus, I came to the realization that our modern "fast food," instant gratification society has all but eliminated what I can only refer to as God's secret sculpting chisel, *"The process of time."*

As a result we have severely limited God's method of transforming us into the beings He wants us to be. A sculpture does not simply pop out of a rock. It takes time, dedication and patience to form a masterpiece. The artist patiently chips away at it, one piece at a time, until he or she achieves the image visualized in their mind.

Modern man, however, has become conditioned to instant gratification. Just like Pavlov's dog, we begin salivating every time "the bell rings," or the "red light" of consumerism goes on. Did you know that dogs are unable to process time? That is why they are so happy when you come home. It is also why dogs never get bored. Their feeble minds do not know if you were gone for ten minutes or ten days. Thus, they go temporarily insane every time they hear the sound of your car engine roaring up the street.

This is untrue of we fellow humans. We can actually feel the pain and dissatisfaction of having to wait. Thus, we allow our flesh to rule over our spirits, instead of allowing patience to perfect us through the unique process God has initiated just for us—time.

I remember back in the day there was a song by the rock band *Queen* whose lyrics rang out, "I want it all . . . I want it all . . . I want it all . . . *and I want it now!"* This may as well be America's anthem. I have often times fallen prey to it myself, as no doubt you have at one time or another, as well.

I also remember while growing up being conditioned by *Burger King's* famous jingle, "Have it your way . . . goes double now . . . have it your way at *Burger King . . ."* If you are a little older than me, you no doubt remember Frank Sinatra's most famous anthem, "The record shows . . . I took the blows . . . and did it my-y-y-y-y way-y-y-y!"

As a result, here we are several decades later and the "Me generation" has been so conditioned by the media to "keep up with the Jone's,"—check that, I just dated myself, the young generation's have probably never heard of the Jones'—to "Keep Up With the Kardashian's," that we begin foaming at the mouth and drooling uncontrollably at every one of the twenty thousand or so television commercials that is thrown at the average human being on an annual basis. "If it feels good do it." Right and wrong is in the eye of the beholder. It has to be true. It's on the internet!

Do you remember the lyrics from the old sixties rock song, "and if you need somebody to love... then... love the one you're with..." Sounds like a cool concept except for the fact that the "love" being encouraged by *Crosby, Stills and Nash* is outright fornication. There is no need to wait for actual love in the new normal of pop culture. Do it now. As the pop icon *Shakira* so unabashedly vocalized, "Wherever, whenever..." and the beauty of today's post-modern culture is that we do not have to wait another minute to obtain anything. Have it your way and get it right now for only three easy payments plus shipping and handling. We even have mail order brides. That's right. They are also on the internet!

The Microwave Culture

I remember when my children were a bit younger, my wife and I drove to our local Ford dealer to look at a new mini-van. We had three children and the car seats were a bit of a tight squeeze in the back of our Mitsubishi Galant. So naturally, we just could not stand such an "inconvenience." I cannot help but think of Mary, the mother of Jesus, as she had to travel from Nazareth to Bethlehem via donkey, and oh yeah, she was nearly nine and one-half months pregnant. Do you think that was comfortable?

So we sashay into the closest automobile dealer we could find and to my great amazement there was a brand new minivan in my garage within a matter of hours. I had not even paid for it yet. No down payment, no first month, no collateral, just a credit application and a signature. What a country, I thought. Only in America!

The reason I find this utterly amazing, and more than a bit amusing, is that at the time I was barely making enough money to survive. That did not seem to matter to the microwave culture, however, me included. I wanted it and I wanted it now. As incredible as it seemed to me at the time, they did not seem to mind giving it to me either—at a "reasonable" rate of interest, of course.

As a result, here we are several decades later, salivating without even a napkin to wipe the drool from our pop culture chins. On both the personal and governmental levels we are in debt up to our ears, with credit cards bursting at the seams and angry at the attendant of our local McDonald's drive-through because our order took thirty-five seconds rather than thirty.

Is it any wonder that our world's economies are in shambles? What happened to fiscal discipline? What makes us believe that every problem needs to be immediately repaired without ever counting the cost of our children's futures? Can you believe that the prevailing economic theory in practice at the time of this writing is to actually *spend* the nation's way out of trouble? What? Can this actually be true? Sadly enough, we have implemented it to the tune of eighty-five billion, with a "B," dollars *per month!*

Can you imagine if you ran your household or business that way—when you are running a deficit, spend everything in your pocket? then clear out the checking account and borrow some more. The only folks I know living that way are either enrolled in *Gamblers Anonymous,* the *Betty Ford Clinic,* or have the title Senator, Congressman or President before their name. Are we gambling away the nation's future? How can we not be?

How long would it be until the bank foreclosed on your home and you were living in the street if you ran your life in like manner? In America, the process is about three years. That alone promotes irresponsibility in the microwave culture. Three years to a modern human may as well be a lifetime. "Shoot, I don't even know if I will be alive in three years," is the way one person voiced it to me. "Why pay the mortgage?"

To a Senator, it is one and one-half terms. In other words, a political lifetime. They could be voted from office in such an egregious time span. I guess they better give away some more free stuff before the voting public forecloses on *them*. Public service has become a career for those whose primary skill-set is the unique ability to charismatically deceive. Some do it for more than forty years. Ask Senator Charlie Rangel. He wrote the nation's financial laws, then proceeded to break them. He was found guilty on eleven of the thirteen accusations. Was he held responsible? No, he was reelected!

No wonder our country is failing. Rather than act responsibly, Congress simply counterfeits more currency. They give it a fancy name, "quantitative easing," knowing that the apathetic masses will have no idea, nor even care, what it really means. They can then proceed to spend away. Ah, another election won. Can someone please call Ruffy the crime dog? I think "someone's" hand is in my pocket. Apparently, crime does pay.

At some point, however, the government and its "leaders" are going to have to pay the piper. You know the old saying, "Nothing is for free." No one seems to care though. It satisfies today's need. It only takes one minute to heat up in the microwave.

Hurry Up

Then there is our prayer life. Lord have mercy! It has also been infected by the microwave culture. We treat God like He is the manager of the very same *McDonald's* that was late with our order. We then put the blame at His feet when our "drive through prayer" takes even a little longer than expected.

If He does not participate in the microwave culture with us, which, by the way, *He will not do,* we claim that He either does not exist or that He does not care. "How could a loving God allow *me,* the god of my own existence, to suffer?" Can you imagine what God must be thinking? It is like He is watching a rerun of the 1980's movie, *Back to the Future,* with the Biff's of the world knocking on every ignorant pop culture forehead and contemptuously proclaiming, "McFly..."

There was a church not too far from where I live that actually implemented a twenty minute service. You drove in, got out of your car, went inside, and came back out. Those participating had the gall to label it a "worship service." That is not worship. It is yielding to a failing and apathetic culture that believes God is only worth a mere twenty minutes of your precious time per week.

In the microwave culture, God has been reduced in importance to less than a half hour per week. On the other six days, twenty-three hours and forty minutes, the Bible is left unopened, prayers are left unspoken and worship is replaced by staring into a pictorial box. In other words, God is efficiently packed into the spiritual casket that has become our twisted, sin propagandized minds.

> *"And even as they **did not like** to retain God in their knowledge, God gave them over **to a debased mind,** to do those things which are not fitting..."*
> **—Romans 1:28**

As a culture, we completely ignore Him and futilely attempt to claim that it is *He* that does not care, while we, either consciously or unconsciously, remain wholly ignorant of His ways. Therefore, when witnessing the ensuing chaos that is degrading our culture, look in the mirror and point the finger at yourself. It is actually *we* who do not care. Sometimes myself included! Yet, for some reason God still loves us.

"But God demonstrates His own love toward us, in that while we were still sinners, Christ died for us."

—Romans 5:8

I am so thankful that God does not think like a man.

Patience is a Virtue

As you progress in God culture, you will find that God is a different type of Manager than even the most competent and efficient executive. He is not daunted by our immature rants and tantrum filled outbursts. He does not care if we throw His Word in His face, if we actually know it, and claim that *He* must do what *we* say. God has no one to answer to. God has no supervisor. He *is* the Supervisor! He knows exactly what is best for His "business," and His business is you.

Therefore, He will take His time and build His "temple" in the exact manner He desires. Not too fast, and not too slow—but just right, tailored to the exact manner and measurements that you require—and all in the process of time.

Yahweh does not use microwaves. He has no drive-through. He is eternally patient and infinitely longsuffering. The only timeline He ever follows is His own, which is an absurd thought since He resides in eternity where time is irrelevant. If you allow Him, He will make you all you have ever imagined you could be—but all in *His* time. Your timeline is not only inaccurate, it is irrelevant. It does not even exist to Him. So learn to go with the flow and recognize when God is sculpting you into forever. Therefore, with time now on our side, let's have a quick look at our next secret, *"The process of time."*

Time Traveler

Time is unlike anything in God's universe. It can only be tamed in the now. When past it is gone and when future it is impending. The process ever moves on and into infinity. Its future is unknowable and the process is unchangeable. Unless that is, your name is Yahweh. Yahweh holds the keys to the process of time. He can amend it, stop it, and even fast forward it. *Your* only choice is to submit to it, and even more importantly, however, if we want to enter His gates, we must submit to Him.

Eternity is a long time. Forever never ends and believe it or not, you get to choose your own fate. God will not choose for you. He gave Christ to heal you, but *you* must choose Him. Millions, billions, and beyond even trillions of years will pass in eternity. In eternity, time is un-ending. Although I have tried, I cannot rap my head around eternity. No beginning and no end is a mystery. It is a secret that can only be unraveled as we enter His eternal presence. Your everlasting destruction, by the way, is also permanent if you choose to discard Him.

Some will ask if that is a warning. Although hell was amongst Jesus' favorite topics, pop culture Christianity has been precluded from proclaiming the horrors of hell. It may scare you away from the church. As you may or may not have noticed, contrary to the teachings of Christ, popularity has become the church's new measure of success.

I, however, am perfectly aware of the fact that I will not win any popularity contests, and, therefore, I will have to be the one to say it. You bet it is a warning! If you reject God you *will* go to hell. Although the modern day pop culture church has attempted to keep this a secret, it is absolutely *not* a secret of the Father. Jesus continually broadcasted this truth loud and clear. Therefore, someone must sound the alarm and pray that you are able to hear and receive it. The politically correct microwave culture will not just remain silent in this regard, it will attempt to convince you of its non-existence.

Therefore, as you read on and into the future, my hope and prayer is that through the process of time you will begin to understand God's purpose for your life. Even reading the end of this chapter and book requires you to participate in the process of time. Not even Evelyn Wood, the speed-reading expert from the 1970's, could instantaneously absorb its content. What does God have for you? He alone holds the key. So let's move on and into the future where you will find not only your destiny, but the mystery of His infinite goodness.

I Knew It All Along

Do you realize that you have no idea what your future holds? I can honestly say that the only human being to ever grace this beautiful planet knowing exactly what His fate would be was Jesus Christ of Nazareth. He was born for the cross. For every other human spirit, your destiny on planet earth can only be revealed through the process of time.

Did David know he would be king? Did Joseph know he would rise to the position of second only to Pharaoh? How about the New Testament? Do you think Stephen woke up knowing he would be martyred that fateful day? Did Saul of Tarsus have a clue that after persecuting the people of *"the Way"* (Acts 22:4) he would author two thirds of the New Testament as the Apostle Paul—and that He would serve the same people and God he so savagely attacked? Of course not.

Take me for example. Do you think I had any idea when I was partying with my beer buddies and head banging at Metallica concerts that I would be writing a discourse for the purpose of leading people to Christ thirty years later? That was never revealed to me in the mosh pit. Even if it had been, I would have never believed it. I would have written it off as absurd.

However, God knew what He was doing. He always did. I was visiting my parents on the eve of this discourse and my mother happened to run across something she had saved from my childhood. Having grown up

Roman Catholic, and according to tradition, I made my confirmation in the sixth grade. I have to tell you that what my mother showed me blew my mind. Apparently it occurred during one of the few Catechism classes I did not skip. To this day I have no recollection of writing it.

She laid before me a report that I had written in regard to my confirmation name, Stephen. In addition to that being my Great Grandfather's name, there it was on paper right before my eyes—quotes from the Book of Acts, regarding Stephen the martyr. There were writings, which I now believe to be prophetic, about my life being filled with the Holy Spirit, blessings from the Lord . . . the list went on and on.

I would imagine that at the time I had written it, it did not mean all that much to me given my lack of recall. That is not unusual. Even Caiaphas, the High Priest, had no idea that he prophesied when declaring, *"that it is expedient that one man should die for the people."* (John 11:50 and 18:14) Notwithstanding the inspiration of the Holy Spirit, in sixth grade I knew absolutely nothing about God or His Word. The fact remains, however, that I *did* write it, and in the process of time God brought it to pass. Had my mother not saved this project I would have never believed that I had written such a document at the age of eleven. I believe God preserved that document not just to prove His existence to me, but He revealed it at exactly the right moment to give me the courage to press forward with *this* project.

Slow Cooked

In truth, God was at work in my life even before then. He was working in my life before I was even born. Whether you realize it or not, the same holds true for you. It simply took the process of time for the Lord to manifest His glory in my life. At an earlier age I simply was not ready to deal with the trials He has in store for me and the difficulties associated with bringing His will to pass.

As you begin to seek your ultimate destiny, you will find He has always been there for you as well—prodding you along one step at a time, until you are prepared to embark upon your own personal journey. Therefore, let's take a look at some biblical examples of how the Lord uses patience, in conjunction with the process of time, to perfect His people and implement His incorruptible and unwavering plan.

Let's pick up in the book of Exodus. This takes place after Moses has already fled to Midian. Approximately forty years have passed and Moses and his lovely wife Zipporah are building a family together—but something else is happening. In a far-away land, and in what Moses thought was a long defunct life, God has resurrected His plan for the children of Israel.

> *"Now it happened **in the process of time** that the king of Egypt died. Then the children of Israel groaned because of the bondage, and they cried out; and their cry came up to God because of the bondage. So God heard their groaning and God remembered His covenant with Abraham, with Isaac, and with Jacob. And God looked upon the children of Israel, and God acknowledged them."*
>
> *"Now Moses was tending **the flock of Jethro** his father-in-law, the priest of Midian. And he led the flock to the back of the desert, and came to Horeb, the mountain of God. And the Angel of the Lord appeared to him in a flame of fire from the midst of a bush..."*
>
> **—Exodus 2:23–25 and Exodus 3:1–2**

Although we have examined the burning bush incident on numerous occasions, there is still much more to the incident. I will begin with the fact that Moses was out in the desert of Midian learning to tend sheep. This was certainly God's will, but it was definitely not His ultimate plan. The prior forty years was about Moses' learning to be faithful in the "little things" before being entrusted with something greater (Matthew 25:21,

Luke 16:10). Talk about slow cooked—our Father loves the *Crock Pot,* which, by the way, has only been in existence since 1971. I would have thought it was much older. Anyway, slow-cooked is always how God operates in your life. It is the chisel that sculpts your character.

He will never "throw you to the wolves" without first preparing you. He will give you little tasks which build into greater and greater responsibilities with the process of time. God certainly had a flock for Moses to tend, but it was not a few sheep in the desert of Midian. God's flock was about five hundred thousand disgruntled Israelites who would constantly grumble and complain for the next forty years. My goodness, I cannot help but empathize with Moses. Most never consider how Moses must have suffered in those forty years. The pressure he was under would have been crushing.

Tending to Israel was no simple task. It required training on the part of Moses. Godly training always comes in the form of minor tasks that escalate into greater responsibilities as time goes by. How you handle such tasks, and the trials associated with them, determines your future standing in the kingdom of God. What "little things" are you being faithful to right now? Take stock of how God is working in your life.

Secondly, it was certainly no mistake that God led Moses into the desert of Midian right in the midst of Mount Horeb, the dwelling place of Yahweh. God had separated and saved Moses from birth and it was about time for Moses to fulfill his destiny. He had completed the "process of time."

As a young man Moses was much too reactionary to lead Israel. His intentions were good, but his decision making capability had a bit to be desired, if you know what I mean. Rising up and killing the Egyptian guard was a decision based upon pure emotion. To be a leader, Yahweh requires you to be led by His Spirit, not the lusts of your flesh. Thus, God exiled Moses, but not for the purpose of punishment. God exiled Moses to purify him.

It is not as if God was starting over with Moses. Moses was being processed. Just like you and I, he was still under construction and had to be perfected by the process of time. Therefore, we must conclude that God was simply finishing what he started. The same holds true for you and I when we experience what we perceive to be troubles, difficulties, trials, tribulations or however you would like to categorize them. Therefore, you can live your life *"being confident of this very thing, that He who has **begun** a good work in you **will complete it** until the day of Jesus Christ."* (Philippians 1:6)

Think about it, God was not surprised by Moses' faux pas. He was not confused on His throne—trying to figure out plan "B." With God there is no plan "B." Plan "A" works every time. It is infallible. Therefore, when God speaks, have faith and obey Him.

God knew exactly what Moses was going to do and when he was going to do it. He did not make him do it. This is an important distinction for us to make. Just like Adam, and just like all of us, Moses had freewill. God, however, knows the what, where, when, why and how of every situation. He knows the same thing about you, as well.

Where God was leading Moses, to be the leader of the "flock of God," would require a man with his emotions in check. This is true of any and all leadership positions. Moses had forty years to replay and unpack the fit of pride leading to his emotional hijacking. The Midian experience was the chisel in the hand of God. Moses had to be stripped of both his Hebrew and his Egyptian pride in order to submit to Yahweh. There was no other way to bring him into the fold. Therefore, Yahweh chipped away at Moses for forty long years before He sent him back to Egypt. Only this time, it was not the Prince of Egypt that showed up, Moses had been transformed into the image of God.

Consider the following, when Jesus was driven into the wilderness and tempted by the devil, He returned in the power of the Holy Spirit. As we discussed earlier, just like Jesus, Moses found himself in the wilderness as well. He underwent the same transformative process which can only be perfected by pain, suffering and the process of time. I know that is not a popular message in today's post-modern, pop culture church, but it happens to be true. Check the scriptures for yourself. The majority, and dare I say all, of God's prophets were persecuted in one way or another. The transformative process known as time, when united with faith produces the power of the Lord God Almighty. You may not like it, but the truth remains that it is God's way. Do not fret about this, however, *"weeping may endure for a night, but joy comes in the morning."* (Psalm 30:5)

Do you recognize the process of time in the above statement? The order is set for a specific reason. The Lord is disclosing His process to you. Joy is non-existent without weeping. It is the weeping that ushers in the joy. Therefore, when you trust God in faith, the pain you are experiencing right now is designed to ultimately bring you joy in the forever.

Listen to what I purposely did not disclose and see if you can recognize the process of time. Here is the whole verse of Psalm 30:5, *"For His anger is **but for a moment**, His favor **is for life**; weeping may **endure for a night**, but joy **comes in the morning.**"* I will gladly swap temporary pain for an eternity in His presence.

Time Spent In the Wilderness

Do not make the mistake, however, of comparing your prescribed circumstance and time period to someone else's. Learn from Jesus and Moses. The testing that took Moses forty years in the boring Crockpot of Midian to complete, took Jesus only forty days in the intensely heated Pressure Cooker of the Spirit driven, temptation filled, wilderness! The result was exactly the same. Jesus returned from the wilderness in the power of God (Luke 4:14) performing signs, wonders and miracles. So did Moses.

What was the difference? Are you wondering how Jesus could be approved by the Father in only forty days? Think about it, and contrary to what most believe, it was *not* the fact that Jesus was divine. Although

Jesus was, and is, God manifested in flesh and blood, He was one hundred percent human, with real emotions, fears, and concerns. Just like all of us, Jesus possessed the ability to experience every difficulty that is common to the human experience, including fear, worry and temptation.

> *"Then He said to them, 'My soul is **exceedingly sorrowful,** even to death. Stay here and watch with Me.' He went a little farther and fell on His face, and prayed, saying, "O My Father, if it is possible, **let this cup pass from Me;** nevertheless, not as I will, but as You will."'*
> **—Matthew 26:38–39**

The reason Jesus expedited His wilderness experience is that unlike so many of us, if not all of us, Jesus remained intimately connected to the Spirit of God at all times. Moses did not. There was no Egyptian guard incident in Jesus' life. Jesus diligently maintained His relationship with Yahweh through constant prayer, worship and unmatched knowledge and understanding of the Word of God. Jesus always obeyed the Father. Even when, as noted above, He did not want to. Make a note of that and remember that obedience is the difference between living a life of obscurity in the presence of God and one of power and authority in the kingdom.

Jesus was one hundred percent in control of His will and emotions. How could he not be, there were no sin, nor trust issues to get in the way. The duration of your time in the wilderness depends upon your trust, which depends upon your connectivity to God. You cannot be connected when sin is obstructing your path. The secret to reducing the process of time and living a holy life is as follows: *When trust is high the speed of God's plan is high.* When trust is low, you are sent into the wilderness to be sculpted.

The process of time had perfected Moses. That does not mean he became flawless. He continued to make mistakes, i.e. striking the rock rather than speaking to it. (Numbers 20:11) Time, however, had matured him. He left Egypt a rowdy and reactionary young man, unable to lead even his own emotional mind. He returned a mature adult, anointed with the Holy Spirit of Yahweh, prepared to lead a flock of five hundred thousand men, women and children. He had been sculpted by the process of time. He was now able to intelligently utilize the power of God Almighty, thus perfectly fulfilling the will of God.

The question, therefore is, where are you in the process of time? Are you still in the wilderness, or have you matured, having been tested by fire and proven faithful in the little things that have come your way? Are you properly managing your family life and your work life? If God were to call you right now and have you declare; "Let my people go," would you be prepared? That is what declaring the gospel is. Have you been perfected or are you still incomplete? Are you feeling that there is something left undone?

If so, do not fret. Chances are that you either have not submitted to God or you have not fulfilled the process of time. Either way your trust in God is still low. Therefore, have fun in the wilderness . . . but while you are there, keep in mind that you are merely one decision away from deliverance.

Joy In the Midst of Pain

The secret to reducing the process of time lies in the following; *when troubles arise, do you seek the Lord?* Do not forget that *He* is your deliverer. **"Faith isn't the ability to believe long and far into the misty future. It's simply taking God at His Word and taking the next step." —Joni Erickson Tada**

Faith is the difference between success and failure in the kingdom of God. Faith develops trust. Dr. Phil, or whoever your therapist may be, is not your Savior. Jesus is. *He* is your healer. Therefore, let's return to scripture and watch how trusting your Father can change any situation, no matter how bleak the circumstance may appear.

*"Now there was a certain man of Ramathaim Zophim, of the mountains of Ephraim, and his name was Elkanah . . . and he had two wives; the name of one was Hannah, and the name of the other Peninnah. Peninnah had children, **but Hannah had no children.** This man went up from his city yearly to worship and sacrifice to the Lord of Hosts in Shiloh."*
—1 Samuel 1:1–3

Going to temple once per year may seem like small potatoes to the casual reader of God's Word. Keep in mind, however, that Elkanah's place of worship was not the local church or synagogue. There were no cars in Elkanah's day. There was not a temple or synagogue on every corner. In fact, Elkanah did not even have streets to travel on. Elkanah had to hike to other cities, and God only knows how far away they were. Suffice it to say, that Elkanah was "of the mountains." Homeboy had to go mountain climbing to get to "church." It is sort of convicting to consider that I barely get out of bed some Sunday morning's. You are about discover, however, that God is rather fond of commitment and dedication.

"And whenever the time came for Elkanah to make an offering (to go mountain climbing), *he would give portions to Peninnah his wife and to all her sons and daughters. But to Hannah he would give a double portion, **for he loved Hannah,** although the Lord had closed her womb."*
—1 Samuel 1:4–5

Once again, this does not sound like anything special upon first glance, but keep in mind that in ancient Israel your self-worth as a woman, and a wife, was predicated upon your ability to produce children—particularly, male children. The phrase, *"for he loved Hannah"* is significant in revealing the character of Elkanah. Like Jesus, Elkanah was a God culture revolutionary. He did not measure the worth of his beautiful bride according to the same measure as the rest of the world.

I would love to say this was also true for Elkanah's other wife Peninnah, but it was not. The love of God was simply not in her. She viewed Hannah merely as competition for her husband's love and attention. In fact, not even Hannah perceived her own self-worth. She wholeheartedly believed the lie. Like blind Bartimaeus, Hannah considered herself broken.

Jehovah Shalom, however, the God of peace, who causes nothing to be missing and nothing to be broken, was about to acknowledge this young ladies humble spirit. If you have not already realized it, you are about to discover that God loves the underdog.

> *"Therefore I take pleasure in infirmities, in reproaches, in needs, in persecutions, in distresses, for Christ's sake.* ***For when I am weak, then I am strong.***"
> **—2 Corinthians 12:10**

As I stated earlier, for many of us the process of time includes pain and suffering. A masterpiece is formed by skillfully hitting and chipping away until you get the exact visage you desire. It is not always a gentle process, particularly in the beginning when all you have is a chunk of marble or rock. Sometimes the unfinished product appears to be an absolute mess, completely unrecognizable. The same is true with the process of time. Therefore, I would encourage you to regard how God sculpted Hannah. The process of *your* time may be similar.

> *"And her rival (Peninnah) also provoked her severely,* ***to make her miserable,*** *because the Lord had closed her womb. So it was,* ***year by year,*** *when she went up to the house of the Lord that she provoked her, therefore she wept and did not eat."*
> *"Now Eli the priest was sitting on the seat by the doorpost of the tabernacle of the Lord.* ***And she was in bitterness of soul, and she prayed to the Lord and wept in anguish.*** *Then she made a vow and said, 'O Lord of hosts, if you will indeed look*

upon the affliction of your maidservant and remember me, and not forget your maidservant, but will give Your maidservant a male child then I will give him to the Lord all the days of his life."'

*"Then they rose early in the morning and worshipped before the Lord, and returned and came to their house at Ramah. And Elkanah knew his wife, **and the Lord remembered her.** So it came to pass **in the process of time** that Hannah conceived and bore a son and called his name Samuel."*

—1 Samuel 1:6–8 and 19–20

Gone but Not Forgotten

Samuel, Hannah's son, went on to be one of the great prophets in the history of Israel, in addition to becoming the closest advisor and confidant to the great king David. Just imagine Hannah's joy, and do not forget Elkanah either. He was dealing with the situation as well. It was not pretty folks. If you want to talk legacy, think about all the little girls throughout the world named Hannah. Have you ever heard of a girl named Peninnah? Me neither.

The Bible does not say much about Hannah and Elkanah after this incident. In fact, just as death steals us from the pages of history, Hannah and Elkanah disappear from the pages of the Bible, never to be heard from again.

Although they are gone they are not forgotten. Their memory remains with every namesake. They live on in the legacy of Samuel and in the spirit of every human who recants their pain and dedication in the Word of God and overcomes their troubles as a result. Most importantly, because of their love and dedication to the Lord God Almighty, they live on in "forever." They had passed the test. Time tells all.

As we move forward, let's reveal another, and perhaps the greatest secret of all. It is time to visit the deceiver of the brethren, the infamous angel Lucifer. Do not fear. Although Jesus has completely stripped him of any and all power, I realize that most of you are not quite ready to face such a malicious foe. Therefore, while disclosing his purpose, I will keep him at arm's length—for now. As you follow me back in time you will discover that the Emperor has no clothes. Therefore, it is time to get excited. The Lord is about to open a door for you. What was once lost has now been found. Lying at the end of this discourse are the keys to the kingdom of Almighty God.

—— **CHAPTER 8** ——

The Devil Inside

(THE SECRET OF THE STRANGER)

"For the flesh lusts against the Spirit, and the Spirit against the flesh; and these are contrary to one another, so that you do not do the things that you wish."

—Galatians 5:17

You may not realize it, but there is a war raging inside every human being. The battle for good and evil is not only in the perpetual struggle for political power that results in global imperialism, cultural hegemony, and crimes against humanity. The ultimate battle for humanity rages from within the heart of every human being and apart from our Savior Jesus Christ, all of humanity has been effected by the wages of sin. Through Original Sin, the enemy of our souls, Lucifer, has infected every single human being alive.

Before we get too far into the character Lucifer, however, we must revisit his methodology. How does he captivate mankind? Keep in mind that he was very close to God at one point in ancient history. In fact, he may have even covered the throne of God with his once majestic wings. Therefore, he has a deep understanding of both the physical and spiritual laws which have been implemented by our King.

As the millenniums have passed, Lucifer has had plenty of time to witness God's laws in action. He has become intimately familiar with humanity's reaction to their intricacies. Therefore, he has quite an advantage over the unredeemed mortal man. In his iniquitous state of existence, and by the power of freewill, he has become an expert at corrupting humanity's perception of God. Therefore, to begin this discussion, let's examine what may be Lucifer's greatest gift—his ability to deceive. Let's pick up this topic by expanding upon a scripture we covered earlier.

*"**Do not be deceived,** God is not mocked; for whatever a man sows that shall he also reap. For he who sows to his flesh will of the flesh reap corruption, but he who sows to the Spirit will of the Spirit reap everlasting life."*
—Galatians 6:8

Look at the opening statement again, *"do not be deceived..."* When you read that an alarm should resound in your spirit causing you to run swiftly toward your spiritual fire escape ... if you have one. If you do not, there is a good chance you may crash and burn, perhaps, even, for eternity. If you believe you can disobey that which follows this short but unambiguously distinct command, you are sorely mistaken. You have undoubtedly already fallen prey to the *"deceiver of the brethren."* (Revelation 12:9)

Do you know what the problem with being deceived is? Think about it, if you have fallen into deception you are completely unaware your plight. Simply stated, you do not *know* when you are deceived. If you did, you would not be. Therefore, a person can live their entire life with good intentions, perhaps, even, while being a "good" person and remain in deception until their final breath. The impending doom can be eternally disastrous.

Those remaining in such a state will only realize their fate when appearing before *"the Judgment Seat of Christ,"* (2 Corinthians 5:10) or even worse, before *"the Great White Throne"* of God Almighty. (Revelation 20:11) Then it is too late. At the Judgment Seat of Christ, the believer will give an account of his or her life to Jesus Christ. As scary as that may sound, you will at least have the luxury of knowing you are in heaven with the Lord.

Those having rebelled against the Messiah, however, will have a date with the Great White Throne of almighty God. They are devoid of salvation. The Lambs Book of Life will be opened and because your name has been blotted out, your time before God will draw to a close. (Revelation 20:12) You will not be able to excuse your way out of it. The Lord is all knowing and your eternal future is a direct result of the choices you make while living.

If you are feeling a bit uncomfortable right now, that is intentional on my part. The first step to solving any problem is recognizing you have one. Therefore, you may be wondering how we can discover whether or not we are living in deception. How do we avoid this eternal disaster? There is only one way to be sure. You must look into the mirror of the Word of God and see what reflects back at you. (James 1:23–25)

If you look closely, you will see your life in the Word of God. That is by design. The question, therefore, is, which side of the truth are you on? Do your actions line up with the light or the dark side of life? Be honest, we all have a light and a dark side. We are all sinners. Thus, no one can escape the need for a Savior. We all have hidden agenda's that affect our behavior.

Like the legendary artist **Billy Joel** so perceptively observed, **"They're the faces of the stranger . . . and we love to try them on."**

Thank God for Jesus Christ. Our saving grace, literally, is that some of us have been saved *by* grace through faith in Jesus Christ. (Ephesians 2:8–9) Sadly, some have not. This is the only true difference between human beings. Race, ethnicity, and even gender, is merely an illusion of the flesh when viewed from eternity. Those who are yet to submit to God are continuing to dwell in ignorance, deception and disobedience. Those are the only options. Either you do not know, you have been deceived, or you do not care; you are in outright rebellion against you Maker. In the latter case, you have chosen Lucifer.

Ignorance, by the way, is not an excuse. Nearly everyone has access to the truth. Everyone has been created with a moral compass residing within. Whether or not you choose the truth is your call. That is what the Word of God clearly reflects back to us. With that in mind, let's continue on and break the chains of deception.

How Ya Livin'?

Let's take a look at how God views deception. Do you think He is okay with it? Will you be able to stand before Him in eternity and claim, "I am sorry God, I did not know . . ." The answer to this question is clearly spelled out in the Word of God.

> **"Do not be deceived,** *God is not mocked, for whatever a man (or woman) sows that shall he (or she) also reap. For he (or she) who sows **to the flesh** will **of the flesh** reap **corruption,** but he (or she) who sows **to the Spirit** will **of the Spirit** reap **everlasting life."***
> **—Galatians 6:7–8**

Unbeknownst to so many, living in deception is clearly an eternal life or death issue. It always leads to corruption. The Greek word for "corruption" is "phtheiro" and according to the definition of "phtheiro," deception leads to both eternal "destruction" and physical "decomposition." Therefore, not only does sowing to the flesh reap physical death, it also reaps everlasting destruction in the lake that burns with fire and brimstone. The question is, do you believe it; I mean, really and truly believe it? It appears to be a simple yes or no answer. However, the truth is born in the way you live your life.

World culture's have undoubtedly been sowing to the flesh for many years and have clearly begun to reap corruption. The television illustrates this sad truth in a matter of minutes every day. As the disease festers, corruption continues to worsen on a daily basis. Public mass shootings, thrill kills and the recent stream of race riots have become so routine that we actually *expect* to see them on the evening news. That, along with the recent wave of terroristic mass shootings, is no longer shocking.

Have you seen footage of "The Knockout Game?" where young men, and incredibly, sometimes, even women, randomly pick out a stranger and punch them as hard as they can in the face. The object of the game is to see if you can knock someone out with one punch. The cowardly blow reigns down upon the unexpecting victim with no prior warning, sometimes even upon unsuspecting senior citizens more than eighty years old. Can you even imagine such cowardice?

With the exceptions of both slavery and the extermination of the Native American, human life value is undoubtedly at an all time low in American history with the rest of the world beginning to follow suit. A lone gunman on the campus of UCLA is the latest school casualty as of the time of this writing. A few short weeks later, forty-nine were shot in Orlando, Florida and another forty-two were killed in Ataturk Airport in Istanbul, Turkey; to name just a few of the worldwide incidents that now seem to fill the news on a weekly basis. Incredibly, no one is shocked or outraged. We have come to expect it. Even the never-ending news cycle spent minimal time on the majority of such heinous crimes.

The twenty-nine killed in Burkina Faso, a little known country in Western Africa, was not even reported. Why does Africa get so little attention? It sort of makes one wonder how many other incidents go unreported. Is it because the people are black? Is it due to the lack of natural resources (apart from gold, silver and diamonds)? I bet De Beer's cares what goes on—as long as it allows them to continue mining. . . . It appears that humanity has been conditioned to respond to the deception of violence like Pavlov's dog.

On the other hand, perhaps you answered, "Yes," that you believe Galatians 6. You may even believe you have overcome deception. If all you are concerned with, however, is your own self-preservation and narcissistic gain, the truth of your actions vociferates a resounding, "No!" You do not really believe that you will reap what you have sown. Your true beliefs will always be reflected in your actions. How ya livin? is a serious question with everlasting implications.

Is there any true purpose in living simply to gather? Are we a people who "honor God with our lips, but our hearts are far from Him?" (Isaiah 29:13) Only an honest look within yourself can determine your answer. What do you believe? What do you stand for? Is your life based upon biblical principles that put you in line with God's ways, or have you succumbed to pop culture and sinful lifestyles that are filled to overflow with greed and lust?

If you are unsure about where you stand, ask yourself the following questions in regard to biblical values and world views. How do you feel about premarital sex? for example. Is it simply a matter of "boys will be boys?" Is that just the way things are these days?

That is merely the beginning. There are a host of other issues plaguing the human soul. What about violence? Do you believe violence is a means to an end? Do you believe God would prefer to kill those who oppose Him, rather than save them?

Where are you on gay marriage? Do you believe homosexuality is sin? Do you believe what the Word of God says about the issue? Do you even know what it says?

While we are on the topic, how about abortion? How do you feel about terminating a human life? Do you support a woman's right to choose? Do you believe a fetus is merely a lifeless clump of cells and life only commences upon a baby's first breath? Are you aware that your life began in the same manner and that without the breath of God we are *all* merely a lifeless clump of cells?

The leading cause of death in America, by the way, is not heart disease, which unfortunately claimed over 600,000 lives in the year 2015. The CDC (Centers for Disease Control) has deceived you and you have willingly, and without question, complied with their lie. It is not even cancer. Cancer claimed the lives of just over 589,000 people in 2015.

Sadly, abortion has beaten them both by a factor of 2–1. Abortion is far and away the leading cause of death in America. Over 1.06 million lives were lost to America's new wave of murderers wearing a stethoscope. Although it is down from 1.2 million the prior year, that is an absolute genocide—yet you believe the lie that gun control is the real problem. That is what the politician's want you to believe. It keeps the nearly meaningless debate raging and keeps them in power. The 12,942 people who unfortunately lost their lives to gun violence in 2015 is a mere drop in the bucket compared to what the murderers carrying the hippocratic oath have done.

Think about the hypocrisy. Just under 13,000 people, which undoubtedly is 13,000 too many, lost their lives to gun violence. But just over 1 million lost their lives to abortion, with no less than 820,000 of them being merely as a selfish means of birth control. Their mother's simply did not want them. Can you imagine? Why, then, are we even discussing gun control?

With over 1 million murders on the table, do you still think a woman has *the right* to choose? How would you feel about God if He simply wiped out 1 million of America's loved one's? Why then, do you give the doctor's, *Planned Parenthood,* and every abortion loving politician a pass?

If all of this is true, and it is, why is there even a debate going on? The answer is . . . deception. The enemy of your soul does not want you to know the truth. Therefore, if you have answered yes to any of these questions, and trust me, there are many more, your heart is in opposition to God. If you do not believe me pick up a Bible and start reading it. Where else can you find the the thoughts and will of God? The Bible is the only place you can find absolute truth.

Perhaps up to this point you truly have not known or you are afraid to face God. That is okay. In fact, it is more than okay. If you are willing to acknowledge that you have been sowing defiled seed, and if you are willing to change, it is perfect. *"The fear of the Lord is the beginning of knowledge . . ."* and the end of deception. (Proverbs 1:7)

As we previously discussed, most do not realize that sowing and reaping has both positive and negative effects. I have heard it referred to as Karma by some of the New Age or Eastern religions. I am compelled, however, to disclose that there is no such thing as Karma. What we experience are the results of the law of sowing and reaping, which operates in both the spiritual, as well as, the physical realms of the universe. If you believe you can defy this law, not only are you deceived, you are making a mockery of God Almighty. As you might imagine, that cannot end well.

Sons of God

To illustrate this, let's go back in time six thousand years or so, and experience what the world was like in the days of Noah. Humanity seemed to have undergone some sort of transformation which appears to have resulted in mankind actually receiving the devil inside. I will let you be the judge of whether or not you believe God's Word. Be that as it may, the source of evil left an unmistakable mark. If you take the time to look, you will undoubtedly recognize Lucifer's twisted signature at the scene of many of our modern day crimes, as well.

> *"Now it came to pass, when men began to multiply on the face of the earth, and daughters were born to them, that **the sons of God** saw **the daughters of men,** that they were beautiful; and they took wives for themselves of all whom they chose . . . And there were giants on the earth in those days."*
>
> **—Genesis 6:1–2 and 4**

I will not go into too much detail regarding the identity of the "sons of God," as it is one of the great mysteries of the Bible. However, I will give you my opinion and why I have come to such a conclusion.

There are two basic theories as to what transpired. Theory number one, is that the Bible is simply referring to ordinary men and woman, just like you and me. The "sons of God" were the righteous and the "daughter's of men" were the unrighteous. It simply categorizes humanity into those who are in touch with the Spirit of God and those who are not.

The main issue I have with this supposition is that sin has separated all men from God by birth. Until Jesus Christ was resurrected, there was no means of gaining access to the Spirit apart from God having sanctified someone for the office of the prophet. These were far and few in between. Humanity as a whole was yet to be "saved" and, therefore, all men were unrighteous.

Theory number two is a bit more spiritual in its derivation and in my opinion better explains the alteration of man's most basic nature during the days of Noah. Before you dismiss this theory as outlandish, I would like to piece together some biblical evidence for you concerning the matter.

The theory hypothesizes that the "sons of God" were fallen angels who accompanied Lucifer in the heavenly rebellion. We find this heavenly incident evidenced in the Book of Revelation chapter twelve. Let's have another look at what transpired. Keep in mind while you are processing this information that much of the Book of Revelation is not laid out in chronological order. Parts of it are parenthetical. This happens to be one of those chronological parentheses which peers deep into eternity past.

> *"And war broke out in heaven: Michael and his angels fought with the dragon; and the dragon and his angels fought, but they did not prevail, nor was a place found for them in heaven any longer. So the great dragon was cast out, that serpent of old, called the devil and Satan, who deceives the whole world;* **he was cast to the earth, and his angels were cast out with him.***"*
>
> **—Revelation 12:7–9**

If you believe the Genesis account is credible, the "sons of God" may have been the fallen angels who were cast out of heaven. We know them today as demons. Their intention in the days of Noah was to corrupt either the genetic or the spiritual makeup of humanity, perhaps, even both. Consider the devil's ultimate goal of stealing your soul. For what other reason would he send his minions to physically procreate, in whatever manner they were able to do that, perhaps somehow artificially, with humanity? It certainly was not out of love. If this is true, it appears that Lucifer's plan may have actually succeeded!

According to the Word of God, this demonic encounter resulted in **"every intent** *of the thoughts of man's heart was* **only evil continually."** (Genesis 6:5) That is quite a statement. If this is true, it appears that humanity had been genetically altered to think like Lucifer. Mankind had become so corrupt that he could not think one single uncontaminated thought. As a result, evil was all man had become capable of. Humanity had truly received the devil inside.

There is no doubt that this describes both the nature and the end goal of Satan. It is actually the same thing he did in the Garden of Eden. After destroying man spiritually, the logical next step would be to put an end to mankind physically. To this very day he is endeavoring to replicate his amazing feat of the past. Do not be fooled by the media. Do you think the ultimate goal of genetic engineering is everlasting life? The ultimate plan is infinitely more sinister. The secret of the devil inside is that *Lucifer uses people with genuinely good intentions to manifest his twisted will.* Good intentions are not always God intentions.

With that said, there are several instances, in both scripture and Jewish tradition, where angels are referred to as "sons of God." The scriptural reference in the Genesis account is not unique to either. Even Jesus, who is witness to time everlasting had something to say regarding the existence of a demonic presence among humanity.

"Then the seventy returned with joy, saying, 'Lord, even the demons are subject to us in your name.'"
—Luke 10:17

Remember, just like those antediluvian "sons and daughters of men," with the exception of the few here that Jesus gave authority to, pre-Christ humanity had no authority over these malevolent beings. They did not have the use of the name of Jesus nor the power of the Holy Spirit to subject evil to their authority. God was yet to make His abode in man.

"And He said to them, 'I saw Satan fall like lightning from heaven. Behold, I give you the authority to trample on serpents and scorpions, and over all the power of the enemy, and nothing shall by any means hurt you.'"
—Luke 10:18–19

Satan was referred to as the great dragon, the serpent of old, in the Book of Revelation. He and his lesser "serpents" and "scorpions," which are both synonymous with injecting deadly venom, and is connotative to the effects of sin, are the "serpents" whom Jesus is making reference to.

Angel of Light

Let's have a look at an incredible description of Lucifer from Ezekiel 28. In any war it is imperative to understand the nature of your enemy. Therefore, make sure you pay careful attention to what follows. In this particular scripture, we will discover why Satan is so easily able to deceive mankind. Remember, what follows refers to Satan, not Jesus.

> *"You were the seal of perfection, full of wisdom and perfect in beauty."*
> **—Ezekiel 28:12**

Doesn't that blow your mind? It is the exact opposite of how Satan is portrayed by the church, by the media, and even by the majority of biblical scholars. When have you ever heard anyone preach or teach that Satan is, or even was, perfect and beautiful? Do not even get me started on Satan's worldly wisdom. As you are about to discover, from God's perspective he still may be beautiful. They say, "Beauty is in the eye of the beholder." I think "they" are right.

> *"You were in Eden; the garden of God..."*
> **—Ezekiel 28:13**
> ...which definitively places the perpetrator at the scene of the crime.

> *"You were the anointed cherub who covers..."*
> **—Ezekiel 28:14**

As some mistakenly believe, the anointing Lucifer experienced in heaven is not the same as that which encompasses the nature of Yeshua Hamashiac (Jesus the Christ). The Hebrew word translated as "anointed" in this instance does not come from the same word translated as "Christ" (Christos, which is the Greek version of anointed), or even the "anointing" experienced by King David. Those words were *"mashiac"* in the case of Jesus, and in David's case *"mashach,"* which means to rub with oil.

In Lucifer's case, his "anointing" comes from the Hebrew word *"mimshach,"* and it means "expansion." The example given in James Strong's Concordance of the Hebrew/Chaldee language is "to expand with outstretched wings." Isn't that exactly how we picture this once great fallen angel? Hasn't he been spreading his wings and rapidly expanding his kingdom of influence ever since he was cast out of heaven? If you do not believe this to be true simply turn on your television and watch the imagery before your sin-stained eyes.

It Wasn't a Snake!

With that in mind, have you ever wondered how Adam and Eve could have been so easily ensnared by Lucifer? Actually, to be more accurate, Eve was deceived, Adam was merely disobedient. Nevertheless, Adam succumbed to the first ever case of peer pressure and followed along. With that said, how could Eve have become so enthralled by a snake, a creature she and Adam knowingly had complete and total dominion over? Furthermore, how could she have let it get so far out of hand that she completely disregarded the one prohibitive law God commanded.

> *"But of the tree of the knowledge of good and evil **you shall not eat,** for in the day that you eat of it you shall surely die."*
> **—Genesis 2:17**

As amazing as this may sound, somewhere along the line Eve determined that God was the liar. To discover the truth of how this occurred, we must remember that Yahweh used to walk in the garden with Adam and Eve in the cool of the day. (Genesis 3:8) Since sin was not an issue and they were able to see both His form and His face, you better believe He was radiant. *"God has brought you out of darkness and into **His marvelous light.**"* (1 Peter 2:9) *"For our God is a consuming fire."* (Hebrews 12:29)

Do you remember how Jesus shone like the sun when He gave Peter, James and John a glimpse of His glory on the Mount of Transfiguration? (Matthew 17:1–2) In the garden, Yahweh did not need to cover Himself in the pillar of cloud. Adam and Eve knew God intimately and yet somehow modern day Christian's believe Eve succumbed to a talking snake? If you ponder it, it makes no sense, whatsoever.

The truth is that Lucifer is still deceiving us. He has convinced us that he manifests in our lives as something that is easily recognizable as being out of the ordinary. This, however, is untrue. The word serpent, that appears in Genesis chapter three, is a translation of the word, *"Nachash,"* pronounced, **naw-kawsh.** In addition to serpent, the root word can connote several additional meanings such as, "to shine," or a "shining one," as translated by *therain.org.* Before we discuss the other meanings, consider what we just learned about Lucifer from Ezekiel 28 and check out how God continues to describe the true appearance of Lucifer.

> *"Every precious stone was your covering: the sardius, topaz, and diamond, beryl, onyx, and jasper, sapphire, turquoise, and emerald with gold. The workmanship of your timbrels and pipes was prepared for you on the day you were created."*
> **—Ezekiel 28:13**

I have often heard preachers, teachers, evangelists, and those who claim to have had a glimpse of hell, claim that Lucifer and the demons have undergone a transformation of their physical appearance. Although I can neither confirm nor deny this teaching, nowhere does scripture describe such a physical, or better stated, visual, metamorphosis.

According to scripture, Lucifer's appearance was, and perhaps still is, akin to the radiant sparkle of the most luminous precious stones coalescing into the brilliance of the most desirous precious metal of all, gold. In using the description of timbrels and pipes, we can also conclude that the glorious melodies of heaven radiated from the breathtaking appearance of the most fabulous angel of all. In short, Lucifer was majestic.

Although Michael the Arc Angel is greater in power, the radiant beauty of Lucifer is unmatched amongst the angelic host. In fact, he was so majestic that although he was not equal to, his appearance bore the similitude of Jehovah. How else could he have gotten one third of the angels of God to follow him? Check out the description of the throne of God according to Ezekiel, the same prophet giving the description of Lucifer.

> *And above the firmament over their heads* (referring to the "living creatures" around God's throne) *was **the likeness of a throne,** in appearance like **a sapphire stone;** on the likeness of the throne was a likeness with the appearance of a man high above it. Also from the appearance of His waist and upward I saw, as it were, **the color of amber** with **the appearance of fire** all around within it; and from the appearance of His waist and downward I saw, as it were, **the appearance of fire** with **brightness** all around. Like **the appearance of a rainbow** in a cloud on a rainy day, so was **the appearance of the brightness** all around it. **This was the appearance of the likeness of the glory of the Lord.***
> —Ezekiel 1:26–28

Lucifer's appearance actually makes sense when you consider that he was created to be a part of the throne room of heaven. Everything in heaven is majestic. Lucifer undoubtedly once was, as well. What he lacks, however, is the brightness of God as described by the prophet. In other words, the light and the fire of God are non-existent in Lucifer. Lucifer is outwardly beautiful, but inwardly dark. He is deceptive. He does not contain the light, the life, nor the glory of almighty Jehovah.

As you undoubtedly know, things are not always as they appear. Beauty can be vainly deceptive. The Hebrew word, "Nachash" also translates as a "whisper," and is connotative to "the practice of divination." The tiny whisper of the Nachash in the Garden of Eden was the beginning of the occult. Lucifer even counterfeited God's *"still small voice."* (1 Kings 19:12)

Interestingly, the bronze "serpent" that healed the Israelites in the Book of Numbers is also a translation of the word "Nachash" and is where and how the concept of shining is derived. *"Then the Lord said to Moses, 'Make a **fiery** serpent, and set it on a pole..."* (Numbers 21:8) The Hebrew word used for fiery is *"Saraph"* and it means "to burn." The imagery associated denotes the fiery reflective color of copper as it reverberates the suns rays. At the direction of Moses, the Israelites were commanded to gaze upon a radiant bronze Nachash to be healed of the plague with which they had been cursed.

The compilation of these descriptions gives us a clue to what Adam and Eve encountered on that fateful day in the Garden of Eden. The occult is deliberately designed to deceive; it is a counterfeit of true spirituality. The reason there are no counterfeit three dollar bills is because there are no real three dollar bills. Therefore, they would be easy to recognize. Deception always carries the appearance of authenticity. Contrary to popular belief and its portrayal by Hollywood movies, evil most often presents itself as whisper, not a shout.

When we put two and two together we discover that it was not a snake that spoke to Eve on that fateful day in the Garden of Eden, nor do I believe Lucifer inhabited the body of a serpent of any kind. Both Adam and Eve were well versed in their dominion over the *"beasts of the field"* and *"the creeping things of the earth."* (Genesis 2:19) It would have never worked. It would have been easily recognized as inauthentic. Therefore, we must consider Lucifer's most powerful attribute.

*"Now the serpent (Nachash) was **more cunning** than any beast of the field which the Lord God had made."*

—Genesis 3:10

Do not forget what we read above regarding Lucifer. *"You were the seal of perfection,* **full of wisdom and perfect in beauty.***"*

While writing this, I just happen to be at one of the most beautiful places I have ever been. It is a tiny island off the coast of Flores, Indonesia, with an incredible coral reef that is accessible right from the beach. On my third day of snorkeling, and while being completely in awe of the sheer majesty of God's creation, I stumbled across a sea snake. Being somewhat familiar with the species, I knew how deadly poisonous this critter was, but also that it would not attack me. I would probably have to force my hand into its mouth to get bit, but nevertheless, it was headed right for me.

To make matters worse, it seemed to be more curious about me than I was of it. This, by the way, is true of Lucifer . . . until he garners your attention and turns the tables on you. Anyway, as it was skimming the surface toward me, I casually attempted to move out of its way. Did I mention that there were also three Lion Fish just to my left, bravely patrolling the stairs leading up the dock? Although their sting probably would not kill kill me, getting stung would certainly be no party and who knows, getting stung by all three rather large specimens could perhaps prove to be too much for one man to endure. Moving immediately to my left, therefore, was not an option.

Being the quick witted individual that I apparently am (not) I began retreating. That ought to give this peaceful serpent plenty of room to pass—right? Wrong! The snake seemed to have a vastly different plan. To my shock and awe it began to pursue me. When I went right, it went right. When I moved left, it moved left. At this point I am beginning to think, "Perhaps I misread this supposedly docile creature. Have I underestimated, or perhaps even worse, been deceived regarding its nature?"

At this exact moment a strange thought entered my mind. Have you ever noticed the insanity that can enter your thought process when you are faced with peril? I was once in an ambulance falsely believing I was having a heart attack or stroke, and while looking death straight in the eye, my thoughts were not of my family, like so many individuals report. My only thought was, "Why am I having a heart attack while so many obese people, who never exercise, who do not eat properly, nor mange any aspect of their physical lives, escape my physical plight unscathed?" I know it is insane and completely selfish, but that is what I was thinking. *"O wretched man that I am."* (Romans 7:24)

Anyway, as I am attempting to avoid this deadly creature, I once again began to have a conversation with myself. "Isn't this just like Lucifer," I began thinking. "Is this really how I'm going out? Am I about to be a story on *1000 Ways to Die?*" Since I lived to write this chapter, however, I gather that by now you have surmised the answer.

Back to the snake . . . In a panic, I attempted to dive underneath it. Just as I did, it dashed to the bottom. My splash must have startled it. I being a glutton for punishment, however, attempted to follow it down. I guess my curiosity had gotten the best of me, which when looking back made me feel just like Adam and Eve. The snake, however, was too cunning. Just like Lucifer it slithered under the reef and disappeared. I had survived the encounter.

When I got back to shore the owner of the cottages was trimming a few trees. I disclosed the confrontation to him and he replied, "I hate snakes."

I said, "But it was so beautiful." It was a brilliant, shiny, black and white striped color. How appropriate, right? A splendidly radiant snake whose colors represent the light and dark side of life.

He then looked straight at me and stated, "Everything beautiful is dangerous." Although he was no longer referring to snakes, I realized how right he was.

That leads us right back to the Garden of Eden and Adam's now dangerously beautiful problem—no, not Lucifer, I am talking about his wife, Eve. Contrary to popular belief, Adam was not following Lucifer's lead. He was following Eve. Therefore, the even greater problem was in how Lucifer presented himself. I do not believe Eve's encounter was with a talking snake. When we look at the evidence of Eve's confrontation with "the serpent," it appears that Lucifer presented himself as the exquisitely radiant angelic being that he is; full of charismatic charm and twisted wisdom and beauty. In fact, based upon the usage of the word "nachash" it also appears that Lucifer shone like the sun in counterfeit of the glory of God. Unfortunately, his corrupted goal just happened to be the destruction of humanity from the face of the earth. Satan appeared to Adam and Eve just as Ezekiel 28 describes.

Now it makes sense! Why would Eve have become so enthralled by a simple snake when she walked with God every day? The truth is, she was not. She was captivated by another *"still small voice"* (1 Kings 19:12) that whispered in her ear with majestic, but deceptive, occultic brilliance. In the Garden of Eden, Lucifer utilized his greatest and most deceptive skill. Lucifer counterfeited Yahweh.

To Eve's less than discerning eyes, he appeared to be on the same divine level as the God with whom she was so intimately acquainted. Once engaged, she became confused and was deceived by his presence in the garden. What appeared to be good was not God. Thus, the premise of every world religion, as well as, modern day humanism had been sown into the heart of man. "Follow me, surely you won't die."

Good or God?

With that in mind I must bring up one other critical point. My entire life I have believed that Adam and Eve were, and that humanity is, attracted to evil. Although that may be true of some demonically twisted, or perhaps, even, insane individual's, that was certainly not the case in the Garden of Eden. Do not get me wrong, they were certainly attracted to what Satan was offering, and without a doubt, they were hanging around a place they had no business being, but it was not the evil of Lucifer's offer they accepted.

It was actually the good! Check out Genesis chapter three with me. I will show you how and why I surmise this critical truth.

> *"Now the serpent was more cunning than any beast of the field which the Lord God had made. And he said to the woman, "Has God indeed said, 'You shall not eat of every tree of the garden'?"*
>
> *And the woman said to the serpent, "We may eat the fruit of the trees of the garden; but of the fruit of the tree which is in the midst of the garden, God has said, 'You shall not eat it, nor shall you touch it, lest you die.'"*
>
> *Then the serpent said to the woman, "You will not surely die. For God knows that in the day you eat of it your eyes will be opened, and you will be like God, **knowing** good **and** evil."*
>
> *So when the woman saw that the tree **was good** for food, that **it was pleasant** to the eyes, and a tree **desirable** to make one wise, she took of its fruit and ate. She also gave to her husband with her, and he ate. Then the eyes of both of them were opened, and they knew that they were naked; and they sewed fig leaves together and made themselves coverings."*
>
> **—Genesis 3:1–7**

Have you ever made a decision that you thought was good, perhaps, even, God ordained only to find that you had made a mistake? I see it happen all the time with things like big houses, new cars, computer's, hand bags for the lady's, or whatever purchase you made that seemed good at the time . . . then the monthly payment's start coming in. Incredibly, I have even seen it with calls into the ministry. Give *that* some thought for a moment. It is often times at this point that you realize a vital truth. You cannot afford it. You made a mistake. It was not God's voice. It was John's voice, or whatever your name may be. In other words, what you thought was good was not God, and now you have a problem.

This is what happened to Adam and Eve in the Garden of Eden. It is also what makes Lucifer so extraordinarily deceptive and cunning. Just like us, Eve did not perceive the evil intertwined with Lucifer's offer. How could she? In truth, she did not even understand the good of the Garden of Eden.

Think about it. The tree containing the forbidden fruit was the *"the tree of the **knowledge** of good and evil."* (Genesis 2:17) In other words, Eve did not have the knowledge required to make an educated decision. Does that sound familiar? I see the same issue occurring regarding people's opinion of Yahweh and/or the variety of world religion's on a daily basis. People continuously form their opinion's based upon what others are saying without ever having read the religious text accompanying said religion, or comparing it to another religion's claim upon the "truth." Unfortunately, discernment goes out the window when someone has no legitimate reference point. My friend, ignorance is a deadly venom. It always leads to both death and destruction.

> *"My people are destroyed for lack of knowledge."*
> **—Hosea 4:6**

The English word, "knowledge" is a translation of the Hebrew word, "daath." In addition to knowledge, it also connotes having the skill of discernment. In other words, not only did Adam and Eve have no knowledge of evil, they had absolutely no ability to discern between that which was good and that which was evil. In fact, although they were basking in the perfect goodness of Yahweh's Eden, where even His presence would enter the Garden, they were completely unaware of it. They had no frame of reference between good and bad.

Therefore, have a second look at the scripture. Eve was not attracted to the evil of Lucifer's offer. She thought she was signing up for something that was, *"good, desirable and pleasant."* Dare I even say, Godly? That is what she was attracted to. Unfortunately intertwined with what appeared to be good was unrepentant evil; and that is what makes Lucifer so deceptive. He is an expert at camouflage and always packages evil together with good. Evil is always inherent in the deal.

The recent Supreme Court ruling on gay marriage is the perfect example. It appears loving. It appears to be good; but it is outright rebellion against the King of the universe. It is disobedience toward the Word of God and it is exactly what befell both Adam and Eve in the Garden of Eden. Eve fell for the deception and Adam, just like the pop culture world in which we now live, followed right along.

Perfectly Imperfect

With that in mind, let's return to the eye opening narrative of the demon Lucifer recorded by the prophet Ezekiel. As you are about to learn, my analysis of the angel Lucifer is not mere speculation. Check out the following historical account coming directly from the Word of God.

> *"**I established you;** you were on the holy mountain of God; you walked back and forth in the midst of the fiery stones."*
> **—Ezekiel 28:14**

Talk about sowing and reaping! Take note that God clearly communicates that it was He who established Satan. The devil has no authority of his own. Lucifer, however, has sown spiritual corruption, and having fallen from the fiery stones of heaven has reaped hell's Lake of Fire in recompense to his rebellion. Let's move on . . .

> *"You were perfect in your ways from the day you were created, **till iniquity was found in you.**"*
> **—Ezekiel 28:15**

What is your reaction when you read that portion of scripture? Do you have difficulty understanding how God could have created something perfect and later find iniquity within it? To our human understanding that is something of an oxymoron. How can something be perfect and flawed simultaneously?

The answer lay in the truth that God does not define perfection the same way humanity does. This is a secret truth that must be understood to find your place in God culture. To us, perfection means without flaw. To God, perfection means that something, or someone, is functioning exactly as God created it, or them, to be, whether flawed or not.

Satan, man, and the entire universe for that matter, is operating in the exact manner that God intended. Therefore, it is perfect. It functions exactly as He designed it to function. His perfect plan has never gotten a millimeter off track. That is a secret we human beings do not comprehend, but must learn to recognize and trust.

God will only do things *His* way. It is your choice as to whether you want to submit to Perfection or continue on in your own damaged and certainly less than splendid ways. The secret truth is that *God purposely created Lucifer with iniquity implanted in him.*

God has a purpose for Lucifer. One of them is to be the tempter and tester of humanity. In passing and learning from these tests, we discover God's perfect plan for our lives. In temptation and tribulation we are driven to our knees. We finally recognize our own frailty and cry out to God for mercy. As for the rest of Satan's usefulness to God, that is God's business. I do not pretend to know or understand it. I do, however, accept it.

The Devil Made Me Do It

Hang in there for a moment longer. We are not finished with Lucifer yet. The Ezekiel account has much more to say. Just as mankind was transformed by evil, Lucifer experienced quite a metamorphosis of his own.

*"By the abundance of your trading **you became** filled with violence within, and you sinned. Therefore, I cast you as a profane thing out of the mountain of God; and I destroyed you, O covering cherub, from the midst of the fiery stones. Your heart was lifted up **because of your beauty;** you corrupted your wisdom **for the sake of splendor;** I cast you to the ground ..."*

—Ezekiel 28:16–17

You may not realize this, but Satan appears to have been blessed with the same gift of freewill that humanity has, and, therefore, was presented with a similar set of choices. Just like Adam and Eve, and just like every single one of us have at some point in time, he chose to rebel against God. In God's eyes, He was blessed with beauty and splendor, but he chose to throw it in the face of God rather than be thankfully submissive to his Creator.

If this does not sound an alarm it should. He has been influencing us to sow the same seed ever since. He transforms himself into an *"angel of light,"* (2 Corinthians 11:14) exploits our presently corrupt nature and deceives humanity with his iniquitous beauty and wisdom, thus leading us into following *his* will as opposed to the will of God. This is exactly what went on in Noah's day and it is precisely what occurred in the Garden of Eden. It is still transpiring today.

Eve was deceived by the corrupt wisdom of a fallen angel created to be perfectly used in the area of testing the love and faithfulness of mankind toward God. Do not be deceived, however, God is not causing men to commit evil acts. Man is selecting that of his own accord. Man is now contaminated by the same iniquity as Lucifer and has undergone the same metamorphosis. Therefore, we tend to make the same choices. That is the pinnacle of Lucifer's influence. Man is choosing to do things Lucifer's way and not God's way. That is the very definition of sin.

The word "sin" means "to miss the mark." What mark are we aiming at? Of course it is God's mark. The result of our inaccuracy is corruption leading to death. Therefore, all the death and destruction is the outcome of the evil influence so prevalent in the world today. It is the result of the devil inside of every unredeemed human being under heaven.

Just like Satan, mankind is full of pride. In fact, it is Satan's influence upon man which causes pride. It is the sowing of pride that reaped Satan's fall and it is the sowing of pride that reaps the fall of every man as well. Until you recognize this iniquity you will remain a spiritual zombie, walking eternally as the living dead, vying to fill the hole in your spirit with every idol Satan can thrust upon you. With the exceptions of Judaism and certain forms of Christianity, it is the nature of every religion that has ever been practiced upon the earth. Yahweh alone, and all that He encompasses, is to be worshipped. Consider this truth the next time you are tempted to pray to Mary, Saint Michael, or even Allah. Just like Eve, you are staring into the face of the Nachash.

Satan is the originator of pride. He alone is the author of impure religion. *"Pure and undefiled religion before God and the Father is this: to visit orphans and widows in their trouble, and to keep oneself unspotted from the world."* (James 1:27) That is the extent of it as far as religion is concerned.

God's will is simply to draw you to Him, revive you into a living spirit and spend eternity with you in the Eden of the New Jerusalem. The Spirit of God obliterates the "devil inside" of every human being, which is the iniquitous nature you have been born with. Religion has absolutely nothing to do with it.

Therefore, I would encourage you to learn the ways of God and follow them—period the end. It is all about knowing Jesus and having a relationship with both He and the Father. Therefore, stop running. Your Father awaits your return.

"Then Jesus said to those Jews who believed Him, 'If you abide in My word, you are My disciples indeed. And you shall know the truth, and the truth shall make you free.'"

—John 8:31–32

Good Grief!

Let's pursue this topic a bit further. Why would Satan and his demonic angels even care enough to reproduce with mankind? Honestly, what was the point?

In case you are unaware, Satan is unable to actually create anything. His only two abilities, and he happens to excel at both of them, are to lie and to corrupt. God created man. Satan attempts to destroy man through corrupting the greatest gift God endued you with, choice. He tries to corrupt your freewill, and he will lie, cheat and steal in order to accomplish his goal.

But the question still remains. Why does he focus so much upon humanity? Why not corrupt the animals for instance? To answer this age old question, let's once again return to Noah's day and find out. The following takes place just after the procreation between the fallen angels and the sons of God.

> *"There were giants on the earth in those days, and also afterward, when the sons of God came into the daughters of men and they bore children to them. Those were the mighty men who were of old, men of renown."*
>
> *"Then the Lord saw the wickedness of man was great in the earth, and that **every intent** of the thoughts of his heart **was only evil continually**. And the Lord **was sorry** that He had made man on the earth, and **was grieved in His heart**. So the*

Lord said, 'I will destroy man whom I have created from the face of the earth.'"
—Genesis 6:4–7

That, right there, is Satan's ultimate goal. The secret motivation of Satan's evil plan is *to grieve God.* It is not about you, my friend. Satan could care less about you. Apart from jealousy, he has no feelings whatsoever toward humanity. Lucifer's quest to destroy man is a crusade to avenge his hatred of Yahweh. Lucifer's contempt and jealously of God is so intense that he longs to cause God excruciating and eternal pain by destroying the one thing God loves the most—humanity.

Can you hear Satan's insidious laughter? Can you envision his vindictive scorn? He believed he had won the war. His goal in corrupting man always has been, and always will be, to get God to once again utter those four tragic words, *"I will destroy man . . ."*

How does he do it? Lucifer knows that there is no sin in heaven. He used to live there and that is why he was thrown out. He also knows that if he can get you to sin, you will be denied entrance, as well. So what does he do? He sows the seed of sin. When you accept it guess what you reap? Eternal destruction. You experience spiritual death.

But why pollute mankind so irreversibly? What could possibly motivate him to change our actual genetic makeup by having his twisted minions corrupt our nature? This is far beyond iniquity. It is an act so evil that it would bring the eternal end to the glorious and wondrous species known as humanity, and guess what? even that is not about you. It is all about Jesus. It is all about forever. Everything in the universe revolves around Jesus.

*"For by Him all things were created that are in heaven and that are on earth, visible and invisible, whether thrones or dominions or principalities or powers. All things were created through Him **and for Him."***
—Colossians 1:16

Satan was not just attempting to contaminate mankind. His iniquitous sin is far worse than mere gene sharing. *Lucifer was attempting to extinguish the image of God!* That is his dirty little secret. Now do you realize how depraved and wicked he is? He still believes he is at war with Yahweh. He actually believes there is still a chance for him to win, as well. To this day he believes he can overthrow God.

As prefaced earlier, Lucifer knew the Messiah was coming. He knows the intention of God very well. He knows the law of the Kinsman Redeemer and that Jesus alone is the only hope mankind has for redemption. He also knows how much God loves humanity.

If Lucifer could change the image of man to resemble his own twisted and sin marred countenance, Jesus would no longer qualify as our brethren. We could not become His image, and, therefore, Jesus could not become *"the first born among many brethren."* (Romans 8:29) In fact, from Lucifer's twisted point of view, because Jesus was to be born of a woman, that would even transform the Messiah into *his* image. Wouldn't that make him "god" over Jesus? Isn't that exactly what he was attempting in the wilderness of temptation?

> *"Again, the devil took Him up on an exceedingly high mountain, and showed Him all the kingdoms of the world and their glory. And he said to Him, 'All these things I will give You **if You will fall down and worship me.**'"*
> **—Matthew 4:8–9**

Can you imagine? His ultimate goal was an attempt to transform the Messiah into the image of Lucifer. If successful, Jesus would be disqualified from fulfilling the law. Mankind would be lost for eternity. The pain of Yahweh would burn for eternity.

In truth, Satan's plan was an attempt to recreate man. *"The prince of the power of the air,"* (Ephesians 2:2) who through Adam and Eve's act of original sin has become *"the god of this world,"* (2 Corinthians 4:4) was attempting to replace Yahweh. Satan attempted a hostile takeover that would cause him to become the god of the physical universe. Yes, he is that twisted.

Secondly, and this is evidence of his lack of power, he needed a plan "B." He knew his plan "A" might not work. Therefore, his "Plan B" was a ridiculous attempt to trick God into destroying one hundred percent of mankind. Can you imagine how arrogant one must be to believe they can trick the omniscient Creator of all that exists? If successful, his would be divine genocide would preclude the Messiah, the Savior of mankind and killer of the devil, prophesied from Genesis three, from being born into the earth. There would be no Savior.

If God would once again destroy man there would be no womb; there could be no lineage through which Jesus could enter the natural realm, and, thus, Lucifer could prevent the virgin birth. If successful, man would be forever damned. The birth, death, and his now final attempt, the triumphant return of Christ could be thwarted and Satan could avoid eternal fire. With Jesus out of the way the earth would be his for eternity. He would be spared destruction.

Praise God, however, because Lucifer has failed! God preserved a remnant. Noah and his family had not been corrupted by the times in which they lived. God kept a seed for Himself. He sealed them in the ark and brought them to safety. Thus, the image of God had been preserved and the promise of the coming Messiah, the redemption plan of God, remained.

Four thousand years later, the seed sprung forth in the person of Jesus Christ and rescued all those who believe. Today, God is still reaping His harvest.

But evil still persists. Satan *"knows his time is short."* (Revelation 12:12) Therefore, the perpetrator has returned to the scene of the crime. Satan continually lurks in the shadows, longing for victory, and forever yearning

to hear God utter those horrific words that are so sweet to his detestable
ears.

> *"I am sorry that I made mankind. I will destroy man whom I have
> created from the face of the earth."*
>
> **—Genesis 6:6–7**

CHAPTER 9

Lucifer

(THE SECRET OF THE WAR IN HEAVEN)

As you may have guessed by now, I am a movie lover. Although I am certainly not a fan of the Hollywood lifestyle, even I must admit that they make some extraordinary films. Every once in a while, perhaps once in a generation or so, a film is made that even has the ability to change the world in which we live. Films such as *Roots,* for example, brought the horrors of slavery to the forefront of the American public and did wonders for the African American in their struggle for civil rights and equal opportunity. One could make the argument that there would be no President Barak Obama without the incredible film series regarding the forefather's of one Mr. Charles Haley. Such change, however, is not always positive. Movies also have the innate ability to deliver fear and if you are yet to realize it, fear is the number one tool of our enemy Lucifer.

In my opinion there are two such movies that have affected society like no other in history. Of all the horror movies ever made, there are two which have instilled the fear of God into the public, and one of them does not even fit into the genre of "horror." Make no mistake though, it *is* terrifying. Its effects on the lives of millions are still being felt as I pen this discourse. The two movies are *Jaws* and *The Exorcist*. They are without a doubt the two most frightening movies to ever hit the silver screen.

To this day, I cannot set foot into the ocean without thinking of the possibility of being eaten by a shark, particularly when my eyes cannot see or my feet can no longer detect the bottom. Since first witnessing the opening scene of *Jaws*, I have become acutely aware of what potentially lurks below. The image of the young lady bobbing up and down, while being dragged through the dark ocean current has never abandoned my psyche. I am sure that I am not alone.

However, not even *Jaws* affected my life like *The Exorcist*. *The Exorcist* literally scared the hell out of me. I can remember lying in bed and waiting for it to begin shaking and levitating. I could hear the growling and the blasphemous intonations bellowing out of Regan, the satanically possessed young girl upon whose life the film was based. Not too long ago, as I was flipping through the channels I stumbled across it. After about a minute I had to change the channel. Not for fear, however, the devil no longer has that effect on me. Let me explain.

As a child, it seemed logical to me that if I did not want to be eaten by a shark I could simply stay out of the ocean. Oddly enough, the incident the movie *Jaws* was based upon was actually five separate attacks transpiring in the Matawan Creek between July 1, and July 12, of the year 1916. Only one victim survived. Incredibly, the Matawan Creek is only about twenty minutes from where I grew up. It also happens to be fresh water, but is partially a tidal inlet of the Rarity Bay—thus the shark.

In 1916, who would have ever thought the fresh waters of the Matawan Creek could be inhabited by a man eater? Sharks inhabiting rivers and estuaries is a fairly recent discovery. In 1916 four of the five victims were strangely killed while swimming in the refreshing cool waters during a legendary heat wave that drove an unprecedented number of people to the shores of New Jersey. Air Conditioning was non-existent in 1916. The only way to cool off was to find shade or swim in the water.

It is now believed that the culprit was the always underestimated bull shark and not a Great White, as portrayed in the movie. Bull sharks, by the way, have been found as far as 2500 miles up the Amazon River. Is there really any place safe in the world? Your life is fleeting at best. Nevertheless, in my mind's view there was an aspect of control regarding shark attacks. They are one hundred percent avoidable. I could simply stay out of the water.

The Exorcist, on the other hand—I could not escape the dark or the isolation of my bedroom at night. The fact that Lucifer could push his way into my life and there was nothing I could do to stop him did not just scare *the* hell out of me, it ultimately scared *hell* out of me, quite literally. In a strange way, *The Exorcist* led me to God. Talk about "*all things working together for good . . .*" (Romans 8:28)

However, after finding Christ I have come to realize that my fears were unfounded. Satan cannot push his way into my life any more than you can. In Christ, you have more power than Satan. Therefore, Lucifer cannot accomplish a single twisted act without your help. Satan requires your physical body. He needs you to act on his behalf. Without you, he is nothing!

Wars, murder, rape, or whatever crimes against humanity that have become so prevalent in today's world do not just materialize from thin air. Genocide's do not just magically happen, as if someone could conjure up some sort of genocide spell and an entire race of people would magically fall to the ground dead. Lucifer requires a human being to do his bidding. Hitler's *Final Solution* was carried out by human beings. There is no doubt that they were Satanically influenced, but that is exactly the point. Without the *Third Reich*, Satan's demonic plan to kill the Jews was powerless.

Thus, the now rise of ISIS, Boko Haram, as well as, every past regime whose goal was to annihilate the Jewish race. It is the same plan simply using a different set of body's. The same is true of every individual succumbing to Lucifer's twisted will.

When I last saw *The Exorcist* I did not turn it off for fear of reliving my childhood nightmares. I turned it off due to its blasphemous nature. I can no longer tolerate such insolence toward the Lord of glory. I will never watch it again.

As we began to explore in the last chapter, I do not even believe the content of *The Exorcist* is entirely accurate. Demonic manifestations on the level of Regan are extremely rare. They do occur, but more often than not, as we discussed in the previous chapter, Satan disguises himself as an angel of light. (2 Corinthians 11:14) He is much more deceptive that way, and, therefore, infinitely more effective.

Today's emphasis on "tolerance" is the perfect example. Although it seems to be a doctrine derived from love, in many cases it is nothing more than a platform to promote, normalize and desensitize humanity to sin. If you do not believe that, ask yourself why the tolerant will not tolerate the Christian. Imposition is always an act of the enemy.

Knowing your spiritual rights, or in other words, being in Christ, eliminates the fear of Lucifer. Therefore, I am not afraid of the devil regardless of what form he chooses to take. There is no reason to be when the right "team" is on your side. In fact, I am one hundred percent convinced that the devil is much more afraid of me than I am of him. Therefore, I will speak the truth in love and dare the "tolerant" to tolerate *me!* and more importantly God, who, of course, is above all.

I once heard a story about the great preacher Oral Roberts. He woke up one evening to find the devil sitting at the foot of his bed. Satan slowly turned and glared at him with his foulest and most petrifying scowl. Brother Roberts sprang up in his bed, looked the devil right in the face, yawned, and said, "Oh, it's just you..." then lie back down and immediately fell asleep.

I do not know if that story is true or not but I love the principle behind it. The devil simply has no authority over the man whose God resides within. How could he? *"You are of God, little children, and have overcome them, because He who is in you **is greater** than he who is in the world."* (1 John 4:4)

With that said, and based upon what we learned in the previous chapter, the deceptiveness of evil does have a certain appeal to mankind. Believe it or not, evil even has a purpose. Therefore, let's explore the truth of the evil that has so ensnared the world and discover how we should deal with it. Let's peer into the ancient past and have a look at the origin of Lucifer and his demonic forces.

Fallen Angels

If you take an honest look at yourself, you will realize that as human beings we seem to be drawn to the way evil presents itself. How many times have you heard someone say, "Well if I go to hell all of my friends will be there anyway." Although it may be true that your friends will be there, it will not be the ongoing party that most people seem to believe will occur.

I remember a joke that I heard as a very small child. In it, a man dies and goes to hell. As he enters through the gates of hell he notices that all of his friends are there. His favorite music is playing, he sees all of his friends hanging out, playing cards, having a drink or two... It all seems as he expected.

As he takes a closer look, however, he notices something strange. The entire floor of the pit of hell seems to be covered with water up to about the average person's knees. All of sudden he notices Satan playing cards in the corner of the room. Just as the man sits down with one of his friends, Satan stands up and proclaims, "Okay, break time is over; everybody stand on your head!"

The point is, the offer is always prepackaged with what appears to be good. What good is being with your friends and loved one's in hell if you are *"separated from the everlasting presence of God,"* (2 Thessalonians 1:9) *"cast into the outer darkness"* (Matthew 8:12, 22:13, and 25:30) and deconstructed by the "Lake of Fire" (Revelation 20:10–15).

How is that appealing to anyone? I think it has something to do with the curiosity that God has implanted within us, but in a perverted sort of way. Therefore, before we move on, we must reconsider the definition of evil. Evil does not need to be manifest as an act of murder, rape, racism, nor any of the classical definitions of what one may consider to be a demonic manifestation. God considers anything that draws you away from Him to be evil.

Most of the Hollywood films, television shows and even our daily surfing of the internet, for example, leads us away from Jehovah. In many cases, engaging in such activities is merely creating idle time apart from our Maker. Therefore, when it becomes the focus of our lives it is evil.

Idle time is not our only ill. Evil comes in a plethora of forms and lifestyles. Think about it, premarital sex, or what the world now considers to be the most romantic physical relationships, leads humanity away from God's presence. The genre of "Romance," which is really nothing more than written porn, is a multi-billion dollar industry and has garnered an entire classification of the printed word.

That is only the tip of the iceberg. The insatiable desire to accumulate wealth, for example, otherwise known as greed and lust, leads humanity away form God's will. Ignoring God, never reading your Bible, nor acknowledging your Maker leads us away from His presence. Unbeknownst to most, something as simple as not believing in God is an act of evil. (Hebrews 3:12) These are just a few examples of how evil ensnares us. In fact, evil does not need to be so overt. Evil can be present in a single solitary thought. Why, then, do we fail recognize evil's devices? Why is evil so alluring?

The answer is that there is a demonic influence present in the world in which we live. His name is Lucifer. He belongs to a special class of created beings that perform a specific and purposeful function for the Lord God Almighty. They are purposeful, powerful and completely obedient to their governmental ruler. Their goal is to *"steal, kill and destroy,"* (John 10:10) and their target is you.

If you read *Yahweh Revealed*, you will recall our discussion regarding the ministry of angels. That is a great place for us to begin this current endeavor. At the time, I purposely failed to mention that there are two sides to every coin. After coming this far, however, I believe you are ready to progress to a higher level of truth. Not only does God command the ministry of the heavenly host, but as we touched on in the last chapter, Lucifer has his own brand of "ministering" spirits, as well.

They also happen to be angels created by God for the purpose of good. However, it must be understood that just like us, it appears that angels have also been created with the ability to choose. Amazingly, most biblical scholars believe about one third of them *chose* to rebel against God and followed Satan in his attempt to usurp the throne of heaven. The number of dissidents stems from the following verse taken from Revelation 12, where the Apostle John witnesses the birth of Israel, (expressed as "the woman") as well as, the birth and crucifixion of the Messiah (expressed as "the child").

> *"And his* (Lucifer's) *tail swept away **a third** of the stars of heaven* (angels), ***and threw them to the earth.*** *And the dragon* (Lucifer) *stood before the woman* (Israel) *who was about to give birth* (to the Messiah),

so that when she gave birth he (Lucifer) *might devour her child."* (By killing the Messiah)
—Revelation 12:4 — Parenthesis added for clarity

Lucifer's name, by the way, does not mean "morning star" as so many believe. It is actually Jesus who is referred to as the *"Bright and Morning star."* (2 Peter 1:19 and Revelation 22:16) It is also believed that the stars (sometimes referred to as the "heavenly host") of Revelation 12:4, were the angels that followed Lucifer in his rebellion against God. Thus, their being *"swept away"* from heaven and *"thrown to the earth."*

Interestingly enough, the Greek word translated as "swept away" is suró. It means, "to draw" or "to drag" and usually refers to one being compelled to appear before the judge and/or being forcibly dragged to prison. I cannot help but wonder how the angels must have felt once their deception was revealed. Can you imagine the horror as they were being forcibly drawn toward Lucifer while he was being dragged out of heaven? To this day, Lucifer has not changed. Just as Lucifer does to man, he drew the rebellious angels to himself and ultimately sealed their fate. This too, is a counterfeit of the ways of Christ.

*"And I, if I am lifted up **from the earth,*** (Lucifer was sent below to the earth) ***will draw all peoples to Myself."***
—John 12:32

In this case, however, the word Jesus used for "draw" is "helkó." It means, "to draw by inward power." Consider the implications, Satan drags you out of God's presence and *away* from heaven. Jesus draws you toward God's presence and *into* heaven. Apparently the devil is in the details—literally.

As I began to say, Lucifer's name does not mean, "morning star." The name Lucifer means, "light bearer" and may be a reference to his function while still residing before the throne of God. Thus, his ability to *"transform himself into an angel of light,"* (2 Corinthians 11:14) begins to make sense.

He was once the bearer of light. Take note, however, that he being a *bearer of light* does not make him the light. Perhaps this is where the fallen angels were mistaken. That honor is reserved for Yahweh alone.

> *"This is the message we have heard from him and proclaim to you, that **God is light,** and in him is no darkness at all."*
> —1 John 1:5

We also find confirmation of the fallen angel's rebellion and ousting from heaven in the Book of Jude . . .

> *"And the angels **who did not keep their proper domain, but left their own abode,** He has reserved in everlasting chains **under darkness** for the judgment of the last day."*
> —Jude 1:6

The result of this rebellion was a war in the heavens with Lucifer and his new-found followers being cast to the earth with him. Let's revisit Revelation chapter twelve for a brief moment.

> *"And war broke out in heaven: Michael and his angels fought with the dragon; and the dragon and his angels fought, but they **did not** prevail, **nor was there a place found for them in heaven any longer.** (Due to leaving their proper domain) So **the great dragon was cast out,** that serpent of old, called the devil and Satan, who deceives the whole world, **he was cast to the earth, and his angels** (the stars that were swept away) **were cast out with him."***
> —**Revelation 12:7–9, parentheses added for clarity**

We know these fallen angels as demons. Satan is their leader. We see them manifest as ghosts, spirits of the dead, or however you would like to categorize them. In truth, any disembodied spirit you may encounter in this life is either an angel, a demon, Lucifer or the Spirit of God. I do not even see where the Cherubim or Seraphim leave the throne of God to act on man's behalf. Michael, the Arc Angel, and all those under his command have been sanctified for that role.

Additionally, according to scripture, there are no such things as ghosts in the traditional sense. *Casper the Friendly Ghost* is a non-existent entity and there is no scriptural evidence to cause one to believe that our long lost relatives watch over us. The idea is based solely upon humanity's ability to self-soothe when facing a situation that causes emotional distress and pain. Intervening on behalf of humanity is God's job. Why do you think He sent "the Helper," His Holy Spirit to us? (John 14:16 and 16:7) Why would He have us, who have been granted no supernatural power to intercede, oversee the affairs of mankind? He already gave humanity authority over our own lives and look how that turned out. Our intercession comes only through prayer, and it is God, not we, who does the work.

Furthermore, human beings either go to hell or to heaven upon death. We cannot reside in two places at once. (Luke 16:26) Only God has the power to do so. He alone is omnipresent. Not even Lucifer possesses this divine capability. He was thrown out of heaven and cast to earth, and on the rare occasion that He is permitted to appear before God in heaven, he cannot do his bidding from there, nor exist in both places.

> *"Now there was a day when the sons of God came to present themselves before the Lord,* **and Satan also came among them.** *And the Lord said to Satan, 'From where do you come?' So Satan answered the Lord and said, 'From going to and fro* **on the earth,** *and from walking back and forth* **on it...'"** *And the Lord said to Satan, "Behold, all that he has is in your power; only do not lay a hand on his person." So Satan* **went out** *from the presence of the Lord.*
>
> **—Job 1:6–7 and 12**

Think about what you are believing when you credit humanity with such capability. It is an idolatrous thought. Human beings screwed it up in the Garden of Eden and have continued to do so every day forward. We cannot even manage our own affairs and yet somehow we choose to believe we are magically given the power to function as a god upon death, or equally as absurd, as someone's guardian angel? The oversight of humanity is the function of the Holy Spirit who is *assisted* by the angels of heaven.

Woe to You

> "Then I heard a loud voice saying in heaven, 'Now salvation, and strength, and the kingdom of our God, and the power of His Christ have come, for the accuser of the brethren, who accused them before our God day and night, **has been cast down**. And they overcame him by the blood of the Lamb and the word of their testimony, and they did not love their lives to the death."
>
> "Therefore **rejoice O heavens, and you who dwell in them! Woe to the inhabitants of the earth and the sea!** For the devil has come down to you, having great wrath, because he knows that he has a short time."
>
> **—Revelation 12:10–12**

I realized something as I was transposing the above scripture. We have been interpreting and attempting to apply it all wrong. Where we see the phrase, *"for the accuser of the brethren, who accused them day and night before our God,"* we have always assumed that the brethren being accused were we human beings.

However, the scripture cannot be referring to humanity in this instance. The war it is referencing took place in the heavens. It was between Lucifer, God and the rebellious angels. It is actually a picture of the heavenly rebellion of Lucifer and the fallen angels, which transpired *before* he had been cast out of heaven and apparently just after the creation of Adam. Remember, Lucifer was either already in the Garden when Adam was placed there, or he was exiled to the earthly realm just after. I lean toward the idea of just after due to the fact that the earth already had inhabitants. Revelation 12:11 states, *"Woe **to the inhabitants** of the earth and sea,"* while ousting Lucifer from the heavenly realm.

Either way, since Adam and Eve were yet to have their first child we can deduce that the war in the heavens took place some time around or during God placing Adam and Eve into the Garden of Eden.

Can you imagine? Here is God creating this incredible universe on behalf of His most recent beloved act of creation and Lucifer immediately became filled with a jealous rage and attempted to usurp the throne of God. Thank God that He is all powerful. God never hesitated for a second. He instantaneously commanded Michael to put an end to the situation. Therefore, ol' Lucifer and his *Mötley Crüe* of demonic raiders found themselves stripped of all power and authority.

As a result, Adam and Eve found themselves face to face with an already defeated foe for the purpose of undergoing the same test that we all must pass. Who will you serve? Unfortunately, we know how it worked out, or more accurately, didn't work out. We are still suffering sin's effects. Therefore, the scripture citing the war in heaven must be referring to the two thirds of the angelic population that remained loyal to God. It could only be they who overcame Lucifer in the heavenly realm.

Furthermore, humanity does not reside in the heavens. We reside on earth. Isn't that why God created the great blue planet? Isn't the earth man's abode? The Lamb, Jesus Christ, however, apart from His brief period in human flesh, has always existed in heaven. *"**In the beginning** was the Word, **the Word was with God and the Word was God** . . . and the Word **became** flesh and dwelt among us."* (John 1:1 & 14) We know that the angels of God exist in heaven, as well.

Therefore, I must conclude that those being accused by Lucifer in this instance cannot be us. They had to be the angels of God who had not chosen to *"leave their proper domain,"* but kept *"their own abode."* (Jude 1:6) As a result, Lucifer despised them. In showing his true colors, he attempted to turn God against them. By falsely accusing them of treason, Lucifer endeavored to bring death into the heavenly realm. Think about the gall of this "guy." He is a disaster regardless of where God places him.

In this particular instance, it is not *we* who overcame Lucifer by the Blood of the Lamb, it is the angels in heaven who overcame him *"by the Blood of the Lamb and by the word of their testimony."* That happens to be a mind-blowing revelation, but it is also very consistent with the heavenly patterns we see being manifested in the natural realm. We will discuss that shortly.

It is the next sentence of the scripture that solidifies this truth as it proclaims, *"Therefore,"* which is a consequential word based upon what occurred prior, namely, the war in the heavens, where the Lord, the devil and the angels were residing. *"Therefore rejoice, **O heavens and you who dwell in them!"*** That cannot be us. As I previously stated, man was not residing in heaven at the time. Death had not yet entered our realm and, therefore, the whole of humanity, which consisted of a mere population of two, could only have resided in the natural creation this side of the cosmos. God, who knows exactly what will occur in the future, however, was warning all those yet to come.

As you will see shortly, there is no cause for mankind to rejoice over this particular victory. In fact, the opposite is true. As the scripture states, it is now time for man to woe. We need to look out! As a result of the heavenly war, Satan was cast down to the earth. He now resides with mankind where he was able to accomplish what he could not complete in heaven. The presence of Satan brought death into a realm where death did not exist. In the aftermath, he also brought illness, rebellion, and every consequence of sin.

This is certainly no cause for celebration. The hell on earth Satan brought to the natural realm of humanity is the direct cause of rampant and unrepentant evil. Therefore, man must woe. *The accuser of the brethren* (Revelation 12:10) was about to set his sight on a brand new target.

Heaven, on the other hand, is a vastly different story. The heavenly celebration is a result of the wicked nature of Satan and his rebellious angelic following being cast out of paradise. The obedient holy angels of heaven had overcome the devil, thus passing the test that each and every one of us must now face. Do you realize that we are given exactly the same choice as the angels in heaven: Who will you follow? In other words, *"thy will be done on earth, **as it is in heaven.**"* (Matthew 6:10) Why do think Jesus taught us to pray those words? Obedience to God's will always overcomes Lucifer. With heaven having been cleansed of evil, however, the angelic rejoicing burst into heavenly praise of Almighty God.

Therefore, it is now time for you to answer the same question; who will you follow? The answer you *live* will determine your place in eternity. In truth, we must overcome the devil in the same way the angels in heaven did—through Christ. In the preceding verses of scripture, Christ had not yet become manifest upon the earth, and, therefore, in our now sinful state humanity was ill-equipped to handle Satan. This becomes crystal clear when you read the preceding declaration:

> *"Woe to the inhabitants of the earth and the sea!* ***For the devil has come down to you*** *having great wrath."*

Incredibly, God warns the inhabitants of both the earth and the sea. In other words, God was speaking to Adam, Eve, every future descendant and every living creature on earth. All life would be affected by Satan's dissidence. In fact, all of creation has fallen. (Romans 8:20–22) Since Satan is alive and well in the earthly realm, the result is the multitude of horrific and evil acts upon mankind, as well as, the environment as a whole, while his demons continually carry out their corrupt service to the filthy and wretched *"prince of the power of the air."* (Ephesians 2:2) The "air" is a reference to the earth's atmospheric realm in both a spiritual and physical sense.

Playing Hard to Get

Here is some additional information for you to consider. In *God Culture* we discussed how the Father patterned everything in the natural after what exists in heaven. Thus, the model prayer we discussed above, *"Thy will be done on earth **as it is in heaven.**"* We termed the concept "blue printing."

In the preceding passages, we discovered that our battle with Satan is merely a heavenly pattern and the real war took place in the kingdom of heaven. We discovered that it was not man, but the angels of heaven who overcame the devil by the Blood of the Lamb and by the word of their testimony. The question, therefore, is, how is that possible if Jesus were not crucified until after He was physically born of the Virgin Mary? We will get to that in the next chapter.

To discover the answer, we must once again refer to previous passages of scripture and piece the Word of God together. God does reveal it. We simply need to know how and where to look for the answers.

While we are on the subject, have you ever wondered why God makes His ways so difficult to find? Why doesn't He just plainly tell us what He wants us to know? If God is love, why would He create evil and make life so difficult, and in fact cruel, for so many of us? The answer is that in addition to love requiring one to make a choice, it also requires diligence. Believe it or not, the secret of knowing Almighty God can be found in the refrain of the 1980's hit song, *Prove Your Love,* performed by the legendary pop star Taylor Dayne. We must prove our love to Him. Since we have all failed God in this endeavor, our loving Father took responsibility as our Creator and imposed our penalty upon *Himself.* We know it as the crucifixion of Jesus Christ, and that, my friends, is the definition of true love and grace.

God, however, wants you to *diligently* seek Him. (Hebrews 11:6, Proverbs 8:17 et al.) He makes this known all throughout scripture. He *did* tell you what He wants you to know and He *did* disclose how to overcome evil; but He wants us to put some effort into finding Him. It shows that you care. It demonstrates that you really love Him.

If He simply placed everything in front of you it would require no effort, and thus, no diligence, whatsoever. What kind of love is that? You put a great deal more effort into courting your wife or girlfriend, husband or boyfriend. Yet it is God who set them apart for you from the beginning of time.

Is God playing hard to get? I guess you could say that. As you all know, the things in life which are the most difficult to obtain are the things you value the most. God wants you to value Him. In fact, He wants to be that which is of the greatest value to you. That is what it means to give Him first place in your life.

So let's step back in time a few . . . maybe five thousand years or so, to the time of Moses, as the Lord reveals exactly, in detail, how He wants the children of Israel to build the tabernacle which will become His temporary dwelling place on earth. We are about to learn that the Lord God Almighty loves to secretly blueprint His will, and here is one of the most incredible Secrets of the Father; *Lucifer cannot see it!*

CHAPTER 10

Blueprinting

(THE SECRET OF THE HEAVENLY PATTERN)

"For if He were on earth, He would not be a priest, since there are priests who offer the gifts according to the law; **who serve the copy and shadow of the heavenly things,** *as Moses was divinely instructed when he was about to make the tabernacle. For He said,* **"See that you make all things according to the pattern** *shown you on the mountain."*
—**Hebrews 8:4–5**

*"Therefore it was necessary that **the copies** of **the things in the heavens** should be purified with these, but the heavenly things themselves with better sacrifices than these."*

—Hebrews 9:23

When I was a child my grandmother used to do needlepoint. Although I am not the crafting type, the artwork she could produce with a needle and thread would often times astound me. The intricacy and patience required is mind boggling to a man like me. She and my late Aunt, who also inherited a similar talent, would sit on the couch with a basket full of multi-colored threads and from nothing but a pattern on an instruction sheet produce a masterpiece worthy of anyone's fireplace wall.

Keep in mind, however, that none of this was done from memory. That would have been nearly impossible. To accomplish such mastery always required a pattern, whether it be stamped on the cloth or in the instruction manual. Without it, even the greatest of needle pointers would be completely lost.

Think about the great architectural and engineering works of the world. Are any of these *Modern Marvels* possible without first creating a blueprint? The shovel does not hit the ground until a pattern is formed—a guide that is detailed to the rivet for all those involved in the project to refer to and follow. The blueprint ensures perfection. Without it, the building crew would be left with a mere pile of rock, steel and mortar; or perhaps, even worse, the *Leaning Tower of Pisa*. Can you imagine the disaster if today's modern skyscraper leaned a little to the right?

The kingdom of God is no different. The Word and will of God must be properly interpreted and applied to be effective. Leaning a little in either direction ejects you from His will. Doing it your way is not an option to the King of the universe.

If you follow God's method of blueprinting, however, you will ensure that evil, and thus Lucifer, will no longer have dominion over your life.

Following the heavenly pattern will leave you more than capable of executing God's will. With your heavenly blueprint in hand, (found only in the Word of God—the Bible) your destiny is in God's hands. Satan only comes into play when you deviate. Therefore, in order to enter the kingdom of God, we simply need to learn the pattern of His will and start digging. To begin this journey, let's have a gander at God's instruction as given to Moses.

These are Not Crop Circles

> "Then the Lord spoke to Moses saying: 'Speak to the children of Israel, that they may bring me an offering. **From everyone who gives it willingly from his heart** you shall take my offering. And this is the offering you shall take from them: gold, silver, and bronze; blue, purple, and scarlet thread, fine linen, and goats hair; ram skins dyed red, badger skins, and acacia wood; oil for the light, and spices for the anointing oil and the sweet incense, onyx stones, and stones to be set in the ephod and in the breastplate.'"
>
> "And let them make Me a sanctuary that I may dwell among them. According to all that I show you, that is, **the pattern of the tabernacle** and the pattern of all its furnishings, **just so** you shall make it.'"
>
> **—Exodus 25:1–9**

I included this detail, and trust me; there is chapter upon chapter of instructions detailing exactly how the Lord wanted the tabernacle constructed, for a reason. It may seem cumbersome upon your first reading of it, but it is necessary to reveal to you the importance of building your life God's way. You must learn to apply this concept to your life if you want to live a life of victory in overcoming every situation that Lucifer can and *will* throw at you.

God wanted His house and all who served in his house to look and act in a precise manner. Although this still holds true today, it is not religious observances and practices that God requires or even desires. It is not acting a certain way that overcomes evil. It is *being* a certain way that overcomes evil. This too is a heavenly secret.

> *"Therefore, if anyone is in Christ he is **a new creation;** old things have passed away; behold, **all things become new.**"*
> **—2 Corinthians 5:17**

Since Lucifer has no access to this change in image, he has no power over those who are newly created. Lucifer is *not* in Christ. He is not, was not, and never will be the image of God, nor is he in any way connected to God. When you get born again, *you are.* Therefore, unlike you and me, Lucifer has absolutely no access to the power of God.

> *"You are of God, little children, and have overcome them, because **He who is in you** is greater than he who is in the world."*
> **—1 John 4:4**

This is why God requires that we live a holy life of righteousness. God lives in you. God will only dwell where righteousness reigns. Therefore, if you desire to be the temple of God you must be righteous. Think about it logically; why would God dwell somewhere that is not right with Him? Righteousness is not for the purpose of imposing a bunch of rules and regulations. Righteousness sets you apart and above the forces of evil. Evil cannot dwell where God dwells, which means Lucifer cannot be a part of you if you are in Christ. Remember, it was the unrighteous act of Lucifer and the fallen angels of *"leaving their proper domain"* (Jude 1:6) that got them ousted from the presence of God.

Therefore, righteousness places you in a vastly higher spiritual plane of authority. Righteousness places you in the kingdom of heaven which is miles above both the kingdoms of *"the power of the air"* and any that reside in our natural earthly realm. Righteousness gives you direct access to the Father. In fact, *the secret to dominion and authority is found in righteousness.* Why? As I just stated, righteousness gives you direct access to both the heavenly realm, as well as, God's system of operation upon the earth. Lucifer has access to neither, nor does any human being apart from the redemptive work of Jesus Christ.

When Adam and Eve were created they were righteous. They were yet to sin and, therefore, were connected to the living God. Just like Adam and Eve, when we remain righteous we continue on and in the power of Almighty God. On our own, however, we are incapable of righteousness. It is no longer the nature of a sinful humanity that is now born in the image of Adam.

> *"And Adam lived one hundred and thirty years, and begot a son **in his own likeness, after his image,** and named him Seth."*
> **—Genesis 5:3**

That is exactly where righteousness by birth ended. Incredibly, and as you meditate on this concept, consider the absolute absurdity of mankind. Being born in the image of God lasted less than a single generation. Cain, the first ever human being born of a woman, slew his brother Abel without even a thought of the potential consequences. That, my friend, is the influence of Satan and the power of succumbing to sin. Therefore, righteousness by birth never even got to *"be fruitful and multiply."* (Genesis 1:28) Thank God for Jesus Christ.

> *"For He made Him who knew no sin to be sin for us, **that we might become the righteousness of God in Him.**"*
> **—2 Corinthians 5:21**

Therefore, do not be intimidated by the term "righteousness." If you are in Christ, you are righteous. It does not mean you need to be religious. In fact, the opposite is true. Religion does not, and apart from the pure and undefiled religion I mentioned earlier, cannot produce righteousness. Righteousness, or being right with God, is the prerequisite that God requires to become a part of you. It can only be found in Christ, and, therefore, it is really His only requirement for salvation.

Righteousness makes you holy, which simply means set apart to Him. In other words, you have given your life to God and not to the things and ways of the world. Why is that so important? That is how it is in heaven.

*"Thy will be done on earth **as it is** in heaven"* is our next *Secret of the Father.* The secret of righteousness is where the power of God is accessed. Righteousness is the key that unlocks the pattern of the Almighty whose image you have been restored to in Christ.

Certainly you are familiar with the "Our Father?" What did you think it meant? Perhaps you have not thought much about it. *"Thy will be done on earth **as it is** in heaven,* is God's will for mankind.

Interpreted into modern language, Jesus actually prayed, "Father, bring the heavenly pattern into full manifestation upon the earth." I don't know about you, but that changes everything in my considering how to pray for my, and other people's, needs. "Lord, in the name of Jesus, manifest heaven in the lives of my family, friends, business colleagues, acquaintances, and oh yeah, my own life, as well." Why would I pray that? Heaven is perfect. God's intention toward humanity is perfection. Thus, in Christ, He has already created the blueprint of His will for our lives. With that in mind, let's again move forward a few thousand years to the Book of Hebrews and learn even more about the heavenly copy that is the tabernacle.

> *"For when Moses had spoken every precept to all the people*
> *according to the law, he took the blood of calves and goats, with*
> *water, scarlet wool, and hyssop, and sprinkled both the book*

*itself **and all the people**, saying, 'This is the blood of the covenant which God has commanded you.'"*

*"Then likewise he sprinkled with blood both the tabernacle and all the vessels of the ministry. And **according to the law** almost all things are purified with blood, **and without shedding of blood there is no remission of sins."***

—Hebrews 9:19–22

There Will Be Blood

Wow! The tabernacle was one bloody place. There was blood everywhere. It was sprinkled upon the altar, on the horns of the altar, on the book of the law—you name it and there was blood on it. Even the people were covered with blood.

In modern times, this resonates more like a horror film than a religious ceremony. It conjures up visions of Santeria or the image from the movie *Cary*, when a bucket of blood is dumped on her at the High School Prom. All this blood, however, is revelatory. It was a shadow of things to come—a *pattern* if you will. It was the blueprint of what God was going to do in the New Covenant with the blood of Christ for the remission of sin.

Remember, *"according to the law almost all things are purified with blood, and **without shedding of blood there is no remission of sins.**"* Why? ***"For the life of the flesh is in the blood**, and I have given it to you upon the altar to make atonement for your souls; for **it is the blood that makes atonement for the soul.**"* (Leviticus 17:11)

Keep the word "atonement" in mind for just a few seconds. It comes from the Hebrew word, "Kaphar." You most likely know the more modern version as the word "Kippur," as in "Yom Kippur," which is the "Day of Atonement" on the Hebrew calendar. "Kaphar" actually means, "to appease" or "to cover." In other words, the blood of an unblemished bull or goat was not sufficient to remove your sin. It could merely cover it up temporarily to appease God. "Atone," or "atonement," however, is not the word we see associated with the blood of Jesus Christ. In Christ Jesus, we find the Greek word, "aphesis," which means, "to dismiss," "to pardon" or "to release."

In Christ, your sins are not merely covered. The sacrifice of Jesus Christ does not just appease God. The secret of the blood of Christ is that it *releases you from your transgressions.* In Christ, you are pardoned from your sin. Your eternal death sentence has been fulfilled by the only one worthy to release you from the imprisonment of sin's destructive effect—hell.

Therefore, it is only through the blood of Jesus that we can overcome the effects of sin. Perhaps you are wondering, why Jesus? Why not Mohammed, Buddha, or any other so called prophet or religion? It is simple. *"Whatever has a defect, you shall not offer, for **it shall not be acceptable on your behalf.**"* (Leviticus 17:20) Jesus is the only human being to ever walk the planet without being stained with the tattoo of sin. Our Father is perfect. He does require blood, *"**life for life,** eye for eye, tooth for tooth . . ."* (Deuteronomy 19:21) He will not, however, accept anything less than perfect as an offering for sin. Therefore, no man can fulfill the following precept of the law.

*"For the law, **having a shadow of the good things to come,** and **not the very image** of the things, **can never** with these same sacrifices, which they offer continually year by year, **make those who approach perfect.** For then would they not have ceased to be offered? For the worshipers, once purified, would have had no more consciousness of sins. But in those sacrifices there is a reminder of sins every year. **For it is not possible that the blood of bulls and goats could take away sins.**"* (Hebrews 10:2–4) Therefore, only Jesus, the Word becoming flesh (John 1:14) being perfect in every way, could fulfill the heavenly blueprint of atonement.

*"Then he shall **kill the goat** of the sin offering, **which is for the people,** bring its blood **inside the veil,** do with that blood as he did with the blood of the bull, and sprinkle it **on the mercy seat** and before the mercy seat. So he shall make atonement for the Holy Place, because of the uncleanness of the children of Israel, and because of their transgressions, **for all their sins . . ."***
—Leviticus 15:15–16

*"And when he has made an end of atoning for the Holy Place, the tabernacle of meeting, and the altar, he shall bring the live goat. Aaron shall lay both his hands on the head of the live goat, confess over it **all the iniquities** of the children of Israel, and **all their transgressions,** concerning **all their sins,** putting them **on the head of the goat,** and shall send it away into the wilderness by the hand of a suitable man. **The goat shall bear on itself all their iniquities to an uninhabited land;** and he shall release the goat in the wilderness.*
—Leviticus 16:20–22

Because only one man, Jesus, has ever existed without being subject to the blemish of sin, only His unspotted, life-giving blood, could qualify to fulfill the law of atonement by *remitting* your sin. Jesus' blood obliterated the effect of sin. Jesus was Jehovah's freewill offering in fulfillment of His own law. He was the only possible unblemished sacrifice that could ever be acceptable to become the sin offering and bear the countless transgressions of humanity.

Voodoo, Santeria and every other blood sacrificial form of religious worship is merely a Satanic perversion of atonement. They are counterfeits of Christ that are no different than Lucifer imitating God in the Garden of Eden. Jesus Christ of Nazareth is the fulfillment of the Levitical sacrificial system.

When you accept Jesus Christ you are spiritually sprinkled with His blood. Therefore, God sees you through the bloody mess of Jesus Christ crucified for the remission of sin. The shedding of Jesus' blood is fulfillment of the blood sprinkled upon the tabernacle, which included the altar, the Book of the Law, the vessels and the people. All have been purified according to the heavenly blueprint. The result is salvation. In Christ, your sins have been voided out. You are clean.

The Blood of the Lamb

Somehow, however, and as incredible as it may seem, I have another secret for you. *There was blood in heaven.*

> *"And they overcame Him by **the blood of the Lamb** and by the word of their testimony."*
> **—Revelation 12:11**

In light of what we recently learned regarding the war in heaven, do you find this to be as incredible as I do? What was the Blood of the Lamb, the precious Blood of Jesus Christ, doing in heaven *before* Jesus was crucified on the earth? Simply stated, sin had entered the heavens in the form of Lucifer's rebellion. Just as we must be purified by Christ on earth, the heaven's required the blood of the Lamb as well.

Once again, we find a pattern. The *"Lamb slain from the foundation of the world"* (Revelation 13:8) was a foreshadowing. It was a blueprint of the heavenly pattern that would be fulfilled in the crucifixion of the Word becoming flesh. (John 1:14) The blood of Jesus will always overcome Satan. In order to gain a better understanding, let's visit the Book of Hebrews a little deeper.

*"Therefore it was necessary that the **pattern** of these things **in the heavens** should be purified."*

—Hebrews 9:23

Hebrews 9:23 is making reference to the tabernacle on the earth being a pattern of what exists in its perfect state in heaven. Since man's natural realm of existence has been corrupted by sin, it has become necessary to purify the earthly patterns of heaven that are being implemented by our Father, Yahweh. Thus, the sprinkling of the blood by Moses.

Therefore, the pattern established by willingly gathering the materials and constructing the tabernacle is the instruction manual revealing how we must approach God. Coming into His presence is impossible without first being purified by the blood of Christ, just as the people were purified for the presence of God by the sprinkling of the blood at the altar.

The blood of Christ, however, need only to be shed once for the purification of all. Thus, just like heaven, the blood of Christ is both physical and spiritual. It was shed once in the natural realm and since we have also discovered that the Lamb had been slain *"from the foundation of the world,"* (Revelation 13:8) we know that the origin of the blood of Christ is heavenly. The pattern had been formed and all that was left for perfection was the manifestation of Christ's blood on earth. Therefore, the blood of Christ is eternal. It is infinite. It never degrades.

With that in mind, consider the following. Just as the people willingly gave of their sustenance, we must willingly enter the presence of Jesus Christ. That is our freewill offering. We must give Him ourselves, which is an offering of our own personal sustenance. He will not take from us, nor will He abduct us. He and Lucifer are polar opposites. Lucifer only comes *"to steal, kill and destroy."* (John 10:10a) Jesus has come *"that you may have life, and that you may have it more abundantly."* (John 10:10b)

The law, the New Covenant, the crucifixion of Christ, and the ways in which God requires us to approach and relate to Him are *patterns* of the heavenly realm. When you understand this concept and how God has blueprinted the things on the earth after the things in heaven, the excerpt from Revelation 13:8 which proclaims, *"The **Lamb slain from the foundation of the world**,"* makes perfect sense. Even the Lord's holy city, Jerusalem, is a pattern of what exists in heaven.

*"And he carried me away in the Spirit to a great and high mountain, and showed me the great city, **the holy Jerusalem,** descending **out of heaven** from God."*
—Revelation 21:10

A Violent God

Sadly, however, the sin and corruption of man has damaged, and in many cases, destroyed the patterns God has ordained on earth. Humanity is suffering from much more than mere separation anxiety in the physical realm. Apart from Christ, we have been cut off from the presence of God. In this condition, our eventual demise can only result in judgment.

Take note of how rebellious mankind actually is. God created the Garden of Eden ... man was ejected due to disobedience. God sends a prophet ... man persecutes or even kills the prophet. God appoints the law ... man completely ignores and breaks the law. God sends the Messiah ... man has Him crucified ... and on and on it goes until you have reached the point where many kids are not even safe in their own homes and schools. Day after day, we hear reports of psychotic, and, perhaps even, demonically influenced behavior that is resulting in the mass execution of innocent men, woman and children.

Do you see the problem? The judgment due to man abandoning the ways and love of the only true God, Jehovah, has resulted in evil being allowed to run amuck upon the earth. There is no escaping it. We are all infected. Evil has been perpetuated throughout the planet since the dawn of mankind. However, do not make the same crucial mistake as those who are ignorant of the will of God. It is not that God is causing evil to dominate mankind. It is man disseminating evil by ousting God from his life. It is we who are at fault. We are attempting to live apart from God which places us outside of His perfect will. Although satanically influenced, humanity is the perpetrator of evil upon the earth.

Therefore, I would encourage you to analyze where you have been placing the blame and determine what role you are allowing God to play in your life. It is not God who is causing evil, it is man's unwillingness to submit to his creator that has resulted in his inability to procure the authority given to the believer in Jesus Christ. Sin has corrupted man's ability to see, hear, and act upon all things spiritual. Lucifer quite simply happens to be an expert at taking advantage of our iniquities.

As we have witnessed throughout history, if man can see, touch, hear, smell or taste nearly anything, we will corrupt, or perhaps even, destroy it. Therefore, God has hidden His ways from man's five senses, and *from the days of John the Baptist until now the kingdom of heaven suffers violence, and the violent take it by force.*" (Matthew 11:12)

This has never been more evident than today. God and His ways can only be discerned by those who have become alive in the Spirit. This is purposeful on Yahweh's part. Since Lucifer and all those under the power of sin are spiritually dead, it makes God's ways incorruptible. The spiritually dead are incapable of discerning God's will and, therefore, are unable to *"enter the kingdom of God."*

In order to counter the problem caused by man's rebellion, God had a plan. When the time was right, God got violent. Not in the same manner as Lucifer, however. Lucifer's aim is to perpetuate violence against all things spiritual, man included. It is the essence of his self-centered and violent nature. (Ezekiel 28:16)

However, as stated earlier, God is the exact opposite of Lucifer. There is not even a hint of egotism within Him. When God became violent, He lashed out at Himself in the form of the crucifixion of Jesus Christ. God's violence decimated sin and overcame death. Unlike Lucifer, the violence of God procured everlasting life, the exact opposite of Lucifer's violence. Yahweh took *His own* kingdom back by force. The resurrection power of Almighty God forced Jesus out of the grave and back into His rightful seat at the right hand of our Father.

> *"But now Christ is risen from the dead, and has become the first fruits of those who have fallen asleep. For since by man came death, by Man also came the resurrection of the dead. For as in Adam all die, even so in Christ all shall be made alive. But each one in his own order: Christ the first fruits, afterward those who are Christ's at His coming."*
> **—1 Corinthians 15:20–23**

Jesus had become *"the firstborn among many brethren."* (Romans 8:29) That is what it means to be born again. In Christ, we are restored, or as Jesus put it, reborn in the image of God.

Before Christ, our Father hid the kingdom of God. As you may have learned from my previous writings, He did not hide the kingdom of God *from* you, He hid it *for* you. He preserved it from the corruption of evil thrust upon humanity by the fallen angel Lucifer. Our job is simply to unravel the mystery.

Listen carefully to the preaching of Paul. As you read the rest of this chapter, keep in mind what Paul is attempting to reveal to our understanding. Incredibly, even Lucifer has a purpose. God is completely in control of every event going on in the universe.

Driving in Reverse

> *"I now rejoice in my sufferings for you, and fill up in my flesh what is lacking in the afflictions of Christ, for the sake of His body,* **which is**

*the church, of which I became a minister according to the stewardship from God which was given to me for you, to fulfill the Word of God, **the mystery which has been hidden from ages and from generations, but now has been revealed to His saints.** To them* (us) *God willed to make known what are the riches of the glory **of this mystery** among the Gentiles: which is **Christ in you** the hope of glory."*
—Colossians 1:24–27

Couple that scripture with the following and then I will explain. *"My little children, for whom I labor in birth **again** until **Christ is formed in you . . .**"* (Galatians 4:19)

By hiding these heavenly patterns, the Lord has kept them out of the reach of both man and Satan, thus keeping them under guard and rendering them incorruptible. When the right time arose, which is always according to God's schedule, not man's, the *"the Word became flesh,"* (John 1:14) and opened up the mystery of Jesus Christ, the fulfillment of the Word of God. By the infilling of the Holy Spirit which transforms the image of a man, the pattern of Jesus Christ is then formed within us.

Keep in mind, however, that anytime anything is formed there must first be a pattern, whether written or imagined, to shape it. Christ being formed in you is shaping your spirit according to the image of the anointed Son of God. In other words, it is bringing the "kingdom of God," from the spiritual to the natural realm, thus allowing the ministry of Christ to continue through us. This is the same thing God did at creation. He appointed the image then subsequently shaped him in the natural.

Listen carefully to what I am about to say. This is phenomenally eye opening as to what a Christian is supposed to be like. This is what separates a Spirit filled man from a so called "Christian" faker, let alone someone who does not even purport to have Christ. To the natural man, Christ is not just a mystery, He is insanity. The kingdom of God is the exact opposite of how an unredeemed man thinks and functions.

Man's desire is to gain revenge upon his enemies. Where in scripture do we find the apostles protesting in the streets or blowing up abortion clinics? When Peter cut off the guard's ear in the Garden of Gethsemane, he was not *praised* by Jesus for boldly standing up in defense of his faith. Jesus healed His violent attacker and *rebuked* Peter. He commanded Peter, *"Permit even this,"* (Luke 22:51) even though the guards came to take Him captive and ultimately send Him to a horrific demise.

Do you believe the crusaders were justified? This is always the argument to rationalize the Pope's response to the Ottoman's. All of our worldly reactions are merely evidence of our carnality. They are proof positive that we are still functioning primarily in the natural, as opposed to having entered the kingdom of God.

Think about it, God does not *need* a particular land or Temple to dwell in. He *chose* the Promised Land to set up His eternal kingdom. Jerusalem is His will and in *His* time He will once again reign supreme in the holy city. For the present time, however, the Promised Land known as Israel will continue to suffer violence. Perfection will only be accomplished when *"the New Jerusalem descends out of heaven from God."* (Revelation 21:2)

God is not upset that Solomon's Temple is now a Muslim mosque known as the Dome of the Rock. He no longer dwells there. He left the moment the curtain was torn in two. His current abode is in both heaven and the heart of man. He *will* return to set up His kingdom, but all in *His* time. Make no mistake, God will reign supreme in Jerusalem, but not until He is ready. *"The earth is the LORD'S, and all it contains, the world, and those who dwell in it."* (Psalm 24:1) It all belongs to God—but for now we anxiously await His return.

Do you believe God is strong enough to fight His own battles? Apparently most men do not, and, therefore, we attempt to fight them for Him. There is a major difference between proclaiming the gospel of Peace and striving for God.

*"For we **do not wrestle against flesh and blood,** but against principalities, against powers, against the rulers of the darkness of this age, against spiritual hosts of wickedness in the heavenly places."*
—Ephesians 6:12

As a result of our ignorance, man has continually mistaken evil for good. Islamic terrorists do it. So called Christian "radicals" do it. Atheists do it . . . the list goes on and on. It seems that **"Good people can do good and bad people can do evil. But for good people to do evil—that takes religion."—Steven Weinberg**

Jesus commanded us to love and bless our enemies, not to kill them in the name of religion. Can you see the difference? The Lord revealed the *pattern* of His will in and through the life and death of Jesus Christ, and later the Apostle Paul. It is the opposite of what comes naturally to mankind. It is like driving in reverse. It can be done, but man is it difficult.

Our job is to receive, understand, build, and act upon the Word of God with obedience, regardless of how uncomfortable our five senses make us feel or whatever violation is being perpetrated against us. This is no easy job and Lucifer knows it. Therefore, he magnifies our frustration and pain. One must be acutely aware of God's presence to overcome Lucifer and accomplish such a tall task.

It is much easier to fulfill our own needs and forget about everyone else. That is the direction Lucifer attempts to take you. We even have a new term for it. We call it "The Me Generation."

Lucifer uses his influence upon mankind to perpetuate selfishness and greed. The battle for self-preservation, in conjunction with an insatiable desire for power, ultimately leads not only to persecution, but to the grotesque violation of human rights being promulgated throughout the planet. Apart from the practitioners of radical Islam, does anyone believe ISIS is from God? Most Muslim's do not even believe it. Unredeemed men of power are in the palm of Satan's hand. It merely requires a tiny nudge from his twisted little finger to get humanity to carry out his wicked desires.

Think about how easily Hitler executed the Holocaust with little to no resistance from below. However, even in the face of seemingly uncontrolled evil, God still had a purpose and a plan. The result of the Holocaust and the end of World War II was the rebirth of the nation of Israel. Without the war there would be no Jewish state. Since that time, God's chosen people have begun to return home by the millions. It will not be long before they are in the midst of redemption and there is nothing the devil can do to stop it. The pattern has been set. Do not ever forget that God is in complete control. Lucifer is merely a pawn.

Stop Being Selfish

In Galatians chapter four, we see the Apostle Paul describing the purpose of the evil committed against him. He viewed his suffering as a labor of love for the church, which is not a building, but is in you and me. He actually boasted, *"I now **rejoice** in my sufferings, and fill up in my flesh what is lacking in the afflictions of Christ, **for the sake of...**"* who? Himself? No, it was for the sake of the church.

His total and complete death of self was for the benefit of all those who believe in the name of the Lord. Hopefully, after absorbing this book series you will have been included amongst the many entered into the Lambs book of life, as well. My purpose is no different than the Apostle Paul's, and for that matter, the purpose of Jesus Christ.

By willfully entering into affliction for the sake of the gospel, Paul became the image of God's love with Christ as his pattern. In other words, the evil being perpetuated against the Apostle Paul had actually furthered the Kingdom of God. God actually used the influence of Lucifer to perpetuate His kingdom. Isn't that incredible once you finally recognize the truth? It is a recurring pattern. Just as the tabernacle revealed the ministry of Israel, and ultimately the salvation plan of God, Christ reveals the ministry of the church, which is selfless service to others for the purpose of salvation. Persecution and the death of self is simply part of the process.

Continually overcoming the presence of evil are our tests, quizzes and final exam. Ultimately, your life is not about the now. It is about forever. Evil is Lucifer's attempt to turn you against God. He tries to push you out of forever by altering your eternal focus and thrusting you into the problems and sufferings you experience every day. Do not participate. Keep your focus on eternity. Fix your eyes upon the Lord.

> *"Finally, brethren, whatever things are true, whatever things are noble, whatever things are just, whatever things are pure, whatever things are lovely, whatever things are of good report, if there is any virtue and if there is anything praiseworthy—**meditate on these things,**"* (Philippians 4:8) and not the injustices of those Lucifer has riled against you.

I would encourage you to take hold of the following secret that is so vital to your survival within the kingdom of God. *If you remain under Lucifer's thumb of selfishness, your vision will perish and you will eventually turn on God.* You will unwittingly place a twisted crown of hopeless thorns upon Satan's evil and malicious head. You must find God's will in your trials. To remain in abject suffering with no sense of purpose will cause you to surrender eternally. You will remain lost as you simply cannot see the forest for the trees.

The absolute obliteration of selfishness brings our salvation to fruition. It annihilates the greed of Satan. Our proof lies in the fact that Christ willingly and obediently went to the cross and absolutely exterminated any shadow of self-centered egotism when He wrought salvation upon the cross. Unbeknownst to most, He did have feelings of selfishness, fear and doubt. He was human. Why do you think He prayed, *"If it is possible let this cup pass from Me, nevertheless, not as I will, but as You will?"* (Matthew 26:39)

The difference between you, me, and Jesus, is that Jesus overcame self-ishness through unbridled obedience, even in the face of a horrific death. *"Nevertheless, not as I will, but as you will"* always overcomes Lucifer. It is the essence of *"the blood of the Lamb* and it is *the Word of our testimony."* Furthermore, just like the obedient angels of heaven, it also proves that *"we do not love our own lives, even unto death."* (Revelation 12:11)

Please understand that Paul is not saying that you need to be whipped and tortured to be a Christian, and neither am I. The actual pattern he is revealing is the same as Christ Himself lived. It is selfless service to God and man, and the death of self.

This is not a reference to suicide. It is the elimination of selfishness, pride and ego. You must lose your life in order to gain it (Matthew 16:25). **"We turn to God for help when our foundations are shaking only to learn that it is God shaking them." —Charles West**

True love always puts others above itself. That is exactly what Christ did and it is exactly what Lucifer will never do. Jesus overcame evil with good, which is the only way a true Christian *can* live. Any other lifestyle or doctrine of vengeance is utter abandonment from the truth. It is an invitation to partner with Lucifer. The modern world has relinquished the truth and is suffering relentless evil as a consequence. If we do not change the direction of the world in which we live, the result will be judgment. Trust me, *when* that occurs you will not want to be a part of it.

His Body

Therefore, if the pattern of Christ is to be "birthed" into the natural it must come from within us. In truth, Christ rarely ministers in the natural these days. Of course, I am aware of the story's of Christ appearing mostly to Muslim' in the Middle East. These manifestations appear to be occurring in regions that Christians, for the most part, either refuse to, or cannot, enter. Therefore, I believe it is true that Jesus is intervening by supernatural means.

His natural ministry, however, ended the day He ascended into heaven. His ministry has now been passed along to His body, the church. We have been ordained to take up the mantle, just as Elisha took the reigns from Elijah. (1 Kings 19) For today's believer, the Lord Jesus has sent the Holy Spirit to be our helper. The Spirit of God has been ordained to lead us, to guide us, and to be our power source while we await our Savior's return. Apart from the rare occasions I hear about mainly in the Middle East, for Christ to touch any man in the natural it must be done through His body—and that is us. It is *we* who have been given the power and the authority to do good and overcome the evil one.

> *"Now **you** are the body of Christ."*
> **—1 Corinthians 12:27**

You are the conduit from the spiritual to the natural. In order for Christ to minister on earth it must be done through you, His body. Therefore, we need to go to spiritual medical school. It is imperative for the Christian to understand how the body functions. The body of Christ must learn that by *"speaking the truth in love, we may grow up in all things into Him who is the head—Christ."* (Ephesians 4:15) It is the head that tells the body what to do. Your heart cannot even beat without your brain signaling it to do so. You cannot walk, talk, think or even breathe without your head. So it is with any church or Christian that does not obey Christ.

Obedience to our Head is the only way to overcome evil in the world. In other words, if the truth of God is to be spread and the kingdom of darkness is to be overcome, it must be *we* who overcome it, just like the angels did in heaven. Only this time Satan will be cast down to the pit of hell. Once our time has been fulfilled, he will never be let out of his chains to deceive mankind again. In fact, his ultimate destination is destruction in the Lake of Fire. Only then will the world be fully rid of evil.

Mathematics

Therefore, we must be obedient to our Christ ordained mission. We must *"be fruitful and multiply."* (Genesis 1:28) We have been commanded to make disciples of all nations. That means we must give birth to a new generation of believers. Paul clarifies this truth in saying, *"For whom **I labor in birth again** until Christ is formed in you."*

Paul is revealing to us how the heavenly pattern is to be brought into the natural realm for the benefit of all mankind, hence his use of the phrase, *"I labor in birth again ..."* The revelation Paul discloses is that if we are to bring the heavenly pattern, which is the perfect will of God to our fellow man, it *must* come from the inside out, and not the outside in. This is the difference between the power of God and the illusion of Satan. In Christ, you can be transformed. In Christ, you can be born again.

Therefore, we must become impregnated with the Spirit of God. Mary became *physically* pregnant with Christ. We must become *spiritually* pregnant with Christ. Through His death and resurrection, which was the first new birth, He completed the pattern. He was restored to glory.

The Holy Spirit has implanted the same pattern within you. You have been reborn in the image of God. Therefore, when you call upon His name, the Holy Spirit impregnates you. Since *"today is the day of salvation,"* (2 Corinthians 6:2) it is time for *you* to give birth, as well!

To be obedient to our Master we must add to and multiply the people of God by making disciples of all nations. It is only in Christ that evil can be overcome. It is *'by the Blood of the Lamb and the word of our testimony"* that we can overcome Lucifer. (Revelation 21)

Most importantly, however, and what is far and away the most difficult aspect of the kingdom of God for us to implement, is that *"they did not love their own lives, even unto death,"* (Revelation 12:11) and neither can we. Most people discount, or perhaps even, delete this radically important scriptural principle.

In truth, God and Satan use two different and opposing mathematical formulas in order to build their kingdoms. God uses addition and multiplication. Satan uses division followed by subtraction. I would urge you not to become a negative statistic by holding fast to the kingdom of God. Lucifer's greatest power is merely an illusion. Therefore, let's complete the heavenly pattern by turning the tables on the illusionist. In doing so, we will oust him from the earthly realm and into the Lake of Fire. From there, Lucifer will realize his preordained end. Both he and the evil he has perpetuated upon mankind will be vaporized into the smoke filled ashes of forever.

CHAPTER 11

The Illusionist

(THE SECRET OF THE IMPOSTER)

Perhaps you did not expect to learn so much about the devil when you purchased a book about God. You may even think he is not worthy of so much attention and that I am giving him far too much credit by spending an inordinate amount of time discussing his devices. Nothing could be further from the truth. He is counting on the fact that most people are ignorant of his methodology. He has even convinced an untold measure of the populace that he does not exist at all, that he is merely a myth invented in the minds of man to keep society under control—that he is nothing more than a political pawn of the church.

The above ideology is a true description of the deceptive power the devil possesses, which, by the way, is the only real power he has. Deception is his business. Perception becomes reality to the deceived, even when it is merely an illusion. Therefore, consider the following truism; personal beliefs *become* your reality, even if there is absolutely no foundation of truth in them.

Countless crimes have been committed on the basis of the perpetrator's twisted sense of fantasy, often times accompanying to the old cliché, "the devil made me do it." Since the devil does not have the power to *make* us do anything, I must discount the validity of such a claim. Therefore, something else must be going on. Evil is a choice. Evil is choosing to participate in a lie. Unfortunately, deception all too often resorts to violence.

Illusionists, and even con men, have been altering the perceptions of mankind for eons. Your adversary Lucifer, who happens to be the greatest con man in human history, has mastered the technique of illusion, particularly in his impersonation of Yahweh. Through this altered state of reality, he has been tormenting humanity from the day he was sent out of heaven. In believing that the evil present from the world's inception is merely random, you have fallen under his spell. His latest and greatest trick has been to transform the reality of social "tolerance." His twisted view of love has separated man from God.

Do you realize that there is no such thing as coincidence or random acts of violence? If Lucifer can convince you that he is not real, your perception of reality must believe the opposing point of view as well. If Lucifer is not real, neither is God. Both are merely illusions—figments of man's imagination. That is Lucifer's ultimate goal and his latest and greatest magic trick. In the mind's of man he has made God disappear.

Once headed down this twisted path there is no turning back. You must also come to the following conclusions: There is no such thing as spirits, angels or demons, and nothing exists outside of the natural realm. There is no life after death, so live for today—eat, drink and be merry.

Right and wrong is completely irrelevant and exists only in the eyes of the beholder. Morality has no absolutes.

This erroneous supposition thrusts you directly into Satan's sinister grasp. You must, therefore, also conclude that there is no heaven or hell. From that point it is all over. You have lost the war. Your adversary becomes imaginary and you cannot win a battle against an enemy that does not exist, nor would you even bother fighting it. Shadow boxing is nothing more than beating the air. Therefore, you remain shackled by the bondage of invisible chains. Your life is no longer your own. You have fallen prey to the *"prince of the power of the air."* (Ephesians 2:2) You are now involuntarily subject to his every demand.

The Problem With Freewill

So why doesn't God just put an end to the illusion? Wouldn't that be easier for everyone? It is a perfectly logical question when you consider the nature of the society we live in. Do you remember our discussion regarding the "microwave culture?" Obliterating Lucifer would certainly satisfy our desire for instant gratification. It would also eliminate the conclusion that most people come to when duped into the mindset that God either does not want to stop evil, which leads you to question His love, kindness, and mercy, or that He cannot stop it, which leads you to question His power.

Therefore, I must ask; why *doesn't* God put an end to evil? It is simple. You may not like the answer, but nevertheless, it is not very complicated. The answer is that God has a purpose for evil. Evil is designed to drive you back to your Maker. God's methodologies are rarely about living in the "now." God is a "forever" God and He, not Eric Clapton, is the originator of the *"Forever Man."*

Modern man needs to undergo a heavenly makeover. To avoid Lucifer's trap, we must come to terms with the fact that not only *will* God do something about evil, but that He already has. As discussed in the previous chapter, His pattern to overcome Satan has already been executed and is in full effect. The Blood of the Lamb has been shed. It is available for anyone to receive forgiveness of sin and a testimony which always overcomes the devil.

To complete the process, you must begin loving Jesus above all others, including yourself. Jesus Christ must become your *"first love."* (Revelation 2:4) Only then, can we love our fellow man. It is only when we are in Christ that we obtain the ability to place mankind's best interest above our own. Therefore, we must become like the angels of heaven who *"loved not their lives, even unto the death."* (Revelation 12:11)

As previously stated, this is why Jesus taught us to pray, *"Thy will be done **on earth as it is in heaven.**"* (Matthew 6:10) Jesus was revealing the heavenly pattern to us. He was teaching us how to restore what God originally created. His will is for the earth to be patterned exactly as His will exists in heaven. The love of self does not exist in heaven nor does the illusion of race encumbered by the flesh. In heaven, *"there is neither Jew nor Greek, there is neither slave nor free, there is neither male nor female; **for you are all one** in Christ Jesus."* (Galatians 3:28) Eventually, and I know this by having read the end of His book (the Bible), it will be done.

The problem is that up until now you have not known the rules. You are waiting for God to fight a battle that you have been ordained to contest. God gave man dominion and authority over the earth (Genesis 1 and 2) and thus, your Father has appointed *you* to fight its battles.

If this is true, and it is, He will not simply revoke your freewill when things go awry. He has the power to, He also has the right and the authority to, but His integrity will not permit Him. Revocation would mean He did not actually give you the independence and authority you so desperately desire. It would mean that he did not *really* give you freewill. It was all an illusion. That, my friend, describes the other guy. God *did* grant you the power to choose. God is not the illusionist, Satan is.

Do you remember as a child giving something to your friend and in your regret taking it back? What did your friend say? "Indian giver!" That, by the way, is not a compliment. It is not even politically correct anymore, but so be it. God is certainly no "Indian giver," albeit, many of those ignorant to the covenant practices of Yahweh would love for Him to become one.

Yahweh gave freewill to mankind and sometimes that means we have to suffer the consequences. As stated previously, in order for God to revoke this incredible gift, He would have to renege on His spoken Word. God will never do that.

This is cause for joy not mourning. The integrity of the Almighty means that His truth is not just a perception created in the mind of man. It means that God cannot and will not lie (Titus 1:2) and, therefore, you can truly depend on and trust both His written Word, as well as, His spoken Word.

I Want Your Body

Thankfully, God does have a means of redeeming mankind. His way is perfectly legal according to His law and in no way compromises His integrity. It is not based upon mere perception, or illusion, and it also perfectly satisfies His "now" verses "forever" plan.

After the creation of Adam, the command was to be fruitful and multiply. Since God was no longer creating there were only two *legal* ways to enter the domain of the earth, or otherwise stated, the realm of the natural. The only two legal gateways into the physical world in which we currently reside are through the womb of a female, whether man or animal, after its own kind, or through a seed, after its own kind. Incredibly, this scientific fact is exactly what we find set into law in Genesis chapter one.

> "Then God said, 'Let the earth bring forth grass, the herb
> **that yields seed,** and the fruit tree that yields fruit **according**

*to its kind, whose **seed is in itself**, on the earth'; and it was
so. And the earth brought forth grass, the herb **that yields seed
according to its kind,** and the tree **that yields fruit, whose
seed is in itself according to its kind**. And God saw that it
was good."*

*"So God created great sea creatures and every living thing
that moves, with which the waters abounded, **according to
their kind,** and every winged bird **according to its kind**. And
God saw that it was good. And God blessed them, saying, 'Be
fruitful and multiply...'"*

*"Then God said, 'Let the earth bring forth the living creature
according to its kind: cattle and creeping thing and beast of
the earth, each **according to its kind'**; and it was so..."*

*"And God made the beast of the earth **according to its kind,**
cattle **according to its kind,** and everything that creeps on the
earth **according to its kind**. And God saw that it was good."*

*"Then God said, 'Let Us make man in Our image, **according
to Our likeness;** let them have dominion over the fish of the
sea, over the birds of the air, and over the cattle, over all the
earth and over every creeping thing that creeps on the earth.'"*

*So God created man **in His own image;** in the image of God
He created him; male and female He created them. Then God
blessed them, and God said to them, '**Be fruitful and multiply;** fill the earth and subdue it; have dominion over the fish
of the sea, over the birds of the air, and over every living thing
that moves on the earth.'"*

—Excerpts from Genesis 1:11–28

First, I would like to point out that humanity was created differently
by God than every other animal or plant. Unlike the animals, the sea creatures, the creeping things of the earth; and unlike the grasses, the herbs
and fruits; humanity is the only "creature" created in the image of Yahweh.

That one simple fact makes us different than every organism ever created by God. It is also why we were given the authority over the creeping things, the cattle, the fishes and even the environment. Mankind is special to God. We are intended to be His similitude—His image.

Secondly, think about everyone and everything that is alive around you. How did it or they get here? That's right, through its mothers womb or through the seed of an equivalent species. There are no other options. Even a cloned sheep is birthed through the womb. These are the only two doorways for life to legally, which means, to naturally, enter the physical realm.

With that truth in mind, I have a question for you. How did Lucifer get here? Whose womb did he enter through? What seed did Lucifer sprout from and whose kind is he the image or reproduction of? The answer is no one's. Lucifer was cast out of his natural abode, heaven, and exiled to the physical realm of man. It *is* not, *was* not and never will be his eternal home, nor even his intended dwelling place. In other words, Satan does not belong here and contrary to popular belief, he is not equipped to function here either. That is where you come in. Lucifer needs you. As previously discussed, without you he is nothing.

In the Garden of Eden, we find Satan speaking. Satan, however, was not born in the Garden of Eden. Unlike Adam, Lucifer was not created to be there. He has no physical body. He had to wiggle his way in through the conjoined dual realms. The "wall" separating the physical realm from the heavenly realm is flesh. Your physicality prevents you from passing through. Since Lucifer has no physicality, he, just like the angels of heaven, can pass through upon demand. That, however, does not mean that they have the authority, nor even the power to function here. That ability must be garnered through almighty Jehovah. That is the purpose and the function of God's Holy Spirit. He alone grants the authority, even if only on a temporary basis and/or for a specific purpose.

Furthermore, there were not any angels reproducing in the Garden of Eden. Angels are created beings of the heavenly realm. They never received a physical body nor the command to multiply. Thus, *"it came to pass, when men began to multiply on the face of the earth, and daughters were born to them, that the sons of God saw the daughters of men, that they were beautiful; and they took wives for themselves of all whom they chose."* (Genesis 6:1–2) Alas, a physical body!

Keep in mind, however, that even if Lucifer did possess the body of a serpent, he was not born of a serpent. Therefore, he had, and has, no business interacting with anyone born of a woman. Although God sent him to the atmospheric realm of the natural, he was not graced with the one thing required to function on planet earth, or anywhere within the natural realm. Lucifer was not given a physical body. This one "minor" detail left him powerless. Of course God thought it through! God is not a sadist. He would not, and did not, unleash Lucifer without any limitations.

Lucifer, however, knowing that all authority had been stripped from him, had no other choice but to push and deceive his way back into a position of power. It was his only hope of glory. Therefore, when He entered the Garden of Eden, he attempted to interact with its inhabitants. Unfortunately, Eve took the bait. Although he believed this would bring victory over the Holy One of Israel, he had no idea that his new-found power was merely an illusion. He had even conned himself. Thus, he continues his struggle against the powers of heaven. My, how *disillusioned* the illusionist is.

I must reiterate that God did not cast Satan into the natural realm to have dominion and authority over the earth. That privilege had been reserved only for Adam and his descendants. Satan had been cast into the *spiritual* atmosphere of the earthly realm, where until Eve gave him full entry, he had been completely nullified.

*"But **you** He made alive, who were dead in trespasses and sins, in which
you once walked according to the curse of this world, according to **the
prince of the power of the air,** the spirit who **now** works in the sons of
disobedience."*

—Ephesians 2:1–2

That was to be the place of Satan's exile. His domain was to be the
"air," or the earthly realm of the spirit, where he would be of no bother to
mankind. But he, being the malevolent being that he is, could not leave
well enough alone. It is not part of his iniquitous nature to do so. So he
robbed and looted his way across the inter-dimensional border and into the
earthly realm where humanity takes up residence. He forced his way into
the the physical realm and has been pushing his way into the spiritual lives
of mankind ever since his wretched "success" on that fateful day in Eden.
Lucifer has been pilfering from mankind ever since and *you* have been
giving him the authority he should never possess—your own!

Therefore, the only power he actually has belongs to you. It is an illusion. When will you come to your senses and take your power back? We
were never intended to interact with Satan or any other fallen spirit in our
original state of being. We were created to interact with the Lord and with
one another. This is why God used to come into the Garden of Eden to
physically visit with Adam and Eve. (Genesis 3:8) Not even the angels of
heaven, who kept their proper domain, visited with Adam in the Garden
of Eden. Apart from Lucifer, the first time we find angels on earth is when
God placed Cherubim at the East gate of the Garden of Eden to keep
both Adam and Eve from ingesting the eternal fruit of the *"Tree of Life."*
(Genesis 3:24)

Keep in mind, as well, that God did not visit with Adam and Eve in
the realm of the spirit. They could not interact there. Man is incapable of
entering the spiritual realm. As stated earlier, our physicality blocks us from
doing so.

Therefore, Yahweh came *to* Adam and Eve. This is why the Holy Spirit comes *to*, and fills us, as well. It is not the other way around. We were created that way intentionally to keep us in our proper domain. This is why the medium, who attempts to communicate, channel (which is a perversion of the infilling of the Spirit) and conjure up both evil spirits and the dead is considered sinful, and is strictly forbidden from doing so. (Deuteronomy 18:11) They are defying God by attempting to leave their proper domain. It is a seditious act equivalent to the treason performed by Lucifer and his fallen angelic followers.

The action of interacting with spirits other than God is equated with the fallen angels of Jude, *"who did not keep their proper domain, but left their own abode."* (Jude 1:6a) Consider their end when you contemplate disobeying Yahweh in this manner. *"He has reserved* (them) *in everlasting chains under darkness for the judgment of the great day."* (Jude 1:6b)

As a quick aside, it is not that God wants you to be ignorant of the fate of your loved ones. The Word of God gives us plenty of information to make that determination. The problem is that communicating and interacting with the dead propels you into idolatry. You begin seeking answers from the dead, or from fallen spirits, rather than from your Father in heaven. In doing so, you are elevating them into a position of authority above your Creator. In addition to being utterly idolatrous, it also opens the door to deception, and, therefore, pushes you even further from the presence of God.

However, the doorway Lucifer entered was left open (John 10:1–10) in order for *God* and His *ministering* spirits to interact with the fallen humanity He so lovingly created. *"For indeed **He does not** give aid to angels, **but He does** give aid to the seed of Abraham."* (Hebrews 2:16) Had everyone kept their place, sin would be non-existent and the devil would be irrelevant.

Therefore, angels, which are spirits, must come to the natural realm in order to interact with humanity. Yahweh, our Father, functions in the same manner. The Holy Spirit is your conduit to Yahweh on planet earth. The secret to the presence of God is *the infilling of the Holy Spirit*. Until we are separated from the natural realm through the death of our mortal bodies, we cannot enter the realm of the spirit. Therefore, God visited with Adam and Eve in the Garden of Eden (Genesis 3:8) and no one needed to leave their natural abode. Life was perfect.

The Power of Purpose

"In the beginning" (Genesis 1:1) there was no sin separating the two realms. God and man could flawlessly interact. The two realms were interconnected and for purely spiritual beings like God, the angels, the devil and his demons, it still is. As previously stated, God and the angels are inter-dimensional beings. With no flesh inhibiting them, they can simply pass through the two realms. For man, however, sinful flesh placed an impenetrable barrier between us and the presence of God.

Until death sets our spirit free we cannot pass through. Our flesh obstructs us. Thus, Satan was thrust from the spiritual abode of heaven, away from the mountain of God and into the atmospheric dimension of planet earth. With the blockade (human flesh) in place the two were never to interact.

Therefore, humanity was not endued with the knowledge of, nor the power to wage spiritual warfare. Thus, we were given the command not to eat from the the tree of the knowledge of good and evil. In essence, until Adam and Eve ingested the forbidden fruit they did not have the ability, and thus the choice, to participate in evil.

This, however, left one vitally important question. "Do the people I created love me?" Although Yahweh knows the answer, justice requires the test. From our Father's perspective, the question each individual human being must face remains unanswered to this day; will you prove your love by trusting and obeying your Father?

Therefore, God, who is always purposeful, left Lucifer with the keys. He did not lock the door. Unbeknownst to most, our next secret is that *Lucifer was intended to be here all along.* He is an integral part of God's forever plan. As for man, without the Spirit of God dwelling within us we are severely handicapped. Thus, Satan takes full advantage of our rebellion and our quest for independence.

I love Al Pacino's rendition of Lucifer in the movie, *The Devil's Advocate.* He undoubtedly nailed Lucifer's true character. In it, he speaks one of the great truths of a fallen humanity when he proclaims, "Vanity is my favorite sin." The portrayal of Lucifer was dead on—no pun intended. *"The lust of the flesh, the lust of the eyes and the pride of life"* that *"comes **not** from the Father"* (1 John 2:16) will take us down every time.

In discovering this truth, however, you have no need to worry or fear. God was not surprised nor overcome by Satan's dissidence. God uses him to His advantage, and believe it or not, for your ultimate benefit, as well. The secret of Lucifer is that *freewill could never exist without him.* He forces man to choose. Have you ever considered the fact that Satan is the origin of your freewill? Satan has not only considered it, he knows precisely how to use it against you.

Thank God for Jesus Christ. With Christ's death, even the illusion of Satan's cozen power was ripped from him. He was not created for the purpose of possessing the body's of humans and causing the death and destruction that we experience today. When everyone keeps their proper domain, he does not possess even a hint of influence, let alone any true power.

Therefore, the authority given to Adam was solely in the realm of the natural. Adam was given dominion and authority over the earth and all things living on the earth. He was not given any power in the spirit. If you do not believe me search the Genesis account for yourself. Search the entire Bible. Man's authority was created for the natural realm. He did not need spiritual authority. That belonged to God, and Adam was one in Spirit with Him.

Therefore, there was no need for Adam to have authority over *any* spirit. That was not where our proper domain is; nor was any spirit apart from God ever intended to be our companion. Also keep in mind that planet Earth was never intended to be Satan's permanent abode. It is still not. That was reserved for Adam, his offspring and every organism created for the natural realm.

Therefore, since man was not intended to interact with Satan and his demons, we are not born with the spiritual authority to do so. In our fallen state we do not possess the equipment. It must be garnered through the death and resurrection of Jesus Christ. When Christ is left out of the equation, the only result is chaos, suffering, and pain. Furthermore, religion does not possess God's power and Lucifer knows it.

Illegal Alien

Therefore, Lucifer pushed his way into the physical realm and attempts to garner a body through either possession or influence. It is his only way in—a loophole if you will. Perhaps you are wondering what he believes his purpose is? As we discussed previously, it is to dispossess God. Lucifer is still trying to exalt his own power above God's. *"For you have said in your heart: 'I will ascend into heaven, **I will exalt my throne above the stars of God.'"*** (Isaiah 14:13)

His futile attempt to overthrow God is by taking his wrongful place within the spirit of a man. He attempts to dispossess God's abode within the spirit of humanity. He is more than just a petty thief, he is a heavily armed robber.

In so doing, he believes he can thwart the plan of God by preventing the return of the Messiah. As you read earlier, Satan mistakenly believed he could stop Jesus' birth and He now believes he can thwart His return.

Satan believes that if he can turn all men to sin, then God will destroy mankind, just as he did in the days of Noah. Then the earth would be his and he would escape the eternal chains of being cast into the Lake of Fire. Therefore, just like he did to the angels of heaven, he *"accuses us before our God, day and night"* (Revelation 12:10) futilely trying to get God to believe his impetuous lies. His efforts are undoubtedly in vain.

I want you to think about the following in regard to your own life. Adam's failure to use his power over the nachash, who was literally speaking to him in his own place of authority, allowed Satan an entrance into man's world. In essence, by entertaining evil, Adam invited him in. Consider how profound that is. Are you repeating the pattern?

As a result, we have mankind dealing with a spiritual being that he was never intended or equipped to deal with. This is still true today. Without Christ, man lacks the ability to handle him. The outcome is a spiritual scourging by the most vile being in all of creation. It is the equivalent of being a one legged man in a butt kicking contest. Just like the movie *Karate Kid,* Lucifer mercilessly "sweeps the leg." Without ever realizing it, you find yourself flat on your back. You have fallen and you cannot get up. You never had a chance.

In truth, Adam's misguided act of rebellion has resulted in the relationship that is the cause of every evil we have seen in the world throughout history. It is the direct result of Original Sin, and yes, I purposely used the term "relationship" in the last sentence. Without Christ you have not just an unwanted, but perhaps, even, an unknown relationship with the devil. It is forced upon you.

Be encouraged though. Now that you are aware of the problem, a simple, but major alteration of your lifestyle will affect the needed change. I would, therefore, encourage you to accept the sacrifice of Jesus Christ and enter God culture. Do not wait even one more moment. Why not right now?

Once you have done so, I would also encourage you to know your rights. You have a covenant with God. Lucifer does not. Do you realize that Satan is an illegal alien? Since his home country is hell that is exactly where we need to deport him.

Christ gave us the authority to do exactly that. Illegal aliens have no true authority, or rights, within the country's they reside, or, perhaps, even better stated, in which they hide—except California of course. Let's check that, illegal aliens have plenty of rights in America and unfortunately as evidenced by the recent Supreme Court Rulings and demands from the Whitehouse, so does Lucifer. In truth, however, when the people stand against Lucifer, they quickly come to the realization that it is merely an *illusion* of power. It is outright deception. The power belongs to the people—God's people. Do not ever forget that.

I once heard brother Jesse Duplantis say that he can whip Satan with his birth certificate. Do you know what? He can. So can you! Just pull it out of your closet and wave it in Lucifer's twisted, ugly face. He does not have one and, therefore, he is here illegally. You simply need to inform him of what you now know.

Because Lucifer, nor any demon for that matter, was not born of a woman nor sprouted from a seed, they have absolutely no authority over anything pertaining to your life. If you do not know this, however, you will believe their lies and fall into their self-empowering trap. That is when all hell breaks loose, literally, and this time the pun *is* intended. That is when you fall prey to the illusion and actually hand over *your* authority.

"My people are destroyed for lack of knowledge."
—Hosea 4:6

Praise God, you are no longer in the above category.

Citizenship

What about Jesus, how did He get here? Before Adam sinned, God used to walk freely in the Garden of Eden with him. (See Genesis 2) However, God does not dwell where sin dwells, so as a result, natural man has lost his ability to commune with God. How did God lift the restriction? In a single act of utter genius, God reentered the earth in the same manner as those He created to be here. Our holy Father reentered through the womb of the woman Mary, which *was* a legal means of a spirit, or in this case, His Spirit, capital "S," to enter the natural. Even God Himself did not disobey His own law.

If you read either *God Culture* or *Yahweh Revealed*, you already know that in order to function on earth a spirit must be wrapped in an earth suit, which is a physical body. A spirit has no physicality. That is why Satan needs you. You don't think he inhabits people because he likes us, do you? He does not like, love, care, nor have compassion for anyone.

Think about how Adam was created. God took Adam's spirit and *"out of the dust of the ground"* wrapped him in an earth suit. He then breathed into Adam, thus injecting the Spirit of life into Adam, which gave physical life to that which was non-living. Only His mighty power and Spirit can transform the inorganic into the organic. That is the mystery of the origin of life.

God will always obey His own rules. Therefore, it would behoove you to know them. This is why Satan takes possession of a man. He cannot accomplish anything in the natural without first being wrapped in a body. Did you really think all the murders, rapes and even wars, were random acts of violence?

This is why you have no need to fear Satan, or any other demon, for that matter. If he appeared before you in full manifestation of his malice, you could simply laugh him all the way back to the pit of hell where he belongs, just like Oral Roberts did in the illustration I referenced earlier.

He cannot do a thing to you. He has no authority in the natural and since Jesus has taken back the supernatural, he is left completely naked and destitute. He has been completely exposed as an impostor. He is nothing more than an illusionist who plays "three card Monty" for your power. That is, unless you are without Christ. Then it is you who is naked!

Jesus, however, not only entered legally, He also has the right to remain. He can travel back and forth as He pleases. He can set up His kingdom whenever and wherever He wants. According to scripture, He has chosen Jerusalem. Unlike Lucifer, the Lord Jesus has a passport. He described it this way in the gospel of John chapter ten:

"Most assuredly I say to you, he who does not enter the sheepfold by the door, but climbs up some other way, the same is a thief and a robber."

A thief, by the way, steals by stealth. A robber steals by force. Satan does both.

"But he who enters by the door is the shepherd of the sheep."

The door Jesus is referring to is the womb. He is the shepherd.

"To him the doorkeeper (God the Father) *opens, and the sheep hear his voice; and he calls his own sheep by name and leads them out."*

Leads us out of where? He will lead us from the natural to the supernatural, or in other words, from here to heaven.

"And when he brings out his own sheep he goes before them; (Which is exactly what He has done by His death and subsequent resurrection.) *and the sheep follow him, for they know his voice. Yet they will by no means follow a stranger, but will*

flee from him, for they do not know the voice of strangers" or illegal aliens (demons) for that matter.

Now Jesus changes the illustration of the door to Himself.

"Then Jesus said to them again, 'Most assuredly I say to you, I am the door of the sheep.'

Meaning, *you* gain legal entrance into the presence of God through Him alone. He is the entry way to heaven. Now you understand why Jesus proclaimed, *"No one comes to the Father except through Me."*

"All who ever came before Me are thieves and robbers, but the sheep did not hear them. I am the door. If anyone enters by Me, he will be saved, ***and will go in and out*** *and will find pasture."*

This means you can have peace and prosper in both the spiritual and the natural realms of life. Through Him, you have access to both.

"The thief does not come except to steal, kill, and destroy. I have come that they may have life, and that they may have it more abundantly. I am the good shepherd. The good shepherd gives His life for the sheep."
—John 10:1–11

I do not think Jesus could have been any clearer than that.

Alive in Christ

So where does that leave us? It leaves us in Christ. Allow me to explain. Since Jesus entered the earth by legal means, He now possesses the right to redeem man's authority. The Lord is now fully man, and thus, is able to fulfill the Law of the Kinsman Redeemer. He has entered *"the sheep-fold through the door."* Therefore, Jesus has perfectly fulfilled the law of redemption.

In other words, according to the law of the Kinsman Redeemer, Jesus being *"the likeness of sinful flesh,"* (Romans 8:3) has become your brethren. As your Creator, which makes Him your nearest of kin, He has the legal right to take responsibility for man's sin and disobedience and "buy" your way out of the slavery of sin. Therefore, the Word becomes flesh (John 1:14) and God becomes a man in Christ. Jesus then lays down His life by spilling His life giving blood on the cross with the sin of the world thrust upon Him. Through the miracle of death, the Lord turns the tables on Satan, kills man's sin, takes it down to hell where it belongs and leaves it there to be burned in the Lake of Fire. The same supernatural power that created both life and death then resurrects Jesus and voila, restoration and appointment of the heavenly pattern. Thy kingdom has come.

When you allow God to place the same power that raised Jesus from the dead within you by faith in Christ, the same exact thing occurs within your spirit. *"The body of sin is done away with"* (Romans 6:6) and you are spiritually resurrected in the likeness, or image, of almighty God. Thus, you can now become one with the Lord. You become alive in Christ, not dead in your trespasses. You have completed the pattern. Do you see God's wisdom in creating you in His image? There are no illusions in Christ, just extreme brilliance and raw power.

Most never realize that God has always known the entrance way leading into His everlasting presence, which is the narrow gate of Jesus Christ. Jesus was Yahweh's plan from the beginning of eternity. God had the pattern ordained in the Spirit from second number one of creation.

By now you must realize that a biblical hoax is an impossibility. No man could have ever dreamed up nor executed such an elaborate and infinite plan. God, through Jesus Christ, has overcome the devil and will ultimately obliterate all that is sinful. Therefore, let's continue on, there is more to learn about the mystery of evil. It is time to reveal another secret.

CHAPTER 12

Evil!

(THE SECRET BEHIND THE DARKNESS)

In addition to being one of the great mysteries of life, the existence of evil is perhaps the most puzzling, and quite frankly, troubling aspect in all of theology. From the beginning of time, man has been asking the age old question, "Why did God create evil?" Additionally troubling are the following inquiries, does God have the power to stop it? Is He the cause of it, and perhaps the greatest of all, does God have a purpose for evil?

Such questions are not so easily answered, especially in a sentence or two. The quick answer is yes, God does have a purpose for evil, and yes,

God did create it. *"I form the light and create darkness, I make peace **and I create evil,** I, the Lord, do all these things."* (Isaiah 45:7)

Many will argue that God did not create evil. As evidence, they will cite other versions of the Bible that have not translated the Hebrew word "Ra" into "evil." "Ra" can also be translated as "calamity," "misery" or "adversity," all of which can be included in the various forms of evil, by the way, even though most Hebrew scriptures connote the word, "Ra" with moral descent.

In response to such interpretation I have only one question. Did God create Lucifer or not? If you believe God created Lucifer and if you believe Lucifer is the perpetrator of evil on planet earth, than you have no other choice but to accept that God is the creator of evil; particularly when you consider that God purposely implanted the iniquity that caused Lucifer's now infamous rebellion. Any other conclusion would be denial of both God's omniscience and His omnipotence.

Lucifer having been created with iniquity (Ezekiel 28:15) is all one needs to know regarding the creation of evil. Therefore, the true question is not did God create evil? The question is, *why* did God create evil? Believe it or not, Lucifer, now known as Satan, which means, "the adversary," a.k.a. the devil, which also means, "the deceiver," has a vital function in the kingdom and plan of Yahweh. As stated previously, it is Lucifer who forces you to choose between good, evil and God.

Therefore, the question becomes; will you serve God or will you serve evil? Do you love God or do you love yourself, your pride, your ego—in essence, the vanity of your natural life. Keep in mind that the word "Lord" means "to own completely." Therefore, Lucifer causes you to choose your Lord. Who owns you, Yahweh, the King of all kings, or Lucifer, the Prince of Darkness?

Just as good is non-existent without the concept of evil, love is non-existent without the knowledge of hatred. Thus, God placed the tree of *the Knowledge of Good and Evil* in the midst of the Garden of Eden and simply bided His time. Whom will they choose?

Unfortunately, we all know the answer. But why do it? Why place such temptation at the forefront of man's choosing?

As previously discussed, love must be chosen. True love is not a feeling or an emotion. True love is the willingness to put someone else's best interest above your own, just as hatred is the will and/or hope that revenge will be exacted upon your enemy. Your adversary's best interest is non-existent in hatred. True love, on the other hand, is choosing the well being of another over the well being of one's self. That is exactly what Jesus Christ did on the cross. It is also what Lucifer is incapable of doing.

> *"He who knew no sin became sin **that you** may become the righteousness of God in Christ."*
> **—2 Corinthians 5:21**

Don't you find it amazing that God chose *you* over *Himself?* This is why we are required to make the same choice. Choosing not just good over evil, but God over evil, is a part of being in covenant with Yahweh. This is also where so many make an eternal mistake. They choose what appears to be good over God. They choose religion over God. In many cases, and without ever realizing it, they have chosen the "angel of light" over God. Thus, evil reigns on planet earth.

As you can now see, understanding evil, and God's purpose for it, requires time, patience and diligence. It requires spiritual understanding. It also requires knowledge of our most notorious adversary. Therefore, in order to overcome evil, we will now spend some time looking at both the inner workings of Lucifer and the Spirit of God. Let's peer into the nature of both the light and dark sides of life.

Check Mate

As we previously discussed, on an individual basis God uses the devil like a pawn on a chess board, strategically allowing him to work in our lives in order to build character and purify us for what ultimately is intended to be good.

> *"And we know that **all things** work together for good to those who **love God,** to those who are the called according to His purpose."*
> **—Romans 8:28**

In reference to the above, there are two thing we must remember. 1) You must have a forever mindset in order to accept this secret reality, and 2) according to the above principle, you must love God in order to experience His goodness. Take a good look at what I just stated. There are two principles that hold true regarding Romans 8:28. First, if you do not love God, and therefore, have not accepted His call to live holy, and/or if you disobey Him or if you just flat out ignore Him, *"all things"* are *not* working together for your good. In fact, since you have set yourself in opposition to God, *"all things"* may even be working against you. Therefore, when you rebel against Him you will not be in position to experience what God has intended for good. What then is the result? The result is exactly what we see a disobedient world experiencing on a daily basis; chaos, suffering and pain.

Secondly, even if you do love and obey God, if you do not adopt a forever mindset you will fail to recognize God's goodness, even when it hits you smack in the face. As disciples of Jesus Christ, we must come to the realization that even the pain and suffering experienced by the believer on a daily basis works for our good. Although it is rarely immediately recognizable, once you realize that *you* possess God's authority regarding your own life, what Satan intends for evil, God uses to accomplish His will, which can only good from a God *"who is love."* (1 John 4:8 and 16) I have seen this work on many occasions both in my own life and in the lives of other fellow believers in grace. If you sit back and reflect upon your past, it is my guess that you will find this to be true for yourself as well.

As you undoubtedly know, God is not afraid of Satan. God is not surprised when evil occurs, and neither should you be. Evil is a means to an end. In other words, a greater good is accomplished by your realization of the truth that you, let me rephrase that, that *we* need the Lord. In suffering, we seek mercy. Pain, whether it is physical or emotional, causes one to look up. Through evil your choice is laid before you.

For some folks there is simply no other way to get their attention. You may be too hard headed, or as the Bible phrases it, *"stiff necked"* to turn toward Him otherwise. For some, God needs to back you into a corner and just like an unprotected King, put you into checkmate. When there is only one way to turn, you turn to God. **"God didn't promise days without pain, laughter without sorrow, or sun without rain, but He did promise strength for the day, comfort for the tears, and light for the way. If God brings you to it, He will bring you through it." —Author Unknown**

Disaster

However, I am sure that you are still asking; what about natural disasters, famines, acts of genocide, and the like, which are out of one's control? Why would God cause or allow this? What good can be accomplished through such mass suffering?

The answer is that God does not cause it—at least not all of it. Of course God can send a whirlwind. We recently experienced what was deemed to be a "microburst" in the neighborhood in which I live. A microburst normally occurs during a severe thunderstorm when a swath of cold air plummets to the ground bringing with it torrential rain, damaging hail stones and winds that can be in excess of one hundred miles per hour. It is also known, by the way, as a "Rain Bomb." If you have ever been caught in one, you will immediately understand the connotation. I love thunderstorm's, but this was on another level. It was terrifying.

In the aftermath of the chaos, and while having no idea of what just occurred, I checked out a video of a microburst caught on film in Arizona. Its appearance is as if God simply decided to drop a giant bucket of water on a particular geographic location no more tan 3–4 miles wide. You can even see the massive splash as the water hits the ground.

The result in our hometown was tornadic type conditions that littered our neighborhood with fallen trees, damaged houses and plenty of business for the clean up crews. In fifteen minutes there was as much damage to our neighborhood as the infamous Superstorm (Hurricane) Sandy caused in about fourteen hours. It certainly seemed to be an "Act of God."

Having lived through such an experience, I have no doubt that an all powerful God can undoubtedly cause the earth to quake. He can even send famine to the land. God can send other human beings into our lives. He can send judgment into our lives . . . In essence, God can do whatever He wants. God has absolute control and total authority over the whole of creation.

We are not, however, some sort of inter-dimensional marionettes being pulled by God's divine puppet strings. God is not experimenting or playing some sort of twisted and demented game with our lives. God does not orchestrate every aspect of the human experience. He can, and will, use the circumstances of life, both positive and negative, to bring His will to pass. He is undoubtedly aware of our plight but He is not micromanaging every motive, decision or situation life has to offer.

God does not cause every earthquake or tornado that strikes the land. I do not know if God caused the microburst in my neighborhood or not. In fact, having such information is totally irrelevant if the neighborhood refuses to obey God anyway . . . and guess what. Everyone living here was effected—even those that are obedient to the will of God. Give that some thought; then consider how every action potentially effects someone, somewhere, sometime. Disobedience to God has undoubtedly effected the whole of humanity, not just those perceived as guilty.

We seem to forget, or even more likely, have never learned that not just humanity fell in the Garden of Eden. The environment was also effected by sin, and, therefore, is fallen, as well. (Romans 8:19–24) Unfortunately, that little known fact effects every human being walking the blue planet.

> *"Then to Adam He said, **"Because** you have heeded the voice of your wife, and have eaten from the tree of which I commanded you, saying, 'You shall not eat of it':"**Cursed is the ground for your sake;** in toil you shall eat of it all the days of your life. Both thorns and thistles it shall bring forth for you, and you shall eat the herb of the field.*
>
> *In the sweat of your face you shall eat bread till you return to the ground, for out of it you were taken; for dust you are, and to dust you shall return."*
>
> **—Genesis 3:17–19**

The cause of human suffering originates from freewill and choice—both Adam's (Original Sin) and our individual acts of personal sin. Human suffering, particularly human induced suffering, is a perversion of the dominion and authority given to Adam at creation.

Most of us never come to the realization that humanity was never intended to have dominion and authority over one another. Man was created to have fellowship with one another. In terms of who or what our dominion and authority is intended to be exercised over—the animals, yes ... creeping things, yes ... birds, fish and every living thing on planet earth ... the answer is yes ... with only one exception. Man was never given dominion and authority over one another.

Then God said, "Let Us make man in Our image, according to Our likeness; **let them have dominion over the fish of the sea, over the birds of the air, and over the cattle, over all the earth and over every creeping thing that creeps on the earth."**

So God created man in His own image; in the image of God He created him; male and female He created them. Then God blessed them, and God said to them, "Be fruitful and multiply; fill the earth and subdue it; **have dominion over the fish of the sea, over the birds of the air, and over every living thing that moves on the earth."**

—Genesis 1:26–28

Dominion over man was designated for God alone. The kingdom of God is a theocratic government. God alone has dominion over the life of man, and, therefore, it is God alone who has the right to take the life of man. Wars, genocide, homicide or whatever crime against humanity is a perversion of dominion and authority. As such, we see God exercising his right to penalize our perversion as far back as Cain taking the life of his brother Abel.

"And He (God) said, "What have you done? The voice of your brother's blood cries out to Me from the ground. **So now you are cursed from the earth,** *which has opened its mouth to receive your brother's blood from your hand. When you till the ground, it shall no longer yield its strength to you.* **A fugitive and a vagabond you shall be on the earth."**

—Genesis 4:10

In the midst of sin, humanity has perverted the gift of dominion, attempted to place himself in the position of Jehovah, and begun to dominate one another. The chaotically flawed result is derived from the truth that God is perfectly just and humanity is hopelessly flawed. Therefore,

"Power tends to corrupt, and absolute power corrupts absolutely. Great men are almost always bad men." —**Sir John Acton** The one exception being Jesus Christ of Nazareth.

Think about it this way, if a dictator or warlord decides to starve his nation's people, which is often the case in Africa and various other nations, it is not God starving the people. It is the warlord starving his people. In most cases there is plenty of food to feed them. Much of the world, for example, sends food to Africa.

Likewise, it was not God who caused the Holocaust. The extermination of six million Jews was caused by an iniquitous leader who twisted the hearts and minds of a nation ripe for genocide. The Holocaust was a demonic manifestation. Adolph Hitler, and all those who submitted to his Satanic will, were exercising their perverted interpretation of freewill. They perverted the dominion and authority given to man from creation.

In fact, many world leaders are so corrupted by sin that they have given themselves completely to the devil. The devil then forces his hand upon them. Without Christ, their only option is evil. It is all they know. It is *whom* they know. Therefore, it is the power of sin, not God's will, that brings evil upon the oppressed. God's "stamp of approval" is nothing more than His refusal to rescind the gift of freewill. Do not worry, those perpetuating such crimes will stand before Him. Eternity is the real issue at stake.

Read the Label

With that said, it is a common mistake to believe that your actions have no effect upon others. Everything we do or say affects someone, somewhere, somehow, sometime, whether small or great. We are all intertwined. You have heard it referred to as the "butterfly effect," which means even the tiny beating of a butterfly's wings somehow effects the outcome of a situation. Ultimately, God works it all together for good *if* you choose to love Him.

The only problem is that *your* definition of good and *God's* definition of good are radically different.

According to *dictionary.com* the word, "good" has seven definitions:

1. Morally excellent; virtuous; righteous; pious:
2. Satisfactory in quality, quantity, or degree:
3. Of high quality; excellent.
4. Right; proper; fit:
5. Well-behaved:
6. Kind, beneficent, or friendly:
7. Honorable or worthy; in good standing

As human beings, we look at the people around us and attempt to categorize them according to one of these seven definitions. It goes something like this; "Mother Theresa, very good, morally excellent. Adolph Hitler, very bad, none of the above. Billy Graham, very good, Osama Bin Laden, very bad." We then place ourselves somewhere in the middle. "Well I am certainly no Mother Theresa, but I am definitely no Hitler either." That is not the way God sees us. When God looks at man He sees only the following:

*"The Lord looks down from heaven upon the children of men, to see if there are any who understand, who seek God. They have **all** turned aside, they have **together** become corrupt; there is **none** who does good, no, **not one.**"*

—Psalm 14:2–3

Jesus said it this way when He was referred to as good master. *"Why do you call Me good?* **No one is good** *but One, God.* **But** *if you want to enter into life keep the commandments.'"*

—Matthew 19:17

Without Christ mediating for us, God sees nothing but sin. He cannot get past it because He did not create us to be that way. Therefore, no amount of good works can change the image God sees. Apart from Christ, we are all evil. Even a "good" man is capable of incalculable amounts of evil. History has undoubtedly proven that to be true. Good intentions, followed by corruption, greed and evil, is not God's will for humanity. Although it is currently hidden, the following is God's will for mankind. This is mankind's original state of being.

"So God created man **in His own image;** *in the image of God He created Him . . ." "Then God saw everything that He had made, and indeed it was* **very good."**

—Genesis 1:27 & 31

We were very good because we were still God's image. Not even creation had fallen at this point, and, therefore, it was very good as well. We must understand that there is no sin in the image of God, but now there is no man without sin. *"All have sinned and fall short of the glory of God."* (Romans 3:23) There is no evil in God. There is no sin or death in His presence. Apart from Him, however, the only thing sin *can* produce is death. *"For the wages of sin is death."* (Romans 6:23) Therefore, we must conclude that the sinner has been separated from God, and unfortunately, without Christ we all fall into the "lost" category.

Although Adam was created in the image of God, when He sinned *"death spread to all men."* (Romans 5:12) Its manifestation is in the form of death and evil, and yes, even an innocent baby is affected by the corruption of the natural realm, which manifests itself in violence, suffering, natural disaster's and ultimately death.

The Adam(s) Family

Here is what happened. As we previously mentioned, mankind was commanded to be fruitful and multiply. The heavenly image was intended to be reproduced all over the earth, but when Adam sinned he was separated from God. The result severed him from the source of life giving, resurrection power that maintained the image of God in him. In his fallen state he began to multiply ... Adam begot Cain who slew Abel, and then, *"Adam begot a son after **his own likeness,** after **his image,** and named him Seth."* (Genesis 5:3)

That was the end of it. Man was no longer good because he was no longer the image of God. Man became the image of Adam filled with sin, death, and evil, and, therefore, began to reproduce exactly that. Since we are all members of the *Adam(s) Family* sin has become magnified to the current tune of just over *seven billion* people! Now do you get it? Give that some thought. Sin is being multiplied by a factor of seven billion on a daily basis. When seen from that perspective, it is a miracle that there is any goodness in the world at all!

That is why the world produces such incredible unrighteousness. No amount of works can correct it. Only a spiritual change in image can fix humanity. It is this unrighteousness that produces suffering. According to Psalm 14, we have *all* turned aside and have *together* become corrupt, thus, producing the works of evil upon the planet that we see today.

Do you remember the theme song from the Adam's Family? It goes something like this ... *Their creepy and there kooky, mysterious and spooky, there all together ooky, the Adam(s) family* ... When taking a hard look at the world, that seems to be exactly who we have become.

Therefore, in order to be restored to God's image we must accept the sacrifice of Jesus Christ. We must do things God's way and not ours. We must accept Jesus Christ as our Lord and Savior. There is no other way to change our image. There is no other way to please God.

*"For by grace we have been saved through faith, **and that not of yourselves,** it is the gift of God, **not of works,** lest anyone should boast."*
—**Ephesians 2:8**

*"And **without faith** it is **impossible** to please Him."*
—**Hebrews 11:6**

No amount of works, no religion, and no man can save you. It is only by the blood of the Lamb slain from the foundation of the world that you can be redeemed.

*"For if we have been united together in the **likeness** (or image) of His death, certainly we also shall be in the **likeness** (or image) of His resurrection, **knowing this,** that our old man was crucified with Him, **that the body of sin might be done away with,** that we no longer should be slaves of sin."*
—**Romans 6:5–6**

Labor Pains

With that said, we still must answer the question regarding the sufferings of the "innocent." God's will is not to see us suffer. Our Father's will is to redeem each and every one of us. (2 Peter 3:9) Human suffering breaks God's heart, but He ultimately uses suffering as a means of seeking the

Super over the natural. Every man must make the same eternal choice regardless of their circumstance.

> *"Therefore we do not lose heart. Even though **the outward man** is perishing... For our light affliction, **which is but for a moment**, is **working for us** a far more exceeding **and eternal** weight of glory, while **we do not look at the things which are seen**. For the things which are seen are temporary, but the things which are not seen are eternal."*
> **—2 Corinthians 4:16–18**

The words "light affliction" came from a man, the Apostle Paul, who was repeatedly beaten, stoned, jailed and tortured. He used this term as a comparison to contrast the glory of an eternity in the presence of Yahweh with the ongoing, but momentary afflictions of natural life, and not to state that one's suffering is petty. It is understood that the suffering of many is great.

Therefore, no matter whom you are or what your circumstance is, you must keep your eyes on the Lord to lighten your burdens. In terms of eternity, we are not really here for very long, and in reality, it is often times death that sets the oppressed free. The eternal tragedy occurs in our failure to deliver the gospel to those who are enslaved in poverty and oppression, and are outwardly, as well as, inwardly perishing.

Those of us who have been made free in Christ *must* become overtly zealous and desperate in conveying the Word of God regardless of the cost, *especially* to the helpless. We will be held accountable to the Lord in accordance with the blessings and gifts the Lord has given us. Without Jesus Christ, the oppressed truly have no hope.

In terms of natural disasters, most never come the realization as I stated earlier that the entire physical realm has been affected by sin.

> *"For I consider that the sufferings of this present time are not worthy to be compared with the glory which shall be revealed in us. For the earnest*

*expectation **of the creation** eagerly waits for the revealing of the sons of God."*

—Romans 8:18–19

This scripture is absolutely incredible. The entire creation, not just God, the angels and your long lost relatives, await not just *your* conversion, but the earths, and perhaps, even, the entire universe's *re-creation*. (Revelation 21) Paul continues his explanation:

*"For the creation **was subjected to futility,** not willingly, but because of Him who subjected it in hope; because the creation itself **also will be delivered** from the **bondage of corruption** into the glorious liberty of the children of God. For we know that **the whole creation groans and labors** with birth pangs until now."*

—Romans 8:20–22

Therefore, we never know our time. The earth labors with earthquakes, hurricanes, tornadoes and the like. As you have already seen in *Yahweh Revealed*, the earth shall be redeemed just as we are. Until then, however, it continues to degrade into the chaos, suffering, and pain of the entropic human experience. That means baby's will die, the just will be oppressed and evil will continue its reign until Jesus sets all of creation free. Therefore, you must make your choice now. Who will you serve? You never know what tomorrow brings.

With that in mind, I would encourage you to join us in battle. We will overcome that evil piece of garbage, Lucifer, also known as Satan, and the devil. We, meaning Jesus, you and I, will cast the devil out of this planet, just as the angels in heaven did.

If you have paid attention to this book series, you will have noticed that Lucifer's time is short and he knows it. (Revelation 12:12) Therefore, he exhibits tremendous wrath in an attempt to cause you to rebel against God, just as he caused the dissidence of the rebellious angels of heaven. His goal is to drag you into a lifeless eternity which has been reserved for him and all those who follow his wicked ways.

That is why there is so much evil and suffering on the earth. It has been designed to cause you to choose. Will you abandon God? Have you given in to Lucifer? or have you seen God turn your trouble, and ultimately, *you* to His side? Evil will continue until God's appointed time comes to completely eradicate it upon the return of Christ the Lord. In the meantime, God will have learned *exactly* where you stand.

What most never consider is the difference between God's *permissive will* and His *perfect will*. His permissive will encompasses the limits of what He will allow to occur in your life as long as you remain in disobedience, ignorance and/or rebellion toward Him. His perfect will is the manifestation of the blessing that occurs when you obediently follow His lead. The former, results in chaos, suffering and pain. The latter leads to love, joy and peace in the Holy Ghost. (Romans 14:17)

Fit Me In

Keep in mind that there are no mistakes in God. It is not as if God did not think things through, or that He may have overlooked some minor aspect of His predetermined plan. God is perfect. His ways are perfect. The spiritual war that we face every day on this planet is a pattern of what went on in the heavens. Only God knows how long it took. Only God knows how long this present age will last. Just as the devil caused rebellion in the heavens, he is causing rebellion on the earth. This causes a choice between good and evil, between God and the devil.

We must, therefore, learn how to deal with evil and declare our loyalty to God. Your choice is an outward exhibit of whose side you are on. The choices we make, which require faith and trust in God, determine our spiritual futures and whether or not we are worthy to reside eternally in heaven with the Lord. When you take the time to think about it, it is really not that complicated.

On a much smaller and somewhat corrupted scale, we treat the people in our lives in the same manner. We make them prove their worth to us as friends, colleagues, business associates, etc... In other words, we have created our own patterns and fit people into them. "Are you with me or against me? If you are with me we can be friends, if not, forget you."

This makes sense when you realize that as God's image you were originally created to operate in the same manner. I must caution you in this, however. Make sure those who are with you are also with God. Otherwise they will drag you into the pit with them.

If you were God, however, why would you do it this way? Wouldn't it be easier and more merciful to just wipe evil away? especially after seeing the trouble Satan caused in the heavenly realm. Why send him to us?

As we previously discussed, God's intention was not necessarily to send him to us. It was to send him out of heaven. Had Adam and Eve not entertained Lucifer all would be well. One has to believe, however, that even had Adam and Eve kept their proper domain, somewhere along the line someone was going to give in. Think about it, how many billions of people have existed on planet earth?

In truth, God knew exactly what both Lucifer and humanity would do, therefore, He states, *"the devil has come to you with great wrath."* (Revelation 12:12) Secondly, and the secret of Lucifer's purpose, is that *God uses him to connect with you.* Although Satan does not realize it, and just like the movie *The Exorcist* did for me, *Lucifer's purpose is to drive you to God.* I suppose, therefore, the same can be said of evil. If only we could look up and not down—at ourselves and not each other... perhaps the world would be a better place.

Growing Together

The secret to why God created evil lies in the greatest gift God has ever given to mankind. This gift is so boundless and so essential to God that not only is He willing to let you die for it, He, Himself, was willing to die for it as well. The gift I am referring to is freewill. The secret of evil is that *it is necessary for you to have freewill.* We see an illustration of this principle in the parable of the wheat and tares contained in Matthew 13:24–30.

> *"The kingdom of heaven is like a man who sowed good seed in his field; but while men slept, **his enemy came** and sowed tares among the wheat and went his way."*

This is obviously an illustration of God creating goodness and the devil corrupting it with his evil nature. It is very important to note that the scripture says the enemy sowed the tares and went his way. In other words, it was Lucifer who caused all the trouble and neither you nor I actually saw him do it.

Mankind rarely realizes or understands where corruption and evil has come from. Most men only see with their natural eyes. Consequently, when we see evil, we rarely, if ever, perceive the true cause of it. Therefore, most of us never even come close to discerning evil's true purpose. We see the "weed." We know the seed came from somewhere, but we do not always realize who sowed the seed. Therefore, we make assumptions as to who may have caused the corruption, i.e. blaming God, when in fact it was the devil that put the seed in the ground.

Sometimes we just choose to believe that weeds are the way things are and no one sowed it. Perhaps the wind just blew them there by chance. I do not believe there is such a thing as chance or coincidence. The result of such apathy is the fact that mankind continues to water the seed of evil through both ignorance and disobedience to the will of God.

"But when the grain had sprouted and produced a crop, then the tares also appeared."
—Matthew 13:26

It is important to note that you cannot always distinguish between particular crops until they either begin to mature, or actually *do* mature. As a seed, or seedling, two different species may look identical. Lucifer, the *"angel of light,"* takes full advantage of this little known and difficult to recognize reality.

Thank God that He lets us grow. If He uprooted me as a seedling I would have been chaff. Take note of the next sentence. In it, you will see confirmation of the preceding discussion. The majority of mankind's reaction to evil is based upon outright ignorance of both the nature of God, and the devil, for that matter.

"So the servants of the owner came and said to him, 'Sir, did you not sow good seed in your field? **How then does it have tares?'** *He said to them,* **"An enemy has done this."**
—Matthew 13:27–28

We must stop blaming God for the problems of the world. It is the enemy, Satan, who deserves your disloyalty, not the One willing to save you.

"The servants said to him, 'Do you want us then to go and gather them up?' But he said, 'No, lest while you gather up the tares you also uproot the wheat with them. **Let both grow together until the harvest,** *and at the time of the harvest I will say to the reapers, 'First gather together the tares and bind them into bundles to burn them, but gather the wheat into my barn.'"*
—Matthew 13:27–30

God allows evil to remain in order to perfect your eternal character. Keep in mind that no matter how bad you may think you are, God knows the difference between the wheat and the tares. He knows your ultimate destination because He knows your heart. Therefore, He will not uproot you before your time. Allowing you to mature, even while life seems chaotic, causes your roots in Him to strengthen. Evil is a catalyst designed for you to make an eternal decision. Jesus said if you are forgiven of much you will love much, and if you have been forgiven of little, you will love little. (Luke 7:47)

The secret is that *evil is God's method of implementing freewill,* thus causing you to choose a side. Before you judge God, consider the fact that there is simply no other way to accomplish such a task. Freewill and choice are like pain and pleasure. They go hand in hand. You cannot know one without experiencing the other. So it is with good and evil. They are actually soul-mates.

Evil is God's way of calling you home. It is how He develops His love and His image within you. *"Have I therefore **become your enemy** because I tell you the truth? **They** (those bent on evil) **zealously court you, but for no good;** yes, they want to exclude you, (from the kingdom of God) **that you may be zealous for them** . . . But it is good to be zealous **in a good thing** always . . . My little children, for whom I labor in birth again **until Christ is formed in you.** "* (Galatians 4:16–19)

Keep in mind that the Apostle Paul was not referring to "the world's" definition of "good," nor am I referring to the "worlds" sensual, earthly definition of "love." True love is the agape, unconditional love of God. The choice between good and evil, whose true definition is between God and evil, is our Father's way of forming the pattern of Himself within you.

Therefore, *"choose life"* (Deuteronomy 30:19) by choosing Christ. The image of God in you obliterates evil. Do not be deceived, freewill mandates choice. It is a "now" vs. "forever" decision, so choose wisely and carefully. Now that Christ is formed in you, let's move on to another vital secret— the mystery of commitment.

— CHAPTER 13 —

Dating God

(THE SECRET OF THE ANCIENT OF DAYS)

I'll bet when reading the title of this chapter you thought I was going to attempt to put a chronological age to God Almighty, the Ancient of Days. You know, like how old is God? In truth, I could never accurately put a date on my grandmother. You know what I mean? I get into the most trouble when my wife poses the following question, "Who looks older, me or her?" In truth, sometimes I just don't know. If I cannot figure out the age of two human beings, how could I ever figure out the age of the Creator of the universe, who has no beginning or end, if you can even conceptualize such infinitude?

God is timeless and He is ageless. He is eternal. There is not a human alive who can even fathom such an immense juncture of time; if time is even a unit of measure in eternity. It appears that there are no spans to eternity. It is infinite—forever expanding into perpetuity.

God is old *and* He is young. Can you even comprehend that? He is everlasting. He resides somewhere outside of our space-time continuum in the realm of the Almighty. As human beings we are simply incapable of gestating the timelessness of forever.

However, the question I intend to ask is one you can most certainly apprehend. I am not yet convinced, however, that most people are willing to concede to the answer. The answer requires unbridled honesty from within—an honest peek into who you really are and what your true motivation is. When embarked upon, the authenticity of your answer can unlock the power of God in your life. Those around you will be affected from here to eternity, but do not be fooled by its aberrance. Although it sounds simple, it is most difficult to ascertain. The consequence of your answer, however, is eternal. So take a deep breath, because ready or not, here it comes . . .

Test Drive

Are you dating God? Yes, you interpreted that correctly. Are you merely *dating* Him? You know, the way we date various men or woman in an attempt to decide who we have "fallen in love" with; in essence, taking him or her for a test drive to see whether or not we are compatible with them and willing to commit. Do they fit into our lifestyle? Can we trust them? Do they have wandering eyes or will they cheat?

Perhaps you just want to have some fun. When you are finished with that person you will just move on to the next target of your "affection," never having, or, even intending to create a lasting relationship.

Sometimes we just use people. We take as much as we can get from them and toss them aside with no regard to feelings or emotions. But maybe... just maybe... this one is different and you are even willing to live together for a time before marrying, if the institution of marriage is still a part of your ultimate code of ethics.

Is that your idea of commitment? If so, what is to keep you from straying, or perhaps, even, walking out when trouble comes—and trust me, trouble *will* come. If that is your level of commitment, you are most likely "outta there" upon the first sign of distress.

Remnants

If you have ever been treated this way or experienced this type of a relationship, you know how devastating it can be. Scars may be etched into your soul that cause a lifetime of chaos for every human being wandering across your broken path.

The unfortunate truth is that this perfectly describes the relationship many of us have with our Creator. We continually break His heart. We use and abuse Him and when He has answered our prayer we toss Him aside for next time. Although we may live with Him while He entertains our troubles, as soon as something "better" comes along we put Him back in the box.

Yet, He never casts us aside. He waits—lovingly, patiently, and compassionately for us to come to our senses and realize how selfish and foolish we are. When we finally realize that He is the One we have been looking for, He welcomes us with wide open arms. Another prodigal has come home. (Luke 15:20)

A Husband

I would strongly encourage you to consider what I am about to say. God does not want to date you. He wants to marry you!

> *"I will betroth you to Me forever; yes, I will betroth you to Me. In righteousness and justice, in loving-kindness and mercy, I will betroth you to me in faithfulness, and you shall know the Lord."*
>
> **—Hosea 2:19–20**

Marriage, by the way, is personal. It is not a hedonistic relationship between multiple partners, and, therefore, in the Spirit, betrothal to Yahweh is an exclusive relationship between you and the Father. As a collective group, meaning, as the church, we are the body of Christ for the purpose of ministering to those walking the blue planet. When it comes to the individual, however, our Father longs to penetrate your spirit and become one with you. Obedience to His will is the marriage vow each individual must take.

You may not realize it, but the Lord is fully committed to you. So much so, that He died to save you. The question, therefore, is; will you commit to Him? As we discussed previously, love is a reciprocal act. Just as a husband provides for his spouse, your Father in heaven will become your sole provider, regardless of your sex. Only He is perfect. His love never fails. He is incapable of disappointment.

When you commit to Him, He will cause you to *"enlarge the place of your tent."* He will *"stretch out the curtains of your dwelling."* Therefore, *"do not spare, lengthen the cords and strengthen the stakes. For you shall expand to the right hand and to the left, and your descendants shall inherit the nations and make the desolate cities inhabited."*

"Do not fear, for you shall not be ashamed, neither be disgraced, for you will not be put to shame, for you will forget the shame of your youth, and will

not remember the reproach of your widowhood anymore. **For your maker is your husband,** *the Lord of Hosts is His name, and your Redeemer is the Holy One of Israel, He is called the God of the whole earth.* **For the Lord has called you** *like a woman forsaken and grieved in spirit, like a youthful wife when you were refused,' says your God."* (Isaiah 54:1–6)

When you become intimate with your Holy Father, what "the world" has done to you no longer matters. As Joel Osteen declares, "You will no longer be a victim, but a *victor,"* of the circumstances of life.

The Lord will never refuse you. You have both a Father and a Husband in the Lord. If you are a guy take heed. Just because the language is gender specific does not mean your relationship with the Lord is gender exclusive. Gender specification is our limitation, not His. He desires the same exact relationship with you regardless of your sex. In truth, when you are in Christ, *"there is neither Jew nor Greek, there is neither slave nor free,* **there is neither male nor female,** *for you are all one in Christ."* (Galatians 3:28)

Husbandry

That means the Almighty's role in mankind's life as a husband applies to you as well, brother. What is the role of a husband? If you *are* one you know all too well that it is protector, provider, leader, lover, etc...

In ancient Israel, the husband's primary role was to show loving leadership in regard to his wife and children, in effect, over his entire household. He was the overseer of all matters, both physical and spiritual. His wife was to be the helper, not the ruler. My how things have changed! The man was to provide for his household and love his wife, not lord his authority over her. His wife's role was to submit to, and to obey the will of her husband, not to rebel and fight against him. She was to be his helper, not his gerent.

If there was a disagreement she would take it to him privately and subtly, not having the authority to command him. His role was to listen to, and to consider the wisdom of all she "brought to the table." As overseer of all matters, his role was to make a decision based upon the best interest of the family unit, not based upon machismo or selfish pride, with regard only to who is right and who is wrong.

Loving and providing for their needs was his responsibility, and, according to 1 Timothy 5:8, if he did not provide for his own he was considered worse than an unbeliever. Can you see how far we have strayed? How many fatherless and absentee father households are there in America, and throughout the world today?

Did you know that as a husband and a father, the Lord considers you to be the Priest of your household? You are intended to be the spiritual leader. The direction of your family's eternal future rests entirely on your shoulders. Do not be intimidated by this. Your Father is there to help you every step of the way. There is no need to run from your responsibilities. Therefore, I would encourage you to stop dating the Lord and fully commit to Him.

Think about your relationship with the Lord and the role He plays within mankind. Do you honestly believe that He will do any less for you than the imperfect human being you call your father, regardless of how good or bad he is, or was? Perhaps you never knew your father. Many of you may even have had a father who abandoned, or, even, abused you.

Yahweh is incapable of such horrific acts. The role of a loving, providing, Father is the exact relationship He wants to have with you. He *"will never leave you nor forsake you."* (Deuteronomy 31:8 & Matthew 21:20) It brings Him pleasure to provide for you (Luke 12:32). It is His desire to be a protector to you (Psalm 91) and He so ardently wants to be intimate with you that He will penetrate your spirit and become one with you, when and if you allow Him (John 14:20). The secret of the Ancient of Days is that *He is the perfect Father and husband.*

We Become One

All He asks in return is for you to be in unity with Him—to be His physical body in the natural realm. That is why He gave Adam dominion and authority over the earth. It is also why He endued you with the same potential. You are His helpmeet, as well as, His agent upon planet earth. He wants you to respond to His love by obeying His will. By the power of the Holy Spirit, He wants you to be His advocate in the physical realm and to usher in His earthly Kingdom, while at the same time rescuing His beloved children from eternal destruction.

Yes, He does understand that you may be just getting to know Him. He will give you time and earn your trust. In fact, if you remember our discussion from *God Culture* regarding covenant, this is the exact process we saw in Abraham's life. It took time for Abraham to move beyond a promise and into covenant with the Lord. A period of so called "dating" is certainly appropriate.

However, you must take the relationship forward. He wants you to commit as a husband would to his bride. You were never intended just to be a girlfriend to Him. Because He is fully committed to *you*, He wants *your* commitment as well. When you finally submit to His will, He will give you the keys to the kingdom and all that it entails. Yes, being one with Yahweh comes with extraordinary benefits. Benefits greater than any you could ever obtain from natural employment.

Friend with Benefits

Therefore, let's have a look at some of the benefits of being espoused to the Almighty.

> *"Bless the Lord O my soul and all that is within me, bless His holy name!*
> *Bless the Lord O my soul and forget not **all His benefits.**"*
> **—Psalm 103:1–2**

The benefits of the Lord are unsearchable. His riches are priceless. As His espoused covenant partner, which is what a marriage partner is, you have a God given right to receive them. Do you understand the intimacy of marriage? God's relationship with you is a pattern of how you are to treat your earthly spouse.

So called "friends with benefits," which have nonchalantly become far too common in our progressively modern culture, or any form of fornication for that matter, which is pre-marital sex, is a perversion of the marriage covenant. There is no commitment in it.

Science has recently discovered that sex stimulates the release of two chemicals in the brain, vasopressin and oxytocin. The reaction causes an increase in dopamine levels which actually causes two people to become addicted to one another. In essence, like the first thing a duckling sees when emerging from its egg, sex imprints you to your partner. This is why you hear of so many people voluntarily participating in destructive relationships, unwilling, and perhaps, even, unable to escape the abuse. As onlookers we sit back and wonder, why don't they just leave? The answer is vasopressin, oxytocin and dopamine. Like a heroine addict unable to kick the habit, fornication has set the hook.

God, having created humanity, and as such, having full knowledge of our chemical processes, knew the unwanted result would always be a broken heart so intensely scarred that it takes a lifetime to heal—if it ever does. Thus, he prohibits premarital sex and declared marriage to be between *one* man and *one* woman. As always, with the progression of modern science we discover that God's restrictions are always for the benefit humanity. So let's spend some time discussing what you are entitled to as the Lord's covenant partner and the secret to receiving and responding to them.

Your Benefits Package

Let's begin with Psalm 103. The following verses list six benefits every believer is entitled to as a child of the King. Take note of what is contained within the following scripture. I have numbered them for your convenience:

"Bless the Lord, O my soul and forget not all His benefits: 1) Who forgives all your iniquities 2) Who heals all your diseases 3) Who redeems your life from destruction 4) Who crowns you with loving-kindness and tender mercies 5) Who satisfies your mouth with good things, so that 6) your youth is renewed like the eagles."
—Psalm 103:3–5

First and foremost, as a believer in Jesus Christ, your sin, as well as your sins, have been forgiven. What is the difference? Your sin, singular, is the nature you have been born with. You can blame Adam for that; you inherited it from him. Your sins, plural, are those hideous little acts *you* commit that are against God's will, or the righteous acts that you *omit* due to your slothful and apathetic nature. Do not blame anyone else for that one. It's all you!

In truth, what God considers to be sinful may not be so abominable in the eyes of most men. As an example, not believing in Him is the worst possible act you could possibly commit. God considers it to be unbridled evil. Hebrews 3:12, states the following, *"Take heed, brethren, lest there be in any of you **an evil heart of unbelief**, in departing from the living God."*

You may not even be hurting anyone, but the truth is, without belief in Yahweh and His plan for salvation, which is Jesus Christ crucified, He cannot forgive your sin. It is not that He does not want to. God is not being pigheaded or stubborn. Without Jesus Christ, you remain bound to the law which leads to the curse of spiritual death imputed by the realization of sin.

The secret of unbelief is that *you do not have to be a murderer or a rapist to find yourself in hell.* Simply ignoring God will suffice. At the very moment you turn back to Him, however, He will freely and lovingly forgive your sin—immediately, and without even a single question.

You must gain an understanding of this benefit in order to walk in the goodness of God. Any other thought process takes you down the road of condemnation and renders you powerless in His kingdom.

> *"There is therefore now* **no condemnation** *for those that are in Christ, who do not walk according to the flesh, but according to the Spirit. For the law of the Spirit* **has made me free** *from the law of sin and death."*
> **—Romans 8:1–2**

Walk in the Spirit

As we have already learned from previous writings, sin enslaves you. It places you under the authority of, and binds you together, with death. Death is the only fruit that sin *can* produce and sin is the only fruit your *flesh* can produce. (James 1:15 and Romans 6:23) That is why salvation can be garnered by none other than Jesus Christ. (Acts 4:12) Every religion requiring the works of the flesh to lead you down the path of salvation simply binds you together with sin. It is impossible to avoid. We are all fallen.

Because *"all have sinned and fall short of the glory of God,"* (Romans 3:23) your good works will always be accompanied by an indeterminable number of bad works. In truth, the number one, with regard to unrighteous acts of the flesh, is far too many. One mere act of breaking God's holy law renders one guilty, and therefore, condemned. Think about that. One mere sin creates a mountain of condemnation so insurmountable that it cannot be scaled, regardless of the number of works any mere mortal can muster.

Therefore, salvation can only exist by being released from the works of the flesh. To my knowledge, such liberty exists in only one place—Jesus Christ. When you place your trust in Him you are separated from your sin and reconnected to the Spirit of God where sin cannot possibly propagate. Jesus Christ nullifies the law.

Therefore, as the above scripture states, if you find yourself continuing in sin it is simply a matter of fact that you are not walking in the Spirit. You may have accepted Jesus Christ, but you are yet to live His life in you. As a result, you remain enslaved by the death producing fruit of sin, which effectuates fear, anxiety, depression, lust, greed and every form of corruption you can imagine. Although you may even believe that you are in Christ, you have been deceived. You have been imprisoned with no hope of ever gaining the key of absolution. Submission to Jesus Christ is not a suggestion. It is even more than a command, it is a covenant with the King of all kings.

When you finally do submit, however, the Lord causes you to live your life according to the law of Jesus Christ. You become a new creation, completely free from the laws of sin and death. (2 Corinthians 5:17) The prison doors are opened and you are set free. Therefore, *"it is the Spirit Who gives life, the flesh profits nothing,"* (John 6:63) and *"where the Spirit of the Lord is there is liberty."* (2 Corinthians 3:17)

The beauty of the aforementioned benefit is the forgiveness of what is termed to be iniquities, as well. Not only does Jesus pass over your sin(s), He forgives your iniquities. The term iniquity, as translated from Hebrew, means perversion. According to Noah Webster, the word "pervert," means to cause to turn away from what is right, proper or good. In other words, sin has perverted your nature. You were not born good, nor can you become good apart from Jesus Christ.

> *As it is written: "There is none righteous, no, not one; there is none who understands;*

*There is none who seeks after God. They have all turned aside; they have together become unprofitable; **there is none who does good, no, not one.** "*

—Romans 3:10–12

The benefit of forgiveness does not just include forgiveness of the act of turning from God. It includes forgiveness of the root cause of deviating from God, which is *you* and all of your unrighteousness. It is your flesh, acting out *your* will which causes you to turn away from the only thing that is incorruptibly good in the universe, almighty God.

Any time you turn away from Him you have committed a perverted act of sin. Sin by its very essence and definition simply means to "miss the mark." The measure you have missed is that which is right with God. This in turn causes you to be guilty of the sin of perversion against God, which brings with it the sentence of capital punishment. If you die in your sin you *will* be put to death.

Not As You Please

Thank God for Jesus Christ who has pardoned you. Thus, the benefit of forgiveness obtains freedom. In Christ, we have been pardoned and thus, have been granted the freedom to live for eternity.

*"Then Jesus said to those Jews who believed Him, 'If you abide in My Word you are My disciples indeed. And you shall know the truth and **the truth shall make you free . . .**' 'Most assuredly I say to you, whoever commits sin is a slave of sin. And a slave does not abide in the house forever, but a son abides forever. **Therefore if the Son makes you free you shall be free indeed.**'"*

—John 8: 31–32 and 34b–36

With that said, you must gain an understanding of this important concept. Freedom does not mean you can do whatever you want. That will only lead you right back into the bondage of sin. The secret of the freedom granted by your life in Christ means that *you now have the liberty to operate freely in the kingdom of God,* which as defined earlier, is the realm of the Spirit. Incredibly, it is spiritual freedom that garners your earthly freedom. Complete freedom from the law is what delivers you from bondage.

When you walk in the Spirit, which is faith in Christ, you no longer have to fulfill the lusts of the flesh. As a result, you are now free to apply the knowledge, power and authority of God Almighty in your life, as well as, in the lives of all those you come into contact with. You become limitless in your potential and without boundaries. Sin no longer shackles you. You have been delivered from its effects.

As previously stated, however, our newfound freedom is not for the purpose of doing whatever we want. Grace liberates us from our singular earthly desires and gives us the supernatural ability to convey the complete and perfect will of God. Do not feel as if God is trying to take something from you. His will is to give everything His kingdom possesses *to* you. When you become one with Him, *His* desire will become *your* desire, and *His* desire is for you to abide with Him in eternity.

Health Insurance

Benefit number two is Holy Ghost health insurance. *"He heals all our diseases."* I know what your foremost doubt is going to be. You have been programmed to believe this way from the time you were born. "But the Lord does not heal everyone. I prayed for so and so, and they did not get healed." That, in fact, may be true, but it does not mean that Psalm 103:3, *"He heals all our diseases,"* is any less true.

Let's have a look at the word disease. When broken down to its roots, it reads as follows: dis-ease. The prefix "dis" means *"not,"* and the word "ease" means the *freedom from labor, pain, or physical annoyance; tranquil rest; comfort: freedom from concern, anxiety, or solicitude; a quiet state of mind: freedom from difficulty or great effort; facility: freedom from financial need; freedom from stiffness, constraint, or formality.*

Now every place you see the word "freedom" within the above definition, change it to "not free," or "enslaved by," which incorporates the prefix, "dis." As you will see, "disease" involves much more than an illness of the body, such as the physical breakdown of an organ. It may involve a breakdown of your entire spirit, soul, *and* body, thus causing you to be bound in some form, or, as otherwise stated, "not free." In fact, spiritual infirmity quite possibly may lead to physical ailments of the body. Listen to what the Word of God says about simply receiving communion in an unworthy manner, meaning without examining one's own heart.

> *"Therefore whoever eats this bread or drinks this cup of the Lord in an unworthy manner will be guilty of the body and blood of the Lord. But let a man examine himself, and so let him eat of the bread and drink of the cup. For he who eats and drinks in an unworthy manner eats and drinks judgment to himself, not discerning the Lord's body. **For this reason many are weak and sick among you, and many sleep (died)."***
> **—1 Corinthians 11:27–30**

The problem is that we walk only according to what we can see. In essence, we engage the manifestation and not the cause. Our dependence is focused solely upon eliminating the symptom. Usually through our doctors and/or our bank accounts, and rarely, if ever, by discovering the root cause of the issue.

Whether spiritual, physical or emotional in its nature, this usually leads to the ingestion of some form of narcotic in an attempt to cover the symptom. This, however, does not eliminate the root cause. The symptom is not where the the problem lies. The symptom simply makes one aware of the problem. It is a means of recognition, not the source of the cure.

Therefore, when you enter into God's covenant and not just a dating relationship, His resurrection power will be the only medicine you need. God is the source of all life. Of course He can heal your disease. The Spirit of God can even overcome death. Disease is, therefore, no problem for God. He *will* heal you from *all* of the aforementioned disorders. The question is, do you trust Him enough to lay down your physical life. Until you do, your bank account will be your god.

I find it interesting that the majority of miracles occur where people have no health insurance, or where people have no money in their bank accounts—if they even have bank accounts. When God is all you have, who else can you depend on? Who else can you trust? If I do not have health insurance or access to a doctor, I only have two choices. I can remain ill or I can rely upon God to be my medicine.

A dear friend of mine recently asked our congregation if they truly believed they could feed our entire congregation with one loaf of bread and a few fish. While several reluctant hands went up, the keyword here being reluctant, the rest simply stared at him like a deer caught in the headlights. After an uncomfortable pause, he truthfully stated that it is impossible. Why? Contrary to your immediate thought, the reason is not due to one's lack of faith. It is because you can open your wallet and buy food. Therefore, you do not need to rely upon God to provide the miracle. My friend, God's supernatural strength begins where ability runs out. Functioning in the realm of the Spirit requires that God be the *only* source of your deliverance. Luxury is not just a major hindrance to experiencing the power of God, it is often times the death of it.

> "Then Peter said, 'Silver or gold I do not have, but what I do have I give you. In the name of Jesus Christ of Nazareth, walk.'"
> **—Acts 3:6**

Our health insurance seems to cut God out of the equation. In truth, we simply have not allowed God access into this area of our life and thinking. When you make Him your doctor, your psychiatrist, chiropractor, etc . . . He will deliver upon His promise.

Do not get me wrong, I believe in doctor's and I believe in taking care of one's health. Where doctor's have failed, however, God has been a continuous source of healing in my life, both physically and emotionally. Just like any treatment or medicine, God does not always heal in an instant. You need to periodically take your medication, which requires dedication to the Word and Spirit of God.

Sometimes healing requires a process. Sometimes it is instantaneous. Sometimes you may even be on medication for a lifetime. This is not bothersome to me. I intend to be on the Word of God forever anyway. Ingesting the Word of God is a lifetime commitment. Ultimately, however, if God decides to call you into eternity, that is His business and decision. Until Jesus returns, we are all headed to the grave at some point. The good news is that all those who die in Christ are going to receive a new body upon the resurrection.

Nullified

Benefit number three, is the redemption of your life from destruction. I will never forget being seventeen years old, drunk, and riding in the passenger seat of my best friends Formula 400 death machine—doing about seventy-five in a fifty mile per hour zone and never even slowing down through a series of about eight traffic lights. By all rights, I should have either died that evening or wound up in jail for the killing of an innocent soul, or souls, with the projectile weapon known as an automobile in the hands of an intoxicated driver. Either way, whether through death or the tragedy of a young life confined to prison, my life should have ended that night—but it did not!

I have often thought about that night and many others like it in the thirty-five years or so that have since elapsed. My only explanation is that the Lord had always been showing me the grace and mercy of benefit number three. He had, and always has, redeemed my life from destruction. Let's examine what that means.

The word "redeem," means "to buy back." You may ask, "Bought back from what?" Before we can understand all that entails, let's look at what we have been redeemed from—destruction. The word "destroy," is defined as follows: *to reduce (an object) to useless fragments, a useless form, or remains, as by rending, burning, or dissolving; injure beyond repair or renewal; demolish; ruin; annihilate; to put an end to; extinguish, to kill; slay; to render ineffective or useless; nullify; neutralize; to defeat completely.*

What I find interesting is that only the words "demolish," and "annihilate," connote our view of what destruction actually means. Redeeming our lives from destruction does not only mean that we have been saved from certain physical and spiritual death. It contains so much more and gives us tremendous insight into God's ultimate purpose for our lives. What I am referring to is the words "useless" and "ineffective."

When I was driving around drunk or getting high, or perhaps something as simple as not serving the Lord, I was completely useless to God. By living in sin, and that does not only mean living together with someone before marriage, I had been rendered ineffective. I was nullified and neutralized—completely defeated by the enemy of our souls, Satan—and I was happy to participate.

Ambassadors

Without ever realizing it, I was already in a state of destruction. I was born that way. We all are. It is the side effect of the condition known as sin. Thank God He is not satisfied with having His creation in a useless state of existence. That is not what we were created for. We were created to serve both God and man. We have been created for greatness—to serve as Yahweh's ambassador to the world.

> *"Now then, we are ambassadors of Christ, as though God were **pleading** through us: **we implore** on Christ's behalf, **be reconciled to God.**"*
> —2 Corinthians 5:20

Can you hear the desperation in God's voice? Don't you find it amazing that God is pleading for you to come to your senses? Is that the sound of an impersonal and heartless God, as so many in the world have been duped into believing? Yahweh desperately longs for your return. Is that the nature of an ogre, or some existential, emotionless, floating energy source? To assure you receive your invitation into His everlasting kingdom, God has appointed other families members to secure your rescue.

According to the above scripture, when we are in Christ we become ambassador's to a dying world. Do you know what an ambassador is? It is *a diplomatic official **of the highest rank**, sent by **one sovereign**, or state, to another, as its resident representative; a diplomatic official **of the highest rank** sent by a government to represent it **on a temporary mission, as for negotiating a treaty.***

This is what you have been created to be. This is who you become when you make Christ your Lord and Savior. God wants to use you to plead with a lost world on His behalf. He is begging mankind to make a peace treaty with Him and He wants to use you as His emissary to accomplish the mission.

When you make Jesus your Lord you will be redeemed, or repurchased, from *something* which has been rendered completely useless to God, to *someone* who is the highest ranking official within the governmental rule of Yahweh. Apart from the King Himself, that makes you the highest official in the universe. Are you still afraid of the devil? Your mission is to aid the King of all kings, who presides over the most powerful government in all of creation, in the redemption of mankind—one person at a time. You are

His diplomat sent to negotiate the treaty signed by the blood of Christ for the redemption of humanity.

The beauty is that God has created you to do it in a manner that is unique to the incredible gifts he has placed only within *you*. You will reach people that only *you* can reach and as time draws to a close, the mission is nearly complete. Once the Lord returns, He will usher in His one thousand year reign on the same earth in which we now live. I do not know about you, but I find this to be of an incredibly exciting nature. You thought serving the Lord was going to be boring? Game on brothers and sisters!

While obeying His will, He bestows His fourth benefit by *"crowning you with loving kindness and tender mercies."* Think back for one second to what you just read. You read that you have been appointed as an ambassador, the highest ranking official, who has been sent on a governmental mission. Who is the second highest ranking official in any monarchy? and make no mistake, the kingdom of Yahweh *is* a monarchy. We do not get an equal vote on the outcome. It has already been determined. In other words, who is next in line to be king—or queen, for that matter? It is the prince or princess. It is those who are born into the bloodline of the king.

Guess what my friend? When Jesus is your Lord you are wearing the crown. In Christ, you become part of the "bloodline." You have been "born again" by the blood of the Lamb into the family of God. He "grafts" you into the vine of Israel and you become the direct descendant of Jesus Christ. You have been *"born of water and the Spirit."* (John 3:5) You are a prince, or a princess, of Almighty God.

Along with any crown comes power and authority. Therefore, He crowns you with His love, kindness and tender mercy. He expects you to do the same to all whom you meet. He has given you His authority to show—let me rephrase that, to do, and to love, to be kind, to be tender, and to be merciful to all whom you meet.

Fly Like an Eagle

Finally, *"He satisfies your mouth with good so that your youth is renewed like the eagles."* Have you ever seen an old eagle? I just saw a bald eagle in nature for the first time. It was majestic. Do you know what? I have no idea how old it was. All I could tell was that the eagle was soaring amongst the clouds, majestic in nature, swift and bold in flight, and absolutely unmatched in the animal kingdom. Whether it was young or old never occurred to me, nor did it matter.

Many people have never actually *seen* a Bald Eagle in real life? I am not talking about on television, in books, or even in a zoo. Have you ever seen one with your own eyes in nature? It is unparalleled in its freedom as it soars amongst the clouds, majestically gliding along the thermals.

The truth is, unless you were as fortunate as I was, or you are one of the few who live in areas where they are somewhat common, spotting an eagle is pretty rare. In fact, at one point in time the magnificent Bald Eagle was in danger of extinction. I have often times felt the true believer in God Almighty was suffering the same fate. Just like Elijah, however, I know I am wrong about that. God has set aside a remnant. He always does.

Tell me the truth. Do you believe God is out to benefit you? Has He satisfied your mouth with good? Step back for a moment and consider your speech. What is coming from your mouth? Is it good or is it unbelief and perversion? I challenge you to take note of your words.

For your youth to be renewed, your mind must be renewed. *"But be transformed by the renewing of your mind."* (Romans 12:2) Unfortunately, or fortunately, depending upon your perspective, your mind cannot be renewed until your mouth is renewed. *"My son, give attention to my words; incline your ear to my sayings. Do not let them depart from your eyes; keep them in the midst of your heart; **for they are life to those who find them, and health to all their flesh.**"* (Proverbs 4:20–22)

What comes from your mouth is what comes from your heart. You must transform your heart by renewing your mind. You must renew your mind by satisfying your mouth with the Word of God, and not evil and perversion. In doing so, He brings health to all your flesh, thus renewing your youth.

These are just some of the benefits of becoming the covenant partner of Yahweh and not just some casual acquaintance that comes to Him in jest. It is time to stop dating. No more living together with God. He has been courting you, and, therefore, I encourage you to become one with Him. You will never regret it.

My friend, I have a secret.

"Your husband is your Maker, the Lord of Hosts is His name."
—Isaiah 54:5

---------- CHAPTER 14 ----------

The End Times

(THE SECRET OF PROPHECY)

Are we in the end times? Asking the question is not a debasement of faith. It is a legitimate question, and even more so, a very real concern. Refusal to *recognize* the signs of the times, however, is another story. Voluntary blindness is an act of hypocritical rebellion. (Matthew 16:1–4) In truth, every generation of disciples for the last two thousand years has expected the appearing of the Messiah. Yet, Jesus continues to tarry. Does His delay reduce the authenticity of His claim? Is the second coming of Jesus Christ a hoax? To the contrary, and like so many of the secret's we have recently learned, the exact date and time of His appearing is merely a secret of the Father.

"But of that day and hour no one knows, not even the angels of heaven **but My Father only."**
—**Matthew 24:36**

It is not that our Father has forgotten. Due to His merciful nature, the Lord is incessantly longsuffering and merciful, not wanting anyone to perish. The Lord God desperately awaits your turning.

"The Lord is not slack concerning His promise, as some men count slackness; but is longsuffering toward us, **not willing that any should perish,** *but that* **all** *should come to repentance."*
—**2 Peter 3:9**

Did you notice that the above scripture proclaims that God is not willing for *any* of His beloved children perish? Our spiritual demise is not His desire, nor His will. Think about it, if the Lord were to return at this very moment nearly 5 billion people, assuming all those professing the name of the Lord are genuine, would be damned to the Lake of Fire. The real number is probably closer to 6.5 billion. Therefore, out of love our heavenly Father patiently waits. Out of mercy, He delay's His return.

As He does, He prods us along, using the circumstances of life to point us in His direction. In love, He does not leave us lost in the woods of the world with no pathway home. Like a trail of breadcrumbs and broken branches in the forest, His Word acts as a sign post to guide us through the wilderness of life. Our ultimate destination is the heavenly abode prepared for us in eternity.

Ascertaining Him, however, requires both faith and knowledge. We must learn to distinguish the secret pathway of His Word amidst the chaos of everyday life. As we do, His hand over creation becomes readily apparent.

Therefore, to discover the truth of His coming kingdom, let's have a look at the signs of the times in which we now live.

The Prophets of Old

To begin, I would like to take you on a journey into the ancient past to gaze upon the visions communicated to several of the prophets of old. As you are about to witness, when viewed from the hindsight of technological advancement, these visions prove to be absolutely astounding. They are more than just breadcrumbs and sign posts. They are as megaphone's, or to use the ancient biblical narratives, they are trumpet blasts through the deafening silence of a muddled world.

As you read what follows, keep in mind that modern technology was not just lacking at the time the visions were recorded; the idea of what we have accomplished was beyond all the ancients *"could ask or even think."* (Ephesians 3:20) Therefore, the ancients did not possess the language to support what the prophet was actually witnessing. Still, the archaic visions you are about to discover are not just uncanny; from the 20/20 vision of modern-day hindsight they are astounding. They are as clear as crystal.

Nahum's Chariots

Let's begin with the Old Testament prophet Nahum. The vision you are about to witness is simply breathtaking. When seen from a modern-day point of view, it could not have come from anyplace except the mind of Yahweh. To discover just a smidgen the Bible's incredible prophetic foresight, let's take some time and go *Back to the Future.*

> *"The shields of his mighty men are made red, the valiant men are in scarlet. The chariots come **with flaming torches** in the day of his*

*preparation, **and the spears are brandished.** The chariots rage in the streets, **they jostle one another in the broad roads; they seem like torches**, they **run like lightning.***
—**Nahum 2:3–4**

Keep in mind that Nahum is witnessing a future event. Although God is showing him the destruction of Nineveh, I believe He is also showing Nahum the future of technology in the times of the end. In Nahum's day, the concept of the automobile, the internal combustion engine, the harnessing of electricity and the speeds at which man can be transported in our modern day "chariots," was unfathomable.

Therefore, they did not possess words like, automobiles, exhaust systems, and the like. Gentleman such as Swiss engineer François Isaac de Rivaz, Karl Benz, Henry Ford, and even Thomas Edison were yet to exist. Hence, there were no break-lights or headlights on a chariot. The prophets of old could only describe what they were seeing with readily available language, using words such as "chariot," "torch" or even "lightning" to describe the incredible sights they were witnessing.

That, therefore, begs the question; what did Nahum see? To gain understanding of this astounding vision of the future, let's take a look at Nahum's chariots. For clarity, I will begin by working backwards within the vision. What you are about to witness is the ancient past manifested in the world we currently live.

*"They **seem like** torches, they **run like lightning.***"
—**Nahum 2:4**

Notice that Nahum did not say, "They *are* torches," or, "They *have* torches." He said, "They *seem* like torches." The word translated as "seem" comes from the Hebrew word, *"mar'eh"* and it means, an "appearance," "shape," or "comeliness." In other words, the scripture says the chariots "appear" to be like torches and "run," (Hebrew word *"ruts"*) which means to "dash," like lightning.

As stated earlier, Nahum did not possess the linguistic capability to describe in exact detail what he was witnessing. Yet, after careful study I believe he somehow managed to get pretty darn close. Indeed, he nailed it on the head. Keep in mind that ancient Hebrew contained roughly eight thousand words at the time of Nahum's vision. If you compare that to the estimated forty-five thousand words modern Hebrew possesses today, the archaic language becomes clearly understandable. As you will see, Nahum's vision, as well as, Daniel's and several others, were incredibly accurate.

Modern English, by the way, contains just over one million words. Most do not realize that as technology progresses, so does language. The word "computer," for example, is a fairly recent addition. You can now "Google" anything you want and everyone on the planet knows what you are referring to. There were nearly one thousand new words added to the Oxford Dictionary in 2015 alone. Therefore, the vision was unlike anything Nahum could accurately describe with regard to the mechanical technology of his day.

Consider what is required to propel our modern day chariots, which, undoubtedly, would appear to be as swift as lightning to the ancients—the internal combustion engine. Is it possible that Nahum was describing a modern day automobile or aircraft and that which is expelled from the exhaust system? When you view a torch, they produce flame and smoke. In the case of many high performance vehicles, such as race cars, as well as, the modern-day fighter jet, you can actually see the flames erupting from the exhaust.

As I was driving last evening, however, it really hit me. As I was approaching a construction zone the masses of traffic simultaneously hit their break lights. In the midst of the chaos a massive flash of crimson illuminated the night sky. As streams of light illuminated my vehicle from every direction, I believe I saw an integral part of Nahum's vision. We have harnessed lightning in a bottle. Modern man has mastered electricity.

As the cars *jostled* their way through the muddled chaos, and with their head, tail and break-lights ablaze as far as the eye could see, *"they seemed like torches."* As the congestion dissipated and the motorists engaged the throttles of their flame powered chariots, *"they ran like lightning."* Then, in an instant, with the thunderous roar of a thousand "hooves" pounding the earth, the blazing chariots were gone.

As incredible as that vision is, there is much more. Do not forget that *"the spears are brandished."* Consider today's modern military vehicle as compared to a chariot. From a moving chariot you could merely toss a singular spear or shoot a lone arrow. It was hit or miss. The pneumatic tire was yet to exist. There were no suspension systems to stabilize your ride and smooth out the imperfections of the landscape. Today's military weapons are technological wonders. In addition to nearly flawless accuracy they can launch endless rounds of ammunition as the modern day spears known as bullets, missiles, etc... annihilate the enemy. Yes, *"the spears are brandished."* I have no doubt that Nahum witnessed the incredible technology employed at the end of days.

The Day of the Lord

If you are as amazed by Nahum's prophetic vision as I am, the following revelation gets even better. In the following passage we will have a look at a vision that is specifically identified as "The Day of the Lord." This, by definition, is the time of the Lord's coming. In that day, the Lord has committed to judging sin and eradicating evil. Therefore, let's have a look at this incredible vision of the future by the Prophet Joel. If I am correct, Joel was witnessing our present-day world.

"Blow the trumpet in Zion, and sound an alarm in My holy mountain! Let all the inhabitants of the land tremble; for the day of the Lord is coming, for it is at hand: A day of darkness and gloominess, a day of clouds and thick darkness, like the morning clouds spread over the mountains."

"A people come, great and strong, the like of whom has never been; nor will there ever be any such after them, even for many successive generations."

"A fire devours before them, and behind them a flame burns; *the land is like the Garden of Eden before them, and behind them a desolate wilderness; surely nothing shall escape them.* ***Their appearance is like the appearance of horses;*** *and like swift steeds, so they run.* ***With a noise like chariots, over mountaintops they leap,*** *like the noise of a flaming fire that devours the stubble, like a strong people set in battle array.*

"Before them the people writhe in pain; *all faces are drained of color. They run like mighty men, they climb the wall like men of war; every one marches in formation, and they do not break ranks. They do not push one another; every one marches in his own column.* ***Though they lunge between the weapons, they are not cut down.*** *They run to and fro in the city, they run on the wall; They climb into the houses,* ***they enter at the windows like a thief."***

"The earth quakes before them, the heavens tremble; the sun and moon grow dark, and the stars diminish their brightness. *The Lord gives voice before His army, for His camp is very great; For strong is the One who executes His word. For the day of the Lord is great and very terrible; Who can endure it?"*

—Joel 2:1–11

Let's break down this vision of what can only be described as modern-day warfare.

> **"A fire devours before them, and behind them a flame burns;** *the land is like the Garden of Eden before them, and behind them a desolate wilderness."*

The vision Joel has seen is not just a slash and burn technique. It is utter destruction. In fact, it is so precise that Joel may even be describing today's modern day smart bombs that are so accurate when guided by laser technology and GPS, that they *"enter at the windows like a thief."*

The destruction laid waste by this army is indescribable. It is so great that Joel uses the term "devour." The enemy is not just destroyed, they are swallowed up. It must be noted additionally that this fire *precedes* the onslaught of the soldiers being sent to the battlefield. In Joel's day, this was an impossibility. The only way to set the land ablaze was to enter the land and torch it while you were presently there. To succeed required an army.

That is not the case in Joel's vision. In the above account it appears more as if the land is being carpet bombed in preparation of attack. This is a 20–21st century tactic. The technology to do so was impossible prior to air travel. That begs the question, why assume air travel is involved?

> *"With a noise like chariots,* **over mountaintops they leap."**

As noted above, the technological terms of today were unavailable to Joel. Therefore, he had to describe what he was seeing using the language and descriptive terms available in his day. Once again, we see the usage of the term, *"chariots."*

These "noisy" chariots, however, have the ability to leap over mountaintops! There is no doubt that the prophet Joel was witnessing modern-day warfare and the miracle of flight. Incredibly, Joel's vision even surpasses Nahum's vision in technological wonder.

As wondrous as the translation mountaintop is, the word translated as "mountaintop" does not do justice to what Joel had witnessed. "Mountaintop" comes from the Hebrew word, *"Har."* Not only does it mean "hill" or "mountaintop," it can also mean the entire "hill country!" Joel's incredible leaping chariot's had the technological capability not just to bound over mountains, but to transverse the entire hill country. Joel's chariots could fly!

Why then, didn't the translators use the phrase "hill country?" Think about it. What translator would have ever gotten away with it at the time the Bible was translated into English? They would have been ridiculed into oblivion and King James may have even taken their heads. Particularly, when you consider that at the time the translation was completed, the year 1611, they too had never seen an airplane.

There is no doubt that the prophet Joel was gazing upon the armies of our modern day, employing airplanes, and by the way these move, helicopters, fighter jets, or both. Interestingly enough, the Hebrew word for "leap" also means "to skip," and/or "to dance."

Several years ago I had the privilege of going to Annapolis, Maryland to watch my daughter compete in the Patriot League Indoor Track and Field Championships. As I was walking down the main drag toward the Naval Academy, I saw something dash past the corner of my eye. It startled me at first. What could have possibly skipped past my field of vision that quickly? About a second later I heard the roar of the jet engine pass by. To my incredible delight, I was also there for the Naval Academy's graduation week and the famed Blue Angel's were bandying about the skies.

As I came nearer to the port of Annapolis I was able to catch a glimpse of the entire sky . . . and there they were. The wondrous Blue Angel's were performing incredible feats of aeronautical acrobatics at mach speeds. The formation's were perfect. Periodically, these incredible aircraft's would break rank and skip off in the opposite direction. Sometimes straight up, sometimes down, to the left, to the right . . . The incredible thing, however, is the absolutely perfect and precise choreography of the aeronautical demonstration's. It was as if they were doing a dance.

Is this what the prophet Joel was witnessing? What else could dance about the skies, leap over mountains, transverse the entire hill country, and devour the land before them. I have no reservation in claiming that Joel's flying chariots undoubtedly brandished Weapons of Mass Destruction hurling death from above upon the defenseless masses below.

These weapons were so powerful and so destructive that *"the earth quakes before them, the heavens tremble; the sun and moon grow dark, and the stars diminish their brightness."* If not modern-day weaponry, what else could have caused the massive explosions that caused the earth to quake and the heavens to tremble? The technology was simply unavailable, and in all honesty, not just unheard of, but incomprehensible in Joel's day. In Joel's vision, as the smoke plumes into a billow, or perhaps, even, a mushroom cloud, the heavens tremble as the sun, moon, and stars appear to be blotted from the sky.

"Before them the people writhe in pain; all faces are drained of color."

In what appears to be a nuclear detonation, those not devoured in the blast zone writhe in pain as the effect of radiation ravishes what is left of their bodies. In the midst of illness and nausea the color drains from their faces as the fallout of judgment is pronounced. *"For the day of the Lord is coming, for it is at hand: A day of darkness and gloominess, a day of clouds and thick darkness,"* has come upon all those who rebel against the Lord.

"For the day of the Lord is great and very terrible; Who can endure it?"
—Joel 2:11

End Time Jet Setters

This brings us to what may be the most incredible vision of all. For this is one that each and every one of we modern-day human beings experience every day of our lives. Let's witness the incredible End of Days vision of the prophet Daniel.

> "But you, Daniel, shut up the words, and seal the book until the time of the end; **many shall run to and fro, and knowledge shall increase.**"
> —**Daniel 12:4**

Prior to speaking this one seemingly insignificant sentence, Daniel received a vision from the Lord regarding the last days. In it, the Father reveals the rise and fall of nations, cultures, and the rise of the infamous beast that will one day rule much of the earth. Daniel sees the anti-Christ. As Daniel is ordered to seal the vision for a later time, the Lord gives him an incredible timeline of when the scroll is to be opened, thus causing these extraordinary secret events to come to pass. The mighty Yahweh echoes, in *"the time of the end; many shall run to and fro, and knowledge shall increase."*

Upon first glance it does not appear to be much. It is not very descriptive when compared to the prior revelations we have witnessed. Without understanding, it can even be categorized as ambiguous or vague. Is it really ambiguous, however? When we step back and analyze what was sealed into the scroll, and when we apply Daniel's vision to our present-day lives we discover something that can only be described as mind boggling.

In Daniel's day, long journeys could be described as nothing less than arduous. They could not just hop in the car, go to the airport, jump on the next available airplane and fly to wherever in the world they wanted to go. In ancient times, you either walked, or at best, went by horse, camel, donkey or ship. These journeys could take days, weeks, or even months.

Needless to say, crossing an ocean was not only perilous, it was nearly impossible.

On nineteen occasions in my life, I have boarded an airplane and flown as far as I could possibly fly without entering the one hundred eighty first degree of the earth's curvature and beginning my return trip home. Each journey required less than a twenty-four hour period. In the incredible times in which we live, we can cross oceans in a matter of hours.

In fact, I recently learned that golfing legend Arnold Palmer holds the speed record for spanning the entire globe in a Learjet—fifty-seven hours, twenty-five minutes and forty-two seconds, a record that still stands to this day. Incredibly, it would have been faster had he not stopped in Sri Lanka for several hours to ride an elephant! We now have the ability to go anywhere in the world we desire; and it is not just me who has the opportunity to do so. In *"the time of the end; **many** shall run to and fro."*

In the 1940's and 1950's, air travel was a luxury of the wealthy. Flights were expensive and far and few in between. In our day, nearly 20,000 flights leave America's busiest airport in Atlanta, Georgia, on a daily basis alone.

On my first trip to Indonesia in 1990, air travel was reserved only for the upper class of society. On my last trip, the flight from Jakarta to Bali was filled with every societal class ranging from the super wealthy to the "lowly" serving class. In fact, it was blindingly obvious that it was the first ever flight for several people as they were completely unable to locate their assigned seats. I recently heard one of Indonesia's wealthy elite complain that they were forced to share their row with one of their maids in coach, a humiliating experience in such a class conscious culture. The first class seats had all been filled.

There has never been a time before us when men can *"run to and fro"* throughout the face of the earth. The end is near and that is only the first half of Daniel's timeline. The second criteria is stated simply as *"an increase in knowledge."*

Consider what the invention of the computer has done for nearly every man, woman and child throughout the globe. It was not long ago that a computer in every household was a pipe dream to an entrepreneurial college dropout named Bill Gates. Nowadays, the average American household contains not just one, but several computers, multiple smart phones, and various other technological devices.

On my last trip around the globe, I brought two computers, a smart phone, an iPad and a hot spot, just so I could stay in touch with what now has to be the instantaneous customer service required for me to remain competitive in business. On my first trip, I merely brought my luggage. Today you can surf the web on your wristwatch. The knowledge streamed into every home via the internet is simply astounding.

According to *Tap Into Industry Magazine,* prior to 1900 the doubling of the information available to humanity occurred approximately every one hundred years. Today, it is estimated to be every twelve months, and according to the same article, if the Lord tarries, it is soon to be every twelve hours. Knowledge is increasing at the speed of light. As it does, every second that passes brings the return of our Lord closer.

Therefore, let's continue to examine prophecy. Like a living timeline, our Father has left us an unmistakable chain of historical mementos along the pathway of the human experience. With the context of the visions above, let's peer into the future from the perspective of Jesus Christ of Nazareth. Through His eyes, we get more than just a peek at the end. He gives us a strategy to recognize, and thus embrace, the coming of His day.

Not Yet!

"Now as He (Jesus) sat on the Mount of Olives, the disciples came to Him privately, saying, 'Tell us, when will these things

be? And what will be the sign of Your coming, and of the end of the age?'"

*"And Jesus answered and said to them: '**Take heed that no one deceives you.** For many will come in My name, saying, 'I am the Christ,' and will deceive many. And you will hear of wars and **rumors** of wars. See that you are not troubled; for all these things **must** come to pass, **but the end is not yet.** For nation will rise against nation, and kingdom against kingdom. And there will be famines, pestilences, and earthquakes in various places. All these **are the beginning** of sorrows.'"*

—Matthew 24:3–8

Incredibly, of all the topics Jesus could have began with, His primary concern commences with the issue of deception. In particular, He alludes to the religious, or perhaps, even, better stated, the spiritual deception that is so prevalent in our world today. Notice that Jesus did not say, "Many will come in My name saying, *'I am Jesus.'*" He actually said, "Many will come saying, *'I am the Christ.'*"

Think about it for a moment. Anytime someone rises up and says, "I am Jesus," they are immediately dismissed as a nut job—and rightly so. Consider some of the folks who have made this claim: David Koresh, leader of the Branch Davidian's, his followers were later engulfed in flames as then Attorney General, Janet Reno torched their compound, thus, killing everyone inside; Jim Jones, of *The people's Temple,* who led a mass murder/suicide, killing nine hundred eighteen people in the *Jonestown Massacre* in 1978; the Reverend Sun Myung Moon, although he has not killed anyone, he has amassed a fortune from his followers said to be worth several billion U.S. dollars.

Even Charles Manson got in on the act. He then instigated two sets of horrific murders. The first claimed five victims including up and coming actress Sharon Tate. The second took the lives of supermarket executive Leno Labianca and his wife Rosemary. Inspired by *The Beetle's* famous

White Album, the assassin's infamously painted the words *Helter Skelter* at the scene of the crime in the victim's blood. These are merely a few to make the contemptible list of false Jesus'. There were, and will continue to be, countless others.

The devil, on the other hand, is not so stupid. For deception to be effective it must be more than just obscured. At the very least, it must be somewhat believable. Therefore, Jesus being fully aware of Satan's ploy, intentionally clarified that many will claim to be *"the Christ."* I do not believe this is a reference to people claiming to be Jesus. Where is the deception in that? Anyone can open a Bible and discover Satan's ploy. However, a false Christ is another story.

The word "Christ," is the Greek form of the Hebrew word, "Messiah." It actually means "anointed." In ancient Israel, when a leader was chosen the people would anoint that person with oil. In other words, they would pour oil from head to toe over the "chosen one" and symbolically separate them to God. The oil, being poured from the head down was representative of the Holy Spirit. Jesus Christ, means Jesus, "the anointed one," which therefore means; Jesus is the one filled with the power of the Holy Spirit. Like the oil of the anointed, the Spirit of God was in Him, on Him and all around Him.

With that in mind, consider what you hear coming out of the pulpits of the world's churches and ministries on a daily basis. How many preachers claim to be anointed of God? Do we, or even they, realize they are saying, "I am Messiah." Some even claim to be "the anointed," or "the Messiah," over their flock.

I am not saying that they are not. To the contrary, I am certain that many have been chosen by God to lead His sheep. That is between them, God and their congregation. I *am* saying, however, that we, the people in the crowd *must* be extremely selective in whom we follow and must put into practice the spiritual gift of discerning spirits. (1 Corinthians 14) In fact, if we are following anyone other than the true Anointed One, who is Jesus Christ of Nazareth, we have already fallen prey to deception. How many of today's "Christians" are following a church Pastor or ministry leader, and not the Lord?

If something does not seem right, chances are it is not. Therefore, it must be checked against the Word of God. Humanity was never intended to be gullible. We are called to be as *"wise as serpents and as gentle as doves."* (Matthew 10:16) We are to *"test all things, and hold fast to that which is good."* (1 Thessalonians 5:21)

Therefore, *"beloved, **do not believe** every spirit, **but test** the spirits to see **whether they are from God,** for **many false prophets** have gone out into the world."* (1 John 4:1) They still do! It is every Christian's personal responsibility to implement the instruction of God into our lives. We must *"be sober, and be vigilant; because your adversary the devil walks about like a roaring lion, seeking whom he may devour."* (1 Peter 5:8) It is imperative for us to learn how to recognize deception. We live in a world chock full of wolves in sheep's clothing. As Jesus' return draws near the deception of false Christ's will surely intensify leading all the way to the rise of the anti-Christ.

There is, however, one false Jesus that every person must be on the look out for. He is the Muslim version of Jesus who is also scheduled to make his debut. Do not be deceived, however. He is not the real thing. To learn more on this vital topic, I would direct you to Joel Richardson's incredible book entitled, *The Islamic Anti-Christ.* In my opinion, it is a must read for every Christian wanting to prepare for the rise of the Bible's most notorious foe.

How Did He Know?

Incredibly, Jesus' second warning turns to world news. How did Jesus know about the rise of CNN, Fox News, Al Jazeera, and the BBC? How did Jesus know about the 24/7 stream of news entering our living rooms on a daily basis? How did He know that every day of our lives would be filled with *"wars and rumors of wars?"*

Not only has modern day warfare become more frequent, it has become more efficient in its killing. Technology has allowed us to produce Weapons of Mass Destruction that can literally destroy the entire planet, as well as, innumerable masses of people in the twinkling of an eye.

I do not believe Jesus statement was a reference to the number of wars or even the incredible number of deaths, although the 20th century was the bloodiest in history. The key to Jesus' warning is in the phrase, *"rumors of wars."* There have always been wars. That, in and of itself, is not unusual. This, however, is more than humanity experiencing war.

In the end of days mankind can make war simultaneously all over the planet. Of those we do not participate in physically, we can now participate in vicariously. It is now possible both to see and to hear about wars all over the earth. Rumors have become international in their scope. We hear of everything today. Nothing is hidden.

In the Greek language, the word used for rumor means, "to hear." Consider the implication. In ancient times you would have no idea if one nation was warring against the other until the enemy was at the gates or a courier brought back word. That could takes weeks, or even months, assuming he made it back alive.

Back in the day, you could actually implement a successful sneak attack. Today, the rise and implementation of satellite technology allows us to hear of every conflict on the planet as soon as the first ship hits the water or the first plane leaves the runway. In fact, it is even greater than that. Through satellite technology, we can now watch from above as the enemy moves their weapons into position. We can now foresee the *intention* of war.

With the rise of world news in conjunction with the internet, modern man can immediately hear of, and sometimes even witness, every event as they simultaneously unfold. We can obtain information about potential conflicts before they occur. Not only was this technology non-existent in the past, it could not have been comprehended in Jesus' day. Yet, Jesus was able to clearly disclose the future of technology, as well as, the events taking place two thousand plus years later, using only the language and terminology of His day.

If Jesus were not God (we have covered why He could be none other in previous writings), or at the very least, a prophet of God, how did He know? Additionally, and this is directed to all of my atheist friends, if Jesus did not exist, how did this revelation make its way to the pages of the Bible? I do not know of any other book that has made such incredibly accurate predictions. Do you? These are merely a few of roughly two thousand prophetic utterances that have already come to pass. With a mere five hundred yet to be fulfilled, I have no doubt that the end is near.

With that as our reference point, Ephesians 3:20–21 now has new meaning: *"Now to Him who is able to do exceedingly abundantly **above all that we ask or think,** according to the power that works in us, to Him be glory in the church by Christ Jesus **to all generations,** forever and ever. Amen."* God has been doing the unthinkable from time everlasting.

Check Your Twitter Feed

As you will undoubtedly recall, it was only a short couple years ago that the entire Arab Spring was organized, planned and implemented via, believe it or not—Twitter! Talk about rumors. Can you imagine the rumors flying back and forth on a second by second basis while that was transpiring? The Arabian Desert must have been electric. By the time the old regimes, unfamiliar with modern technology, figured out what was going on, it was too late. Anarchy arose in their midst like the sandstorms of legend. The arid regions burst into flames and the old guards were decimated. God is real my friends! Entire governments are collapsing like the walls of Jericho via rumor. But do not fear. The end is not determined by rumor.

Does God's preeminence come as a surprise to you? It should not. Those of us acquainted with God culture should be expecting such events to occur. According to Jesus, it is not just that these things may happen. The events we are witnessing *must* come to pass. They are a part of God's eternal plan.

If you have been wondering why the Lord tarries through all of this, here is the revealing of another secret. *In chaos we desire mercy.* Thankfully, our loving Father is incomparably longsuffering and allows us the opportunity to repent. With more souls to save, the time of the gentiles is not yet fulfilled. (Luke 21:24)

As a believer in Jesus Christ, the events we are witnessing are cause to rejoice. Not due to the people's suffering. No one wants to see that. We rejoice in the opportunity to be a witness to the glory of the Lord that is about to be revealed in the return of the long awaited Messiah.

Although Jesus clearly communicated that the end is not yet, I believe there is very little doubt that we have, at minimum, entered the *"Beginning of Sorrows."* (Matthew 24:7) The 20th century produced two World Wars (Nation rising against nation), the rise of regional global terrorism (Kingdom against kingdom), and unprecedented amounts of bloodshed. Still the question remains; how close are we to the end?

To answer this, let's revisit Matthew 24.

> *"For nation will rise against nation, and kingdom against kingdom. And there will be famines, pestilences, and earthquakes in various places. All these are the beginning of sorrows."*
> *"Then they will deliver you up to tribulation and kill you, and you will be hated by all nations for My name's sake. And then many will be offended, will betray one another, and will hate one another. Then many false prophets will rise up and deceive many. And because **lawlessness will abound, the love***

*of many will grow cold. But he who endures to the end shall be saved. And **this gospel of the kingdom will be preached in all the world** as a witness to all the nations, **and then the end will come."***

—Matthew 24:7–14

If you are like me, that portion of scripture sets your eyes ablaze. It makes me declare the proverbial, O.M.G., what's left to fulfill? Betrayal, hatred, and the false prophets disguised as government and religious leaders have brought the masses to their knees.

When you look around our modern world there is no denying that many are offended by Christianity. The attack on the conservative Christian is clearly evident. The same nation that imprints *"In God We Trust"* on our money is looking to remove any mention of Him from our Pledge of Allegiance. If our allegiance is not to God, who exactly have we pledged our allegiance to? Our money? Agnosticism or atheism? Perhaps, even, Satan? Here is a news flash. The government cannot save your soul. Here is an atheist news flash. You have a soul.

Who is Who?

I find it interesting that America has become much less offended by the religion that slaughtered three thousand U.S. citizens and reduced the symbols of our money god to rubble in the process, than by the Christianity on which the nation's principles were founded. Yet the "Religion of Peace" gets a pass. Why? It is simple. The secret of recognizing the end times is that *lawlessness abounds.* The false prophet Mohammed has deceived billions, literally, and the religious violence so prevalent in the Middle East is beginning to manifest itself all throughout the world. It is a prelude to judgment. It is the beginning of the end. The Islamic Caliphate will be resurrected in fulfillment of the final world kingdom and the last world war focused upon Jerusalem will be the result.

Does it offend you that I used the phrase, "false prophet" when citing Mohammed? Let me explain my reasoning. Most of you have been duped by the media to believe that Christians, Jews and Muslim's all worship the same God. There is a bit of an anomaly here, and I must report that the problem is not with Jehovah.

On the eve of this writing a woman at a metro station in Russia opened a duffle bag, pulled out the bloody, severed head of the four year old child she had been employed to nanny, waved it back and forth before a crowd of stunned onlookers and proclaimed, "Allahu Akbar!" which means, God (Allah) is the greatest. In fact, "Allahu Akbar" is the cry we hear with every murderous act of terrorism perpetrated by Allah and his followers. Why is that a problem?

Many of you have also been misled to believe that such acts of violent jihad is a perversion of the religion finding its root in the pages of the Qu'ran. Was this woman perverting the Religion of Peace? To answer this, take note of the following Qu'ran verse, and keep in mind that there are at minimum 164 others just like it.

> "I am with you: give firmness to the Believers: **I will instill terror** into the hearts of the Unbelievers: **smite ye above their necks** and smite all their finger-tips off them."
>
> **—Qu'ran 8:12**

Not only was she following the command of Allah in conjunction with the actions of the prophet, (which carry equal weight, by the way) she was praising Allah as the greatest of all god's for inspiring her murderous act. As we have already discussed, this is diametrically opposed to the doctrine of Jesus Christ, who proclaimed not only, *"Thou shall not murder,"* (Exodus 20:13) but also commanded us to, ***"Love your enemies and pray for** those who persecute you, **that you may be children of your Father in*** *heaven. He causes His sun to rise on the evil and the good, and sends rain on the righteous and the unrighteous."* (John 5:44–45)

The problem with claiming that we all follow the same God is that He would need to be schizophrenic, hypocritical and a liar for this to be true. So, who is the god that this woman, and all of the jihadist's, are praising as the greatest of all god's? I believe Jesus was crystal clear in His assessment of those perpetrating such malicious acts.

> *"**You are of your father the devil**, and the desires of your father you want to do. **He was a murderer from the beginning**, and does not stand in the truth, **because there is no truth in him**. When he speaks a lie, he speaks from his own resources, **for he is a liar and the father of it.**"*
>
> **—John 8:44**

> *"They will put you out of the synagogues; yes, **the time is coming that whoever kills you will think that he offers God service.**"*
>
> **—John 16:2**

There is no doubt that Jesus saw the future of humanity. Do not forget that this was written some two thousand years ago, six hundred years prior to the rise of those whose service to god is murder—with no mercy toward the unbeliever. Therefore, Yahweh's law, and Yahweh's love cannot possibly be in Allah. That also means that the prophet (Mohammed) who originated such doctrine in both word and deed cannot possibly have come from the same divine source as Jesus Christ of Nazareth, whose divine ability to see the future is undeniable. If you are still unsure, let's compare doctrine's and match them to their proper "God" source. It looks something like this:

Jesus preaches peace and love for everyone and anyone, male or female, Jew or gentile (which includes Muslim's) and all who call upon Him will be saved. Jesus died for you to forgive your sin. When reviled, He never retaliated, nor encouraged His followers to retaliate. When He was violently attacked and eventually crucified as a common criminal, He forgave those who viciously slaughtered Him, even while they were driving the nails through His hands and feet. He perfectly fulfilled God's law and He *"ever lives to make intercession for you."* (Hebrews 7:25) When you receive Him, regardless of what your past looks like, you are guaranteed eternal life. The God we are speaking of is named Jehovah. By the essence of His love, He proves that He is the one and only true and living God.

On the other hand, Mohammed preaches violence and imperialism. He promotes good-will toward Muslim's only. All others are Kafir (unbeliever's, a.k.a., infidel's) and must be eliminated. He backed up his words with his own personal acts of violence and murder. Neither he, nor his god, Allah, died for you and through his own words he incites violence against all non-Muslim's. You must wage jihad and die for *him*. He offers no guarantees of paradise, treats women with contempt and subjects your good and bad deeds to a scale. You must pray for *him* every day of your life, while he offers no assurance of eternal life in return. By his intolerance and insolence toward the people of Jehovah, he proves to be the imposter, the false god Lucifer who deceived one third of the angels of heaven. Today, you also know him as Allah.

With that in mind, can you tell me where I am mistaken? One perfectly fulfilled the law and one defies the law. The conclusion, therefore, is abundantly clear.

Lawlessness

Since lawlessness is a major aspect of the end times, let's, therefore, spend a little time on the definition of lawlessness. We must keep in mind the fact that Jesus' audience in Matthew 24, where we find the discussion, were His Jewish brethren. Therefore, He was not making reference to Roman law, just as we should not make the mistake of basing this prediction upon our own societal laws.

Jesus is making reference to the laws of God, the Pentateuch, to be more precise. With that in mind, consider what is happening in our current societies and cultures. We are experiencing much more than just religious anarchy.

We are witnessing a revolution of the human value system. The Word and ways of God are under attack. *"The kingdom of heaven suffers violence, and the violent take it by force."* (Matthew 11:12) Apart from the rapid rise of radical Islam, homosexuality, for example, is not just running rampant, it is being encouraged by the governments under whose authority we now live. The legalization of same-sex marriage by the United States Supreme Court, as well as, various other once Christian influenced society's and culture's, is just the beginning. Homosexuality is being forced upon the public and "we the people" have cowered from the violent. Sexual deviance has become an epidemic. Pornography is being disseminated at epic proportions and, therefore, sexual sin has been reduced to nothing more than trivial.

The "sexual revolution" has been adopted by children throughout ever regressing age groups. Tragically, it is being cheered on by the likes of Beyonce Knowles, a former church girl who has fallen prey to the seduction and greed of Hip Hop and Hollywood. Incredibly, her pop culture husband not only supports her public display of sexual vulgarity, he flaunts her before the entire world to lust after. He panders her about like a common hooker.

In the early 1960's, Elvis Presley could not even show his gyrating hips on television. They would only film him from the waist up. Today, overt sexuality is applauded. Lawlessness is abounding. Pop culture pimps out the promiscuous darlings of the pornographic Hollywood culture and even Kanye cannot keep up with the Kardashian's. Bruce has run amuck with Cait and a brand new form of public lewdness is gracing our twisted airwaves. Lawlessness does not just abound in modern day society. It has become the norm of our society.

No wonder the Bible and the Torah have been ousted from the public square. Peering into its truth would bring the sinner face to face with the God they so vehemently deny. Someone would actually have to tell the Smith's that there son, Jaden, is living in sin. Check out the following quote from Jaden when asked about his new "love" interest, rapper Lil B; *"I was nervous at first but he broke me right in and now I love getting my pelvic bone pushed back, thank you based God."*

Surely you can see how incredibly perverted this young man has become. Apart from the "pelvic bone" comment, I did not even know what "Based God" meant until I looked it up on *Urban Dictionary.* Its definition is far to vile to repeat here.

Incredibly, however, the battle his mother has chosen to fight is having no black actors nominated for the 2016 academy awards. Her son loves getting his "pelvic bone pushed back" while wearing a dress and a flower in his hair, and she is concerned about the academy awards? Honestly, who cares about Hollywood when your child is self destructing? What about parenting?

Indoctrination is the world's answer and it always starts with the youngest members of society. Jaden is the perfect example of what the fruit of our new found culture produces. I guess it is just easier for his parents to sacrifice him to the gods of homosexuality and fame . . . and they are revered for it. Rather than someone standing up and speaking the truth to them, they have become the darlings of Hollywood.

Have you ever considered why our nation's government's and pop culture's are so desperate to eliminate biblical values? Think about it, what do you think the purpose of any religious upbringing is? If you change the heart of the young, you change the future of the world. When you steal God from the children, and in particular, Jesus Christ, lawlessness is only one generation away. Although their methodologies differ, both Hollywood and ISIS have proven this in less than a decade.

Do not be fooled my friend, it does not require anything nearly as radical as ISIS to change the heart of the masses. Just ask your baby boom, 1960's radical neighbor or government leader. It may even be you. Therefore, just peer into the nearest mirror. Purity has not only been expunged from the Western home, it has also been eradicated from the second most influential aspect of your children's lives—their schools. As evidence of our lewdness, condoms are being distributed by the educational institutions that not only support, but encourage and teach the sexual deviance that is so quickly becoming a major part of the curriculum. In our pop culture society, oral sex is no longer sex, and homosexuality is merely an "alternate lifestyle." I was amazed to recently learn that oral sex is now considered third base!

Our lawless culture has legalized abortion and reduced it to the simplicity of the *Morning After Pill*. Our politicians lie to the public as they slip their hands into your uninformed pockets and commit grand larceny in the name of the "public good." Here is another news flash. *"No one is good but One, that is, God."* (Mark 10:18)

Even our own churches have committed the atrocity of factionalizing the body of Christ, giving place to the devil and eliminating sin from its dialogue. We now have homosexual and lesbian Pastors en masse. It appears that many modern-day churches are nothing more than a congregation of Sunday morning atheists idly gracing the skeletal remains of what was once a living, breathing, church body.

Yes, lawlessness abounds! As the cancer progresses, the love of many has grown cold. The evidence pervades our airwaves on a daily basis as we witness a heartless humanity slaughtering our precious children in their very own classrooms—that is, if they are fortunate enough to make it out of the womb and into our rapidly declining schools. *Planned Parenthood* would much rather suck out their brains, cut them to pieces and profit from the legalized slaughter of the innocents. A baby is not alive until it takes its first breath, right? We are passing our children through the modern-day fire of Molech (Leviticus 18:21) and, therefore, judgment cannot be far off.

On the day of this writing, a disgruntled former newscaster massacred his former colleagues as they broadcast the news on live television. Whatever happened to the good old days when the suicidal killed only themselves? Today's Godless, pop culture politicians and mentally ill, liberal community organizers from both sides of the aisle have devalued humanity to the point of creating a suicidal class of murderers only brave enough to pull the trigger on an unarmed public. Therefore, blame it on the guns. In truth, guns have about as much soul as many of today's Western world leaders that are terrified to mention the name of Jesus, anyway. Do you think the world's Muslim leaders are ashamed of Allah? Something's got to give.

People are shot in movie theatre's, malls, airports, on the streets they live, and sometimes as they sit innocently in their own living rooms. A young girl was recently killed as a stray bullet from the drive-by outside her home transported her to heaven while she innocently sat in her house playing. I could give you a time frame referencing this occurrence, but what would be the point? Pick any day of the week. You will find something similar.

With nearly sixty million innocent babies slaughtered in America's holocaust of abortions, who can deny that the love of many has grown cold. We do not even protect our most valued possession. *"Thou shall not murder"* applies to every human being, especially those who cry out for life from the womb. How did murder become a legalized means of birth control? A baby is not a woman's body any more than your body belongs to *your* mother. A woman's right to choose is merely a lawless society promoting the murder of the defenseless. What differentiates the abortionist from Adolph Hitler? Both dehumanized the innocent to perpetrate the slaughter.

The very same people not just condoning, but promoting this heresy, show up every Sunday and "worship" God for an hour—then nearly panic when they read, *"Not everyone who says to Me, 'Lord, Lord,' shall enter the kingdom of heaven, but he who does the will of My Father in heaven. Many will say to Me in that day, 'Lord, Lord, have we not prophesied in Your name, cast out demons in Your name, and done many wonders in Your name?' And then I will declare to them, 'I never knew you; depart from Me, you who practice lawlessness!'"* (Matthew 7:21–23)

Does the lawless pop culture perform abortions in His name? Do they fornicate in His name, lie, cheat and steal in His name, to satisfy their never ending lust for greed and power? Yes, they do! Incredibly, it is all done in the name of tolerance and progress by church going "Christians." Is that their definition of a wonder? Is killing a baby for comfort their definition of a modern marvel? I would encourage you to wake up before it is too late—before *you* hear the words, *"I never knew you!"*

The Pop Culture Church

For many Christians, Matthew 7:21–23 is the scariest scripture in the entire Bible. For the man seeking self over God, this is as precarious and horrifying as Muhammad's scales. Upon first glance, it appears that we may be unwittingly condemned to hell. If you look closely, however, you will find this scripture contains everything that is happening in today's "pop culture church." Once again, lawlessness is the issue at hand.

The pop culture church loves to prophesy. We love to cast out demons. You can even purchase an "anointed" prayer cloth on television. I saw one preacher fill the alter with the congregation's money and declare, "Money, cometh to me now!" Is that the gospel Jesus died for? Why then when asked for money did Peter proclaim, *"Silver and gold I do not have, but what I do have I give you: In the name of Jesus Christ of Nazareth, rise up and walk."* (Acts 3:6) Wouldn't it have been easier to declare, "Money, cometh to me now!" and fulfill the gentleman's need? Where is that scripture in the Bible? Is that exegeted from deriving the temple tax from the mouth of a fish? (Matthew 17:27) Where does the crucifixion fit into that? Is money the new means of salvation? Think about the absurdity of much of the modern gospel message. It is becoming a hodgepodge of Eastern mysticism and New Age mumbo-jumbo.

As a "church" we love to wave our hands in the air and watch the crowds tumble to the ground. It is not that this practice is inherently bad or evil. It is not. The problem is that while the audience believes they have seen a wonder, nothing really changes. In most cases, when "the believer" gets up off the ground they still refuse to speak the name of Jesus to their next door neighbor. If that is the case, what was the actual purpose of the "manifestation?"

Because the pop culture church is so unfamiliar with scripture, they can only focus upon self-gratification and entertainment. Therefore, all they want to see is what is considered to be glorious, including pulpits that more closely resemble broadway stages than houses of prayer; the vain "prophesying" of charismatic leaders afraid to utter the word "sin;" shallow music, and a plethora of false wonders that usually include the financial prosperity of the "man of God." All too often, it has become all about the "anoin*ting*" and not the One who was "anoin*ted.*" In the pop culture church, entertainment outweighs truth.

The modern day, pop culture church has become nothing more than a self-aggrandizing social club where the true anointing found only in the Anointed One is ceasing to exist. That, my friend, is lawlessness. Jesus never has, and never will, know the pop culture church. Just like the Pharisees of old, it is diametrically opposed to all that Jesus Christ of Nazareth is.

> *"Pride goes before destruction, and a haughty spirit before a fall."*
> **—Proverbs 16:18**

The remnant of true believers does not fear Matthew 7:21–23. What do the *doers* of the Word (James 1:22) see in Matthew 7:21–23? What stands out like a sore thumb to those intimate with the Almighty Creator of the universe, who has made Himself known in the person of Jesus Christ? In other words, what is Matthew 7:21–23 really saying?

The secret is contained in two phrases—*"But he who **does** the will of My Father,"* and *"You who **practice** lawlessness."* These two secret little phrases that have graced your eyes unnoticed are the keys to living your *Best Life Later* in the blessing of Jesus Christ and in the glory of the New Jerusalem, while completely eradicating any fear of falling prey to the Great White Throne judgment.

> *"Then I saw **a great white throne** and Him who sat on it, from whose face the earth and the heaven fled away. And **there was found no place for them**. And I saw the dead, small and great, standing before God, and books were opened. And another book was opened, **which is the Book of Life**. And the dead were judged according to their works, by the things which were written in the books. The sea gave up the dead who were in it, and Death and Hades delivered up the dead who were in them. And they were judged, each one according to his works. Then Death and Hades were cast into the lake of fire. This is the second death. **And anyone not found written in the Book of Life was cast into the lake of fire.***
> **—Revelation 20:11–15**

The Death of Hell

To eradicate the spirit of fear and unlock the secrets to everlasting life, let's examine Matthew 7:21–23 a bit further. Do not forget that *"there is no fear in love; but perfect love casts out fear, because fear involves torment. But he who fears has not been made perfect in love."* (1 John 4:18) Therefore, to get to the bottom of this we must answer the question, what is God's will? As you are about to see, it is much more than healing the sick, performing signs and wonders, giving a prophetic word or living a financially prosperous life. All these things are good, but they are not the Father's ultimate will. They are not the reason God sent His only begotten Son to be tortured and crucified on the cross at Calvary. In fact, much of the fanfare is the counterfeit result of following false Christ's.

Most people never come the realization that the abject destruction of both death and hell is God's ultimate will for both mankind and creation as a whole. In paradise, neither will exist. Jesus's ultimate goal—His primary mission for abdicating glory and suffering a torturous death was to ensure you have the opportunity to to take up residence in heaven. According to Revelation 21, the secret of the second death is *not* the unbeliever being cast into hell. *It is the utter destruction of both death and hell* (also known as Hades). Both will be obliterated from existence! The unbeliever being eradicated by the Lake of fire is the unintended consequence of sin.

*"Then Death and Hades were cast into the lake of fire. **This is the second death."***

—Revelation 20:14

As a consequence of rebellion, the connective phrase "and" joins the unbeliever to the eternal destruction of the lake of Fire. "***And** anyone not found written in the Book of Life was cast into the lake of fire.*" Fire is one of the only forces on earth that can change matter from one form to another. Unfortunately for the unbeliever, it will forever change the miracle of life into the horror of spiritual death, which is the destruction of one's soul from existence. "***Anyone** not found written in the Book of Life was cast into the lake of fire,*" and completely obliterated along with both hell and death.

The Lake of fire is not *synonymous* with hell. It was created for the *destruction* of hell. Unfortunately, or fortunately, depending upon where your eternal destination lies, the inhabitants of hell, which may include our modern-day pop culture church, may face the ultimate consequence, as well.

Show Off!

God's ultimate will for the believer is as follows: *"But, beloved, do not forget this one thing, that with the Lord one day is as a thousand years, and a thousand years as one day. The Lord is not slack concerning His promise, as some count slackness, but is longsuffering toward us, **not willing that any should perish** but that **all** should come to repentance."* (2 Peter 3:8–9)

In one six word phrase, *"not willing that any should perish,"* you will find the summation of the entire will of God where man is concerned. It is the opening act, intermission and finale of the entire production called life. The Bible is the screenplay, Jerusalem is the setting, and Jesus is the star of the show. He is not willing that you, nor anyone else should perish. Your holy Father's sole desire is that you spend an eternity in His presence. Therefore, in order to ensure your place, He will destroy hell along with all of its inhabitants. With rebellion out of the way, life reigns over death. In fact, death ceases to exist.

If that sounds extreme, it is. God was willing to adopt the most extreme measure imaginable. He, Himself died on a Roman cross for your salvation—and all we want to do is *prophesy?!* Oh . . . and demand money from God. How blind are we? How lawless have we become? It is tragic when you think about it.

That leads us to the next logical set of questions. How do we accomplish God's will, and why did Jesus oust these folks from His presence? It certainly appears that they were doing the work of the ministry. Weren't they? If we look at the context of Jesus's message, the answer is no. Let's revisit Matthew 7.

"Not everyone who says to Me, 'Lord, Lord,' shall enter the kingdom of heaven, but he who does the will of My Father in heaven."

—Matthew 7:21

Have you ever known anyone who consistently lives their lives saying one thing but when push comes to shove they do another? Perhaps that is even you as you are reading this book. Jesus had a label to describe folks like this and interestingly enough, we use the same word today—hypocrite! If it *is* you, do not fret about it, and certainly do not fall into the trap of offense over my saying it. Simply recognize it, admit it to God, and change. Just do what brother **Jesse Duplantis** does, **"Admit it, quit it, and *forgit* it!"**

People who fear this scripture are either so caught up in the showmanship of the gospel, or blinded by both ignorance and personal gain, that they forget about that which is most important—*doing* the will of the Father. We can cry out, "Lord, Lord," from now until doomsday, but if we never *do* the will of the Father, Jesus will cry out, *"I never knew you."* Why? Because *we* never knew *Him!* If we did, we would obey His will and keep His Word.

Friends of God

Jesus said, *"You are My friends if you do what I command you."* (John 15:14) That is one big "if." It is also the secret to your life in Christ. Avoiding eternal fire is simple; *live a holy life of righteousness and always speak the truth of the gospel.* Jesus uses the term "friend" only with regard to those who are willing to obey Him. Keep in mind this does not mean you become flawless. It means you live your life according the disciplines of Jesus Christ. In essence, you put off lawlessness and live according to God culture. When Jesus is your friend, you will never have to worry about Him casting you from His presence. Jesus will never abandon His beloved.

The Forgotten (Ignored) Commandment

Therefore, if you would like to be Jesus' friend, let's talk about the commands He requires us to keep. Who wants to hear, *"Depart from Me, you who practice lawlessness?"* (Matthew 7:23) Jesus spoke of two great commandments and one great commission. Love God, love one another, (John 13:34) and make disciples of all nations. (Matthew 28:19) Many believe Jesus eliminated the commandments of God by summarizing the law. In truth, however, He simply classified loving God as the greatest commandment.

> *"Teacher,* **which is the great commandment in the law?"** *Jesus said to him, 'You shall love the Lord your God with all your heart, with all your soul, and with all your mind.* **This is the first and great commandment. And the second is like it:** *You shall love your neighbor as yourself. On these two commandments hang all the Law and the Prophets.'"*
> **—Matthew 22:36–40**

True love cannot be mandated. It requires a conscious choice on the part of the lover. In truth, one cannot love God without loving His Word. Anything outside of God's Word is lawlessness. Therefore, we are given the commandments (God's Word) in order to realize the Lord's desire.

Jesus did not eliminate the law, He summarized it. He broke it down into palatable, bite sized, little chunks in order to connect the believer to Yahweh. In the end, God does not want your love of Him to be forced. Love cannot be commanded.

Obedience can be commanded, but love of God requires choice, just as loving one another requires choice. Love of your brother is not an emotion. It is an act of the will. It is placing your neighbor's best interest above your own. With emotion out of the way, the commandment can and must be obeyed. Unbeknownst to most, the commandments of God are all interrelated. You cannot be obedient to one without obeying the other.

Think about it, if you love your neighbors you will not want to see any harm come to them. Therefore, in order to truly love them, you must make disciples. Jesus is *"the way, the truth, and the life. No one comes to the Father except through Him."* (John 14:6) The true friend of God is willing to forgo his own reputation to save his neighbor from eternal fire. Hell is the ultimate harm.

"This commandment we have from Him: that he who loves God must love his brother also." (1 John 4:21) Do you see how it is all connected? He who loves God must love his brother, and he who loves his brother must share the love of God in an attempt to save them. Why do we ignore the most valuable precept in the law? He who loves Jesus must obey His command to *do* the first two. *"On these two commandments hang all the Law and the Prophets."* (Matthew 22:40) Are you really a friend of God?

These two seemingly easy to keep in theory, but difficult to live in reality, commandments are what separate the true believer from the pop culture Christian. All who live outside *practice lawlessness*. Jesus knows none of them. (Matthew 7:23)

How many "Christians" actually practice this? Incredibly, in the midst of all the evil and deception present in the world, the end has not yet materialized. Because of His love and His grace the Lord continues to wait. He gives us more time. Therefore, hang in there. Nurture your relationship with Christ and make disciples. *"He who endures to the end will be saved."* (Matthew 24:13) We who endures the temptations of this present day life will be known by God. He will never cast His beloved children into the abyss. Now that we have covered lawlessness, let's move onto the end of days.

Technology and the End of Days

*"And this gospel of the kingdom will be preached in all the world as a witness to all the nations, **and then the end will come.**"*
—Matthew 24:14

For the first time in the history of mankind, the gospel can be preached to every nation. The boundaries of oceans, governments, and even hostile regions and religions have been vanquished. The barriers to entry have been reduced to the competency of the filtering mechanisms being implemented by the controlling nation's computer technology.

In fact, I have thus far personally reached people in country's as far away as New Zealand, in country's as hostile to Christianity as Iran, Iraq and Afghanistan, and as apathetic as France, without ever leaving my living room. How is this possible? It's simple. Through the God breathed technology known as the internet.

I believe the internet is vitally important to the end-time harvest that is on the verge of taking place. The blogs, books, television and radio shows, newsletter's etc . . . in current circulation are simultaneously being viewed by human beings all over the planet. I am not being braggadocios. I am conveying the incredible power of the internet when it is kept in its proper domain and used as an instrument of righteousness.

That does not mean we need not preach the gospel face to face. Reaching someone in the flesh is by far the most effective means of communicating the gospel of Christ. I have been a witness for Christ in nations as distant as Indonesia, Italy etc . . . and as close as my own home town.

The point that I am making, is that the gospel *is* being *"preached in all the world as a witness to all the nations."* The only question left to answer is when will the end come? Will it be in the next five seconds, or the next five thousand years? I personally believe we are very close. It is simply a matter of the world's nations becoming more immersed in the truth. As they do, the public outcry against the believer will most certainly intensify, leading to an extreme and prolonged bout of persecution. This will lead to the Great Tribulation and then our Lord will come.

> *"Then they will deliver you up to tribulation and kill you, and you will be hated by all nations for My name's sake."*
> **—Matthew 24:9a**

In America and most parts of the West, we have not reached the point of tribulation—at least not yet. Although, when you consider the number of missionaries being sent into all the world by America, and when you consider our founding, along with our current standing in the eyes of world opinion, one can certainly make a case that we are *"hated by all nations for My (Jesus') name's sake."* (Matthew 24:9b) If this is true, tribulation cannot be far off.

> *"For then there will be great tribulation, such as has not been since the beginning of the world until this time, no, nor ever shall be. And unless those days were shortened, no flesh would be saved; but for the elect's sake those days will be shortened. "Then if anyone says to you, 'Look, here is the Christ!' or 'There!' do not believe it. For false christ's and false prophets will rise and show great signs and wonders to deceive, if possible, even the elect. **See, I have told you beforehand.** "Therefore if they say to you, 'Look, He is in the desert!' do not go out; or 'Look, He is in the inner rooms!' do not believe it. For as the lightning comes from the east and flashes to the west, so also will the coming of the Son of Man be."*
> **—Matthew 24:21–27**

I have no doubt that His time is near. Therefore, I would encourage you to keep watch! If you are ready to end our journey together, I have one final secret to share.

*"Jesus answered and said to him, "Blessed are you, Simon Bar-Jonah, for flesh and blood has not revealed this to you, but My Father who is in heaven. And I also say to you that you are Peter, and on this rock **I will build My church,** and the gates of Hades shall not prevail against it."*
—Matthew 16:17–18

As we come to the end of our journey together, let's have a gander at the greatest secret of all, the Church of Jesus Christ.

CHAPTER 15

Building His Church

(THE SECRET OF REVIVAL)

At last we have come to the end of our heavenly voyage together. I trust that you have come to know the Lord in a new and intimate way. I would like to encourage you to continue pressing forward in your pursuit of the Almighty. There are an infinite number of secrets yet to be revealed, and your heavenly Father has set them aside just for you. You will find them in the *"Secret place of the Most high."* (Psalm 91:1) In truth, this is not the end of your journey with God, it is merely the beginning. Therefore, before I bid you adieu, I would like to address one final topic which is of everlasting consequence, the Church of Jesus Christ.

Someone's Missing

I have noticed that the body of Christ is entrenched in a major problem. The issue has become so debilitating that it has all but rendered the body of Christ as not just ineffective, but in many cases, useless. It has so consumed us, that the church has focused all of its organized effort into it. Yet, somehow, with nearly two billion people diligently pursuing the religion of Christianity, our body seems to shrinking, becoming emaciated by spiritual atrophy while our society's continue to degrade and move further from our Maker on a daily basis. If the body were healthy, how could this possibly occur?

In a healthy body, its naturally occurring immune system would seek out the diseased cells and completely eradicate them. This, however, is obviously not the case with the current state of the "body of Christ," otherwise known as the church. The disease we have contracted has so severely infected our body that we have become maimed, disabled, and lame—completely unable to move.

Just like the lame man who sat at the gate called *Beautiful* (Acts 3:2), as the Angel of God stirs the water of our hearts we have become so paralyzed that we cannot even rise to dip into the pool of Living Water. As a result, the healing of the sin-sick hearts of the world alludes the church. In most cases, the body of Christ has become so desensitized to His *"still small voice,"* (1 Kings 19:12) that we fail to even notice the Lord tugging, pulling and pleading with us to enter His presence. Therefore, humanity remains lame, drifting further away from Jehovah to the point of killing just for the thrill of it, all without ever having heard the true gospel of Jesus Christ.

I do not have to tell you that this is completely outside the will of God. The illness has tamed our hearts, our minds, and our actions. It has caused political correctness to the point that truth has escaped the mouth of the believer. Fear of rejection, ridicule, embarrassment and perhaps, worst of all, "enlightenment," has rendered the modern Christian to be all but useless in disseminating the message of the gospel.

You may be shocked to hear that the plague I am referring to is our coordinated effort to build "the church." What! you may ask? Are you surprised to hear this? Perhaps you are even offended? Do not be. I did not use the words, "build *His* church." There is a major difference between bulling *the* church and building *His* church. The majority of church's have not done much of the latter for many years now. We have become much like the ancients of Babel, attempting to build our own towers that reach the heavens by making a name for ourselves and/or for our churches. The disease has caused us to focus primarily upon implementing progressive religious doctrine, providing entertaining worship and tickling pop culture's ears with enjoyable sermons. As a result of personal kingdom building, we have ceased building *His* church.

Keep in mind that I am not saying that our Sunday worship should be dull or that sermon's should be boring. In fact, I believe the opposite is absolutely essential to attracting and maintaining the body of Christ. Living out your walk with Jesus Christ should take you to places you could only have imagined in your wildest dreams. That never occurs, however, in the presence of a watered down and diluted gospel. Fulfilling Sunday services can only be accomplished in the true presence of our Almighty Father. The church does not need to conform to the world to remain relevant.

> *"For the word of God is **living and powerful,** and sharper than any two-edged sword, piercing even to the division of soul and spirit, and of joints and marrow, and is **a discerner of the thoughts and intents of the heart.** And there is **no creature** hidden from His sight, but all things are naked and open to the eyes of Him to whom we **must** give account."*
> **—Hebrews 4:12**

The Word of God is all sufficient in its power to stand alone and remain perfectly intact. In fact, the progressive gospel, and its desire to speak only half truth's, has caused the church to fade. It has committed the same offense as Lucifer in the Garden of Eden. Therefore, with God no longer the center of the heart of the church, the masses have stopped coming.

The institution we have come to know as the church is too busy focusing on how many people are in the seats, what the building looks like, what is its capacity, where is it located, how much money have we taken in, who is on the council, who could give more—Pastor said this, I do not agree with that . . . and the list of irrelevancies to spreading the gospel of the Lord continues into perpetuity while unwittingly leading the modern-day "believer" down the *Road to Nowhere*.

I get that these are questions that potentially need to be addressed, but much of the church has become nothing more than a name only rock group of *Talking Heads* flooding the airwaves with doctrinal fallacy while the denominational heads plot spiritual treason behind closed doors. How else could you explain the utter defiance of the Word of God by committing such heresies as ordaining homosexual and lesbian Pastor's, covering up child pedophilia, and the countless sins being acted out on behalf of the believer on a daily basis?

The result of such "tolerance" has become the mass exodus of a generation that can access the church's hypocrisy with the click of a mouse. Those who remain have been willingly subjected to the infection of ignorance leading the church to the destruction known as inaction. Compromise was never the intended public answer. Unfortunately, for the lost soul about to enter eternity, nothing of everlasting value is getting done. The Word of God is trapped in the building, and thus, never leaves. Ho could it? In many cases it never entered in.

The body of Christ, and I use the term loosely, has completely taken its eyes off the ultimate Builder of the Church, who is Jesus Christ crucified, and, therefore, has failed to engage His resurrection power when preaching the incorruptible gospel of peace. Several of *Jehovah's Witnesses* recently knocked on my door. Unlike most, I always let them in. Why wouldn't I?

God sends a group of un-evangelized cult members to my door and I am supposed to turn them away and let them walk straight into the Lake of Fire? You don't see that as a problem?

Although I completely disagree with their doctrine, the Jehovah's Witnesses (JW's) shame the body of Christ in their zealousness for evangelism. The one thing they always tell me, which the body of Christ has completely disregarded is, "Jesus commanded us to evangelize. That is what we have been called to do." With this, I wholeheartedly agree. Do you realize that the JW's, a cult of Word twisting cult members, more closely resembles the early church than the current body of Christ? How is that for some food for thought?

You may not enjoy hearing this and it may not tickle your ears, but the current body of Christ has gotten it all wrong. The gospel is not supposed to be pretty. Its power is designed to cut right to the heart of the sinner and cause repentance to spring into eternal life. If Jesus Christ of Nazareth wanted beautiful buildings, He would have instructed us to build and beautify the synagogue. Jesus was Jewish. The temple was the only building He ever spoke of, whether it is your physical body or the Jewish worship center. He never commanded us to reproduce "a church" on every street corner—and then hide inside its walls.

Jesus' reference to "the church" and "the temple," for that matter, had absolutely nothing to do with constructing buildings. The same holds true for the Apostle Paul. It had everything to do with bringing the people of the world into repentance and salvation through the cross of Jesus Christ. The only "building" intended is the construction of the kingdom of God, one person at a time. This was meant to be done anywhere, anytime, and everywhere men continue to have breath in their lungs.

*"These commandments that I give you today are to be **on your hearts.** You shall **teach them diligently** to your sons and shall talk of them when you sit in your house and when you walk by the way and when you lie*

*down and when you rise up. You shall **bind them as a sign on your** **hand** and they shall be **as frontals on your forehead.** You shall write them **on the doorposts of your house and on your gates.** "*
—Deuteronomy 6:6–10

As a side not, take a look at where the Word of God is to be bound on the believer—on your hand and on your forehead. Now check out the devil's perversion of God's command.

*"Then I saw another beast coming up out of the earth . . . He causes all, both small and great, rich and poor, free and slave, to receive a mark **on** **their right hand** or **on their foreheads,** and that no one may buy or sell except one who has the mark or the name of the beast, or the number of his name."*
—Revelation 13:11 & 16–17

Satan always uses a twisted form of God's Word to deceive the masses. Just as he did in the beginning, he will once again counterfeit God in the end. The believer must be intimate with God in order to withstand such *"strong delusion."* (2 Thessalonians 2:11)

With that secret revealed, let's get back to the topic. Worship Center's and church building's, or however you would like to classify them today, are fine, but only when they call, equip, and send disciples of Jesus Christ into our present-day dying world. Yahweh is not a one day per week God. We were never intended to be a one hour per week body. The Lord God is twenty-four seven. As His body, we are intended to be the same. Evangelism was never intended to be the sole responsibility of the Pastor. We, the body, are God's image. Therefore, *"let your light shine before men in such a way that they may see your good works, and glorify your Father who is in heaven.* (Matthew 5:16)

As I was recently watching an episode of the hit show *Tanked,* my jaw nearly hit the floor as I witnessed the lobby of a certain church. Contained within, is a salt water fish tank encompassing nearly the entire entrance way to the sanctuary. It was absolutely gorgeous. It looked like an exhibit in the Baltimore Aquarium. Although it was incredible, I do not have to tell anyone who is a tropical fish hobbyist, as I am, that the cost of this is immense, not just in the construction and stocking thereof, but in the ongoing maintenance, as well.

This is exactly my point. I am sure the intention is to provide an illustration that the disciples of Jesus Christ are to be fishers of men, but how about investing in teaching men how to fish for God rather than providing a useless living illustration, which is more indicative of what many churches have become—beautiful, but useless to the kingdom of God.

The church was not called by Christ to build fish tanks. As previously stated, we were not even called to build buildings. God no longer dwells in them. The only temple He resides in is you! I am not saying that buildings are bad, or evil, or however you may misinterpret the message. They were simply never intended to be the sole focus of the gospel. The building was never intended to be "the church."

There are billions of dollars being spent on the construction of lavish buildings, with outrageous furnishings, while millions, and perhaps, even, more accurately, billions of people never hear the true gospel of Jesus Christ presented in the very same neighborhoods. Why is this happening? The "people of God" never leave the safety of the church walls. As a result, we never truly fulfill the *Great Commission* which is, "*Go, therefore and make disciples of all nations.*" (Matthew 28:19)

We have changed the *Great Commission* into the fantasy tag line from the movie *Field of Dreams,* "Build it and they will come." I hate to be the one to tell you, but this has been proven false. We have been erecting buildings for centuries and the people of the world have not come. In fact, as I stated earlier, they have drifted further from God, not become closer. Many of the once great and lavishly adorned churches of the European continent are either empty or have been converted to Mosques.

Europe has become essentially Godless and Allah is filling the void left in His wake. Although Atheism also runs rampant, the even more troubling matter is Europe's outright hostility toward the gospel. Thus, the stage has been set for the Islamic Caliphate. The rest of the Western world, completely blind to the truth, has been in hot pursuit of their trail, chasing after anything and everything that will prevent them from facing their sin. 4000 churches per year permanently close their doors. 3500 people per day leave the American church due to irrelevancy.

Counterfeit or Genuine?

This is not the case for those nations that seem to be relegated to house churches, where the disciples of Jesus Christ truly risk their lives for the One they love. They are unable to build, and yet there, the people actually *do* come, and not because they have some lavish meeting space or charismatic preacher. They come because the persecuted go out and get them!

Somewhere along the twentieth century line, the Western church decided it was best to resemble the world. I used to feel that way myself. Perhaps if we blend in with the world and do not act too weird or religious we will be accepted. Therefore, we, the church, began to dress like the world, talk like the world and walk like the world. We attempted to make our music sound like the world and we began discussing some of the socially taboo issues of the world. Our ministers even began to get plastic surgery like the world, all in an effort to please the world—but it did not matter. The world rejected the church anyway. The world will always reject conformity. Only a thief wants to be part of a counterfeit operation. After coming this far, I need not tell you who the father of this movement is.

If our chief aim, however, would return to preaching the gospel of the Kingdom the true church would multiply, thus causing every other obstacle that we focus on while "building *the* church" to melt into obscurity.

That does not mean everyone will come. In fact, I am sure the church roles would diminish.

> *"And Jesus asked them, 'Do you want to go away also?'"*
> **—John 6:68a**

That is okay. Those whom answer, *"Lord, to whom shall we go? You have the words of eternal life"* (John 6:68b) will race toward *"the mark of the high calling of God in Jesus Christ."* (Philippians 3:14) In our wake, the only member that really matters, Yahweh, would once again return and the blessing would finally flow *"like rivers of living water"* throughout the body.

Therefore, anyone not on board with the mission would cease to fill the seats. In fact, you would rarely have people in the seats, or in your office, or complaining in your ear, because they would be too busy fishing people into the kingdom of God. Although your church roles would diminish, the ministry would prosper. What is more important to you? I will leave that between you and Jesus.

Those who remain would be a haven for encouragement, instruction, prayer, fellowship and worship. Isn't that the purpose of the institution? Fellowship is a consequence of the church, not the focus of the mission. *His* church was never intended to be a social club.

If our focus became the gospel only, we would not have to worry about all our programs. We would only have one, building *His* church! Nothing else would matter, except discipleship and "child care," due to the constant flow of "babies" being added to the Lord daily. That, by the way, *is* building His church.

How about the prayer team? Let's create a prayer army. Building and grounds committee? Let's create a sanitation crew to clean both the building and grounds, but more importantly, the "good ground" that just received the seed of the gospel. Our church council's should need a board room and yet have one unified voice. This, however, can only happen if the people unify with one purpose under the influence of the Holy Spirit.

Our worship teams should be living bodies of refined in the fire, Spirit filled, true worshippers. The body of Christ needs to unite, functioning and living for one purpose and one purpose alone—the salvation of a man's soul. Salvation is the definition of building His true church which can only be founded upon the Rock of Jesus Christ.

Giving Place to the Devil

The church, however, has acquired a secondary illness. The contagion is so intense that it has effected humanity on both sides of heaven. More deadly than ebola, this newborn illness is spread through every medium available to man.

I first noticed it about six years ago when I heard one of my children speaking to a friend in our basement. As I descended the staircase to greet his acquaintance, I was shocked to find him alone. Yet, the disembodied voice was still vociferating throughout the airwaves of my home. No, this was not an episode of the hit show *Ghost Hunters*. It was far more dangerous than any paranormal experience you have ever heard of, or experienced. The ghostly utterance echoing throughout my basement was coming through my son's *Xbox!*

With shock and awe in my voice, I cried out, "Who are you talking to?"

"Oh it's just . . ." my son answered back, as shocked as I was at my technological ignorance.

That was the moment I realized humanity is committing social suicide. I then began looking around. I began to see the disease manifested in every aspect of human life. Employees work from home. Education can now be accessed on-line. Text messaging has replaced the telephone call. We no longer need to leave home to attend something as essential as church. We do not even have to put a check in the offering plate anymore. On-line giving is much more "convenient." In fact, the entire church experience is available on-line. Socializing is becoming a thing of the past. Isolation has become the norm. As we are now finding out its effects can be deadly. Discipleship is on the verge of extinction.

In its beginning stages, the deadly illness of Isolation appears tame. Within days after being infected, however, the disease takes hold of its victim and quickly spreads to all those within the victim's circle of influence. It targets young and old, and amazingly, it thrives wherever large groups of people once gathered.

When searching for the cure, I came to the realization that there is no antidote available to the unregenerate human being. There is no serum or vaccine able to cure this illness. It is much more than a physical ailment. It is a demonic force. Satan has had an *Extreme Makeover* and now appears as a technological *angel of light*. His brand new strategy has morphed beyond separation. He is now manifest in isolation!

Isolation has only one purpose for existing. Its purpose is to *"steal, kill and destroy."* (John 10:10) Isolation functions as the mighty "king of the jungle" roaming the African plains. *"Your adversary the devil walks about like a roaring lion, seeking whom he may devour,"* (1 Peter 5:8) Step one is to separate you from "the herd."

Isolation weakens the believer. You become as a young wildebeest separated from its mother on the vast African plain. As you drift further from the protection of the herd, Isolation pounces, crushes your spiritual windpipe and drags you to an agonizing and lonely death.

In church circles, we know Isolation by a different and more common name. The demon Isolation has disguised himself for centuries under the alias known as, Denomination. As he separates the body, the power of unity fails and a secondary, even more powerful demon creeps in. His power is even greater than that of Isolation as he prohibits the believer from recognizing any and all truth. His name is Deception! Once the spirit of Deception grabs hold of the believer, the death of the member follows in short order.

As each member is slowly killed off, the organism known as the local church body slowly ceases to function. In the end, it perishes. The entire organism suffers a hideous death. The only evidence revealing that a vibrant living body once existed is the beautified skeletal remains of the church building. All life, however, has perished. The church becomes a *"white-washed tomb."* (Matthew 23:27)

Preparing the Way of God

What is the solution? The demon named Conformity, which is the direction the church has drifted, is only adding fuel to the fire. Conformity is Deception's soul mate. The truth of Jesus Christ is the only cure. Obedience to the will of God is the only solution. Religious ritual has no power. The precious blood of Christ is the only known antidote and vaccine for both preventing and curing the deadly illness. Brotherly love, and *"not forsaking the assembling of ourselves together,"* (Hebrews 10:25) and thus, building *His* church, in the name of, and for the purpose of Jesus Christ, is the only known cure. Isn't this how Jesus fulfilled *His* ministry? Isn't this how He instructed us to build *His Church* in order to fulfill *our* ministry?

> *"'**Go into all the world** and preach the Gospel **to every creature.** He who believes and is baptized will be saved; but he who does not believe will be condemned . . .' **And they went out and preached everywhere,** the Lord **working with them** and **confirming the Word** through the accompanying signs. Amen"*
> **—Mark 16:15–16 and 20**

When self has been eliminated from the equation and the believer in Jesus Christ pursues the kingdom of God with reckless abandon, the Lord confirms His Word with true signs and wonders. It is here that things begin to change. The true manifestation of God in the life of any and every human being changes lives for eternity. *"For the kingdom of God is not in word but in power."* (1 Corinthians 4:20) Therefore, with wondrous signs of glory the true disciple of Jesus Christ never need consider the four dreaded words to be uttered to every dead and disobedient church, *"I never knew you."*

I cannot find anywhere in the Word of God where Jesus sat His disciples down and said, "Behold, go into all the world and build buildings. If you build them they will come. Make them as lavish as you can. Stay inside those four walls and wait. Play some music, read a few Psalms, appoint some greeters, and wait. Do not speak too loud and make sure you do not offend anyone. Otherwise they will go elsewhere."

"Oh, and break yourselves up into divisions. Make sure no one really knows the difference. Everyone's personality and style of worship is different. Go with whatever is working at the time."

"Do not forget that some people like to baptize babies. So pour a little water on their heads. Some others will want to be dunked under water. Don't pay attention to the Word about this issue, either way is fine. Oh, and your churches have to be named after someone—name each group something different, as well. Put a ... let me think ... Saint something in front of it and everyone will revere it."

"Please, above all else, do not scare anyone. Do not tell anyone they could go to hell. That is too harsh and our goal is to get as many people in the seats as possible. Most people do not like being touched either, so forget about that laying on of hands stuff. It might freak people out. But above all, build those buildings. The bigger the better—and wait there. Do not go anywhere. You see there are two things you cannot talk about, religion and politics ..."

Do you hear the absurdity of what we have become!? Religion and politics were the exact two places where Jesus hit the Pharisees smack in the face. Offense was never a consideration in His mind. He and His disciples *went out,* preaching the gospel with boldness and with courage. Never waiting—always going. Today's Christian feels they need a doctorate in theology before they can even open their mouth. It is hog wash. Teach the congregation to speak!

When Jesus knew His disciples were sufficiently trained, even if they did not feel that way, He sent them out, two by two, into the towns and cities. They did not volunteer, *they were sent.* That is how my Pastor, God bless him, taught me to preach. He called me up one day and said, "Go." So I went. Even though I did not want to. I felt totally unprepared. But he did not ask me. He sent me. Out of obedience to both He and God, I went. No one overthought the process. He trusted me, so He sent me.

Leaders, lead your people! Jesus decided when they were ready. He sent them without money and without physical supplies. They were fully supplied with the anointing of the Holy Spirit and the power of God to heal the sick, cast out demons, raise the dead, and above all, preach the good news of the kingdom of God.

I am sure they did quite a bit of preaching in the synagogues, but Jesus never instructed anyone to remain and build church buildings in the neighborhoods the synagogues were in. In case you have not noticed, Jesus preached indoor, outdoor, everywhere and anywhere. His most famous sermon was *on the Mount,* not in the Synagogue.

Furthermore, and particularly when we move into the Book of Acts, the preaching of the gospel was always accompanied by persecution. The early church was unable to remain in one place and build a big beautiful building. It would have been painted with their blood!

With the exception of the third world, do you hear of persecution within the body of Christ today, particularly in the Western world? The answer is a resounding no. In the few places you do hear of persecution, the gospel is flourishing and spreading like wildfire. Meanwhile in the West, we are being pervaded by New Age mumbo jumbo, Atheism, and as of late, something even more dangerous than both—Islam! But don't offend them.

Just stick your neck out for their sword. Soon they will be cutting off your head in the very building you spent so much time and money to build.

Church, awake up from your slumber! Fulfill your ministry. Go! Build His church! Fulfilling the *Great Commission* is the only goal of the church of Jesus Christ. My friends, building *His* church is the greatest of all the *Secrets of the Father.*

May the Lord bless you and keep you.

Conclusion

At last, our journey together has reached its end. My prayer is that you have begun to see your Father in a new and unshaded light. Most of all, however, I pray that you have come to know the saving grace of Jesus Christ of Nazareth, that you have made Him both Lord and Savior of your life and that your destiny now awaits you along the golden streets of the New Jerusalem, where you will forever bask in the radiant glory of the one and only true God of the universe.

Therefore, I bid you adieu. May *"the Lord bless you and keep you, the Lord make His face shine upon you and be gracious to you; the Lord lift up His countenance upon you, and give you peace."* (Numbers 6:24–26)

See you in the New Jerusalem!